Women Labor Activists
in the Movies

Women Labor Activists in the Movies

Nine Depictions of Workplace Organizers, 1954–2005

JENNIFER L. BORDA

McFarland & Company, Inc., Publishers
Jefferson, North Carolina, and London

A version of Chapter Two appeared as "Working-Class Women, Protofeminist Performance, and Resistant Ruptures in the Movie Musical *The Pajama Game*" in *Text and Performance Quarterly* 30.3 (July 2010): 227–246. Reprinted with permission.

A version of Chapter Three appeared as "Feminist Critique and Cinematic Counterhistory in the Documentary *With Babies and Banners*" in *Women's Studies in Communication* 28.2 (fall 2005): 157–182. Reprinted with permission.

A version of Chapter Five appeared as "Negotiating Feminist Politics in the Third Wave: Labor Struggle and Solidarity in *Live Nude Girls Unite!*" in *Communication Quarterly* 57.2 (April–June 2009): 117–135. Reprinted with permission.

LIBRARY OF CONGRESS CATALOGUING-IN-PUBLICATION DATA

Borda, Jennifer L., 1973–
    Women labor activists in the movies : nine depictions of workplace organizers, 1954–2005 / by Jennifer L. Borda.
        p.   cm.
    Includes bibliographical references and index.

    ISBN 978-0-7864-4841-8
    softcover : 50# alkaline paper ∞

    1. Working class women in motion pictures. 2. Labor movement in motion pictures. 3. Motion pictures — United States — History — 20th century. I. Title.
    PN1995.9.W6B67   2011
    791.43'652623—dc22   2010029840

British Library cataloguing data are available

©2011 Jennifer L. Borda. All rights reserved

No part of this book may be reproduced or transmitted in any form or by any means, electronic or mechanical, including photocopying or recording, or by any information storage and retrieval system, without permission in writing from the publisher.

Cover image: Charlize Theron as Josey Aimes in *North Country*, 2005 (Warner Bros./Photofest)

Manufactured in the United States of America

McFarland & Company, Inc., Publishers
  Box 611, Jefferson, North Carolina 28640
    www.mcfarlandpub.com

Table of Contents

Acknowledgments vi
Introduction 1

One. Rising Up Against the Dominant: The Multiple Transgressions of *Salt of the Earth* 15

Two. Working-Class Women, Protofeminist Performance, and Resistant Ruptures in the Movie Musical *The Pajama Game* 47

Three. Recovering Women Activists' Voices: *Union Maids*, *With Babies and Banners*, and the Feminist Historical Documentary 73

Four. Hollywood's Working-Class Heroines: *Norma Rae*, *Silkwood*, and the Politics of the Docudrama 101

Five. Negotiating Feminist Politics in the Third Wave: Labor Struggle and Solidarity in *Live Nude Girls Unite!* 141

Six. Hollywood's Feminist Labor Heroines Moving Into the Twenty-first Century: Have We Really Come a Long Way? 164

Seven. Fifty Years of Female Labor Activism in Film: Mapping the Rhetorical Tensions 189

Chapter Notes 199
Bibliography 213
Index 225

Acknowledgments

I came to this project with an interest in the power of collective action and the unity of effort necessary to overcome gender and class oppression. I have come to realize that such a scholarly endeavor requires a similar level of collective effort on the part of many smart and supportive colleagues, friends, and family, and I am extremely grateful to all who have helped make this book a reality. Specifically, I would like to thank Tom Benson for his generous guidance and insight as my dissertation advisor in the early stages of this project. I also benefitted greatly from the thoughtful advice and enduring friendship of Anne Demo, Heather Norton, David Schulz and Jennifer Young as I worked through the various incarnations that the chapters in this book have taken over the years. I owe a special thanks to Julie Haynes who read through much of this project during the various stages of its creation, who found the last documentary that held the project together, and who responded to each new chapter with excitement and great interest. Finally, if not for Brian Snee, who encouraged me to send out the manuscript as a whole, this decade-long endeavor would never have become a book, so I thank him for his foresight and encouragement. I also am grateful for funding support from the University of New Hampshire, which allowed me to secure photos and assistance with the preparation of the index.

Without the love, respect, patience, and understanding of my husband, Willem Verweij, I would not have had the motivation to continue on this path. Finally, I would like to thank my grandmother, Margaret Borda. For years, she was a dedicated reader of my work and inspired me to continue writing about women's rich political and rhetorical history. It was only after I had begun this project that I learned that she had courageously protested unfair labor conditions as a garment worker in 1930s Philadelphia, and so I dedicate this work to her, a rebel girl in her own right.

Introduction

Some of the most indelible images of women in American film in recent years have been of working women taking a stand for labor reform or fighting to expose corporate corruption. Celluloid scenes of these women have become part of our cultural memories, such as Norma Rae standing atop a shop table holding a make-shift "UNION" sign, Karen Silkwood scrubbed down mercilessly after plutonium contamination, or Erin Brockovich baiting a corporate polluters' legal team with the remark: "By the way, that water was brought in especially for you folks from a well in Hinkley." Other moments of female labor activism captured on film are probably less well-known: Esperanza Quintero giving birth to her son on a picket line for striking New Mexico miners in *Salt of the Earth*, women clashing with police outside of the General Motors sit-down strike in *With Babies and Banners*, or female exotic dancers chanting "2-4-6-8, don't go in to masturbate" outside of San Francisco's Lusty Lady in *Live Nude Girls Unite!* Yet, whether well-remembered or utterly obscure, these films illuminate the interlocking dynamics of gender and class through cinematic representations that depict the challenges facing working-class women, as well as the female laborer's potential for resistance and political power. By considering the historical, rhetorical, and cultural context in which these films were created and received, this book seeks to explore how such films contribute to our cultural discourse and social realities relating to gender and class, and the different ways in which they contribute to our shared history and collective memory of the feminist and American labor movements.

The period from the middle of the twentieth century through the beginning of the twenty-first witnessed many changes, from the rise of consumerism and the rapid growth of technology, to major transformations in world politics (such as the fall of Communism), to cultural shifts initiated by various social movements fighting for equality on the basis of sex, race, and sexual orientation. For women, these decades of change were particularly significant in that ideologies and definitions of womanhood and women's cultural and political status were constantly evolving over that time. The women's movement, first established in the mid-nineteenth century through the campaign for woman suffrage, had receded into history in the years after World War II. During the 1950s, many women were once again defined through their traditional roles of wife and mother, however, another movement was already beginning to rise up among the "desperate housewives" of that generation. By the early 1970s, the notion of women's liberation, both social and political, gained some ground through feminism's second wave, only to retreat once again in light of post-feminist reactions to such gains during the end of the last century. Interestingly, this same period also marked the steady decline of another movement for greater rights and political recognition, the American labor movement. By the mid-twentieth century, the labor campaign had already reached its zenith and had begun to dismantle as the result of growing anti–Communist sentiment. Declining union activism continued through the 1970s, and by the year 2000, the number of workers belonging to unions nationwide had reached a 60-year low.

As a prominent producer of cultural discourses and our socially constructed realities, popular culture has played a significant role in shaping our ideas about various social experiments, their political impact, and their cultural significance. According to Bonnie Dow, whose book *Prime-Time Feminism* traces feminist representations over several decades of television programming, popular media serve the function of "interpreting social change and managing cultural beliefs," specifically by defining what it means to be a "liberated woman" and by contributing to the important cultural work of representing feminism for the American public.[1] This book takes a similar perspective, but expands the focus beyond an analysis based solely on gender to a broader understanding of how cultural conversations produced by the media construct not only our ideas about women and feminism, but also about social classes and, particularly, working-class culture. By investigating representations of *working-class women in film*, my analysis broadens the scope of feminist inquiry while also making it more precise by addressing the ways that gender intertwines with other social identities.

Representations of the female labor activist as she has been depicted in various cinematic incarnations over fifty years are the subject of this book. I analyze nine films: the docudrama *Salt of the Earth* (1954); the musical comedy *The Pajama Game* (1957); the documentaries *Union Maids* (1976), *With Babies and Banners* (1978), and *Live Nude Girls Unite!* (2000); and the biopics *Norma Rae* (1979), *Silkwood* (1983), and *North Country* (2005). These nine films exemplify the strongest and most productive representations of the woman labor activist released during three historical periods, the 1950s, the 1970s, and the transition from the twentieth to the twenty-first century. In these films the labor activist is the main protagonist and women's issues and themes relating to working-class culture are featured prominently. Primarily, I also consider how these films invite female spectators, in particular, to accept a range of ideological perspectives on the role of women in society and how these views have changed over time.

By mapping the constructions of the labor heroine across nine films, I am interested in observing how film functions as a response to certain rhetorical exigencies brought on by our social and political histories. Considering these films together, I believe, establishes a more cumulative sense of the ways film, as an American institution, has responded over the last half century to the feminist and workers' movements, and how our popular culture has articulated for audiences notions of disempowerment, ambivalence, and, at times, resistance on behalf of both women and the working class. Through a comparative analysis, I examine how a variety of films function as social discourses that chart the struggles of working-class women over five decades. More importantly, however, I believe that films have the power to produce focused — and sometimes powerful — images of social protest that contribute to our social history and ideological perspectives regarding progressivism, feminism, and socialist experiments. Therefore, I feel it is important to consider the various contexts through which such films arise, and to consider the differing degrees to which these films, over time, have encouraged an awareness of cross-cultural constructions of power, in this case relating to gender and class.

The rise of the social problem film coincided with the birth of the cinema itself; progressivism had brought the nation's problems out of obscurity, and soon all of the fears and tribulations of that transitional era were being reflected in the country's movie houses. A number of scholars have focused on this historical period as representative of the cinema's power to shape the political issues affecting the lives of moviegoers.[2] Kay Sloan, in her study of the origins of the social problem film, explains, "Films interpreted the nation's headlines in dramatic visual images that at once persuaded and entertained."[3] All of these scholars agree that the social problem film functions as a persuasive appeal for societal change. According to Peter Roffman and Jim Purdy, "While all films have something to say, the social problem film functions to more directly influence the attitudes of the public," and they argue that the real social contribution of these films stems from the "tension between a conventional form and a radical vision."[4]

Throughout its history, the social problem film has found its greatest relevance with regard to issues affecting those at the margins of society. For example, a number of scholars have explored the social problem film and its focus on the struggles of the working class.[5] For the century's first few decades especially, members of the working class were the primary audience for the film industry's products. During the 1920s, however, the rise of Hollywood, the construction of movie palaces, and the introduction of longer, feature-length films turned moviegoing into a middle-class leisure activity. This transition also changed the kinds of films offered to audiences — films became more escapist rather than realist in nature. Although labor-capital films did not disappear entirely over the next seventy years, the images presented of the working class often were much more conservative. Despite the decrease in strong portrayals of working-class heroes in the latter part of the century, films that continue to incorporate working-class themes serve an important function by enlightening the public about social issues related to those at the cultural margins. According to Steven Ross, the perpetual existence of working-class films has "continued to shape, not merely reflect, our visual understanding of workers, their organization, and what it means to be working class."[6] Similarly, John Bodnar's recent study of blue-collar Hollywood concludes that "before, during, and after the conventional story of labor's rise and fall ... Hollywood told another tale of working-class life that was affected both by the variables described by historians and by a more intricate set of emotional factors that they seldom looked at."[7]

One aspect of working-class life that has received the most poignant treatment in films has been labor, especially the activities of labor unions. Cinematic portrayals of labor conflict throughout the history of film have consisted of a mixture of anti- and pro-union messages. Responding to this contradiction, many scholars writing about labor and film have bemoaned Hollywood's inconsistent portrayals of labor issues. Most labor historians agree that "Hollywood film-makers have not been kind to organized labor."[8] Ken Margolies writes that the images of organized labor in Hollywood films range from inaccurate to sordid and "confirm the unorganized workers'—and the public's—worst fears about the labor movement."[9] These scholars argue that most Hollywood films have failed to deal seriously with the working class and the history of the American labor movement, and that the few that have tended to eschew a balanced view of trade unions or downplayed "positive images of the collective potential of working people."[10] There have, however, been exceptions.

A subset of the labor film, those films portraying female heroines, have fared much better under the critical view of labor historians and film scholars. This subset of the social problem film genre—"women's pictures" that chart the heroine's plight as a result of economic conditions—have found the greatest critical success (and sometimes even economic success) among the labor films produced since the silent era. Although most scholars have tended to overlook this genre, those who have considered labor films featuring women largely agree that they tend to present the most sympathetic views of organized labor, as well as a strong sense of the collective action and politics of the American labor movement. What these scholars, for the most part, have neglected to address is *what* makes these films different from the other labor films they have disparaged.[11] Sonya Michel, in her essay analyzing three documentaries about American working women, argues that their effectiveness stems from their "multiple radical messages: class struggle, labor militancy, and feminism."[12] Expanding on Michel's argument, I consider that what makes these films different is how the combined exploration of class relations, feminist themes, and social activism produce poignant and persuasive insights into modern political movements for contemporary audiences. Further, I believe these films are characterized by a paradoxical, yet inherently rhetorical, construction in which largely conventional cinematic treatments of the female labor heroine function in progressive ways that offer a challenge to dominant discourse about these political ideologies.

The focus on working women also broadens our understanding of American women's experience beyond the often monolithic view currently offered by most traditional gender histories and studies of feminist rhetoric. For example, in her study of Progressive Era labor reformer Leonora O'Reilly, Anne Mattina reminds us that inclusion of female, working-class figures in rhetorical scholarship allows for the recovery of public voices not frequently included in the discipline and begins to validate those voices not privileged by class, race, or formal education.[13] This book also expands our knowledge of women's cultural status by investigating an aspect of American women's experience not often accounted for: namely her capacity for radical activism and militant resistance in the face of both economic and gender oppression. Women in labor, especially, have been active in fighting this double oppression through their efforts to overcome patriarchal views that limit women, as well as their struggle to rectify the capitalist domination of the worker. Mari Boor Tonn, in her study of female labor agitator Mary Harris "Mother" Jones, notes the significance of such a vexing cause.[14] According to Tonn, female labor activists are involved in a "constant negotiation between social expectations of women's roles and the competing expectations of their public missions," that is, a negotiation "between reigning ideology and lived experiences."[15] Recovery of women's voices and accomplishments in the face of these contradictions and social obstacles reveals their ability to adapt female experience and use it in transformative ways, as well as their capacity to resist social and political domination.

This focus also reflects the agenda of recent feminist film scholarship that advocates critical readings of popular culture texts more responsive to multivalent feminist agendas. According to Diane Carson, Linda Dittmar, and Janice R. Welsch, such endeavors "in addition to critiquing patriarchy's use of an undifferentiated concept of gender to promote an ideology of dominance ... also question ways films represent and define issues of difference and inequality among women."[16] I believe that such a focus is significant because women of the lower class are often those most acutely affected by societal injustices, which makes their dual struggle against both gender and class biases even more profound.

Greater attention to the contradictory experiences of women and their representation in film also has been the goal of feminist film scholars in recent years. Judith Mayne, for example, advocates a feminist criticism that works to encourage film viewers to understand cinema as symptomatic of woman's contradictory investment in patriarchal society.[17] Mayne argues that scholars need to pay more attention to the "ambivalent terrain" of feminist film criticism, which "means an understanding of patriarchy as oppressive and as vulnerable, and the attendant sense that the work of feminism is to exploit the vulnerability, while knowing full well the dangers of a vigorous backlash."[18] Following Mayne's call for more complex critiques of films from a feminist perspective, I also investigate the ways that gender and class are represented in these films as sites of political struggle and engagement with contradiction — especially the dualities between heroine/victim, domination/resistance, and structure/agency.

Attention to these tensions also stems from my critical assumptions that films serve as a cultural response to our political and social developments, such as feminism, socialism, and liberalism, that sometimes works toward the advancement of progressive social change, and at other times functions to suppress it. In this way, this study also shares the objective of Douglas Kellner's work, which "explores some of the ways that contemporary media culture provides forms of ideological domination that help to reproduce current relations of power, while also providing resources for the construction of identities and for empowerment, resistance, and struggle."[19] Such an analysis takes the perspective of negotiation, which allows for greater discussion of a film's conservative *and* radical potential and its ability to *both* celebrate the dominant order *and* criticize or resist it.[20] In my analysis, I also approach these films through an understanding of popular culture texts that, according to Elayne Rapping, recognizes "their importance as well as their strengths and weaknesses, their power to facilitate change, and their tendencies — because they are part of an essentially stabilizing, conservative institution charged with keeping order and preserving the status quo — to restrict change."[21]

Consequently, a primary objective for this book is to chart the rhetorical limitations and possibilities for cinematic engagement with feminist and socialist politics. By viewing films produced inside and outside of the dominant culture (i.e., the Hollywood establishment), I have found that this collection of films represent a spectrum of meanings that oscillate between dominant ideologies that reinforce the status quo and resistant discourses that advocate feminist, liberal, and socialist philosophies. In particular, I show that the variations in the depth of engagement offered by these films are largely a result of the various political, economic, and ideological forces that distinguish independent films from the Hollywood establishment. Cinematic representations of the female labor activist have been marked by four rhetorical tensions: between the formal stylistics of realism and the classical Hollywood paradigm; between textual representations of the female heroine that celebrate her subjectivity and those that exploit her through objectification; between explicit and implicit ideological critiques of cultural politics; and between the use of real women versus Hollywood stars to fulfill the roles of the main protagonists. Through analysis of these tensions, I demonstrate the various ways that independent and mainstream films function to rhetorically impose, reflect, or challenge certain ideologies relating to gender and class identities for audiences both historically and presently. Within the nine films considered in this project, I argue that these tensions operate to produce a spectrum of representations of the female labor activist that are varied and complex, offering audiences a range of aesthetic traditions that allow for different voices to be heard.

I believe that the powerful meanings that popular culture disseminates, in this case cultural discourses circulating around feminism and labor, must be determined in reference to specific texts, events, contexts, and audiences, because meaning for audiences is created through the meeting of producers, texts, and audiences. Additionally, since, as Martin Medhurst and Thomas Benson note, meaning making "is always realized in a social, cultural, and political situation by viewers," this project extends beyond formal analysis of the films' cinematic conventions to also account for the political, economic, and historical contexts in which the films were produced, as well as the social and cultural interaction between audience and text.[22] I think it is important to assume that the mass media contain persuasive potential, and then to identify how the media reflect and create social and political ideologies through their production, form, and reception, as well as how those ideologies constrain meaning making.[23] In addition to a consideration of how these films have contributed to public discourse, and the cumulative stories they tell about feminism, the working-class, and the organized American labor movement, my goal is always also to determine not only what meanings are created, but *how* they are created.

Because I believe the medium of film acts both as a product and a producer of social discourses, I investigate the complex ways in which such discourses are produced and how films about feminism and the working class act as invitations to meaning making for audiences.[24] In an effort to understand this process, that is, to understand the rhetorical function of these films, I employ three different reading practices. For each film, I consider how the cultural context of production; their form, both in terms of stylistic aesthetics and thematic content; and the way these films construct or position spectators intersect to produce arguments, ideologies, and cultural discourses. In doing this, I begin by investigating how notions of gender and social class are constructed from both the margins and the center by examining the tensions between films produced independently of the industry establishment and those created within the Hollywood mainstream. Specifically, I consider the social implications of the historical context of production for each film, as well as the political-economic imperatives that influenced the filmmakers' creative decisions and how those material conditions affect the style and content of these films.

I also evaluate the rhetorical form and content of each film to determine how film structure and style, as well as story elements such as plot, character development, and setting, function in particular ways and influence how the story gets told. Here, again, the purpose is not to find *the* meaning of the film as constructed by these elements, but to investigate *how* a variety of meanings are produced, allowing for various interpretations. The primary method I use to evaluate the films' meanings is textual analysis. I perform close readings of the specified films and analyze the intersecting ways in which different forms of address function across different textual registers. That is, this study employs textual analysis in an attempt "to locate behind the manifest themes of a film another level of meaning that lies in the structural relationships of the text."[25] This method consists of examining devices such as the close-up or direct address to investigate how they construct meaning, as well as how they organize the female image into a patriarchal position or, conversely, offer textual opportunities for resistance. A textual analysis also allows for an analysis of textual negotiation among the nine films—the critical concern with the generation of different readings that challenge each other, and provoke social negotiation of meanings, definitions, and identities.[26]

Finally, I also consider the films as invitations to viewers, or how the films construct certain spectatorship positions and identities. For this, I borrow from Mayne, who articulates a theory of spectatorship as "not just the relationship that occurs between the viewer and the screen, but also and especially how that relationship lives on once the spectator leaves the theater."[27] I approach the notion of spectatorship with a kind of "double vision" that works from both a historical and a contemporary perspective. Historically, I investigate how the cinema, and particularly these individual films, were contextualized in a given culture, what kinds of films female spectators have been offered, with what kinds of representations they were invited to identify, and what kinds of discourses about gender and class they may have taken from these experiences. I also discuss how spectators in the early twenty-first century are invited to make meanings from their viewing experience with these films, and what can be learned about feminist development and changing class consciousness by looking back at these films from our present political and cultural perspectives.

I argue that all three of these variables — production, form, and spectatorship — are related in this project since I believe that context and form circulate, that is, film forms change over time and function differently within various cultural milieus, which invariably influences how audiences make sense of the films' rhetorical vision in different periods. As such, the combination of all of these elements is important when identifying how the films draw upon discourses circulating in society and incorporate them into the fabric of the film.

The chapters that follow provide a detailed, and chronological, analysis of each of the nine films featuring female labor activism. In chapter one, I examine the film *Salt of the Earth* (1954), which tells the story of the striking workers of Local 890 of the International Union of Mine, Mill, and Smelter Workers in 1951 New Mexico, and the Ladies' Auxiliary made up of their wives, who eventually won the fight. I begin with a discussion of the political and economic contexts that existed in Hollywood before and during the film's production, and the way in which the creation of *Salt of the Earth* constituted a resistance to those industry constraints. I then turn to the film itself and examine how the text's cinematic form, convention, and explicit themes create an aesthetic that transgressed traditional standards of filmmaking, and consequently offer textual opportunities for resistance through the construction of an unconventional female heroine, the employment of a Neorealist style, and the production of a radical story of human struggle and human dignity. I conclude by addressing the ideological influence of these cinematic practices from the perspective of the film's historical spectatorship within the cultural context into which *Salt of the Earth* was released.

Introduction

The analysis of *Salt of the Earth* reveals how the cinematic techniques and conventions of Neorealism are employed to illuminate discourses surrounding gender, class, and ethnicity as interrelated struggles for social justice. I focus specifically on how the film tells the miners' story through an unconventional female heroine, the main character and narrator, Esperanza Quintero. I consider how this focus draws attention to issues of the public and the private, as well as women's voice, autonomy, and agency. As a story about the challenges inherent in motivating individuals into collective action and social protest, I argue that *Salt of the Earth* performs multiple transgressions that invite audiences to embrace a radical paradigm of political thinking.

In chapter two I analyze *The Pajama Game*, a 1957 musical starring Doris Day. The film is about Local 343 of the Amalgamated Shirt and Pajama Workers of America, which threatens to strike for a 7½ cent raise. Based on the novel *7½ Cents* by Richard Bissel, and a subsequent Broadway musical, the film combines a romantic plot line between Babe Williams (Day) as the head of the grievance committee and the factory supervisor, Sid Sorokin (John Raitt), with the organizational intricacies of union activity and a variety of musical numbers. The whimsical and comedic elements of this film are in direct contrast to the militant politics of *Salt of the Earth*.

I begin by situating the context of *The Pajama Game*'s creation within the historical context of the 1950s as the era that transformed the World War II working girl into the housewife, represented the twilight of the Hollywood studio era, and heralded in the golden age of the musical film. I discuss the emergence of the musical as a popular American form and its rhetorical influence as a confirmation of normative values. I then turn to the film text itself to examine how *The Pajama Game*'s formal structures function to expose the labor heroine's non-conformity while, at the same time, confirming the status quo. Finally, I consider Doris Day's paradoxical star persona as another means through which contemporary film spectators may have interpreted *The Pajama Game* and its representation of the woman labor activist.

Through an examination of the star persona and narrative performance of Doris Day, I argue that this film also presents a complex representation of the labor heroine that is a combination of both strength and vulnerability. The analysis of the film investigates how these aspects of *The Pajama Game* influence constructions of the female labor activist, and how the spectator is positioned in relation to the portrayal of the labor heroine in the performance of a musical, as well as the related issues of women's empowerment and class consciousness. I also pay particular attention to the spectacle of the musical and the star image of Doris Day, which I argue both confirmed and resisted the cultural ideal of 1950s femininity.

Chapter three consists of an examination of two documentaries by feminist directors. The first, *Union Maids* (1976), documents the careers of three active union organizers and proponents of radical change in a variety of labor industries during the 1930s. The second film, *With Babies and Banners* (1978), is the story of the Women's Emergency Brigade — the militant organization of working women and autoworkers' wives, mothers, sisters, and girlfriends who led the "outside" protest during the 1936–1937 sit-down strike at the Flint, Michigan, General Motors plant. I analyze these films as feminist representations of both women's history and labor history through documentary, paying particular attention to issues of realism, politics, and representation, as well as the efforts on the part of the films' directors to find a "fit" between cinematic form and female expression. I consider the contexts for production of the documentaries and account for the political and social history surrounding these films, which were made during the height of second-wave feminism, but focus on the circumstances of working women in the 1930s. The central focus of the chapter is the struggle of the filmmakers and their subjects to tell the women's stories when these stories reinterpret the past, as well as contemporary response to these films in the context of several decades of feminist debate over the productivity of the realist cinematic style for gender politics.

I begin with a discussion of the evolution of the feminist documentary as a strategy for representing women's issues and experiences within the second-wave women's movement. I then turn to the issue of how, despite feminist film theorists' intense criticism of the form, the strategies of the realist cinema function rhetorically as an ideal medium for recovering the voices of these radical activists. Within the context of these feminist debates over the politics of representation, I discuss how contemporary viewers are invited to interpret the formal aspects of these documentaries and the way these films use realism to emphasize the dramatic narratives of women's historical past and their radical views with regard to issues such as socialism and feminism. Finally, I discuss how the realist form influences film spectatorship, and specifically how *Union Maids* and *With Babies and Banners* serve a consciousness-raising function within the feminist and labor movements by calling dominant ideologies into question and conferring a political call to continued collective action.

In chapter four I analyze two biographical films based on the union exploits of two female labor activists in the 1970s. *Norma Rae* (1979) is a fictionalized story based on the real-life activism of Crystal Lee Jordan and her efforts to improve working conditions at the J. P. Stevens Company in North Carolina. *Silkwood* (1983) is based on a plutonium plant worker, Karen Silkwood, and her work as a union activist for the Oil, Chemical, and Atomic Workers.

I begin by discussing the transformations that took place in Hollywood during the period of these films' creation, and how the films' directors worked within this shifting political-economic context and strived to balance their liberal agendas with the impulse toward greater commercial success. Then, I turn to the film and examine how the politics of the docudrama form influenced the way these female activists' stories were dramatized as individualistic stories of outlaw heroes. I analyze how these women's stories are told through these biopics and, in particular, the thematic and formal practices that are used to reconstruct these women's lives and activities as public history. I also examine the social, historical, and political context for these women's activism, the context of production for the films, and the influence of the prominent star images of Sally Fields and Meryl Streep in the films' feature roles.

I argue that both films present the notion of women's liberation as a problem with no clear solution. Through an analysis of the films' parallel plotlines and narratives, I demonstrate that the societal norms that oppress women and the lower classes are reinforced through the ideological biases coded into the films' traditional myths about femininity and masculinity, working-class culture, and socially-conscious heroism. I argue that, although both *Norma Rae* and *Silkwood* document the negative consequences of the women's public activism, especially on their personal lives, the films fail to critique the societal conventions that restrict the women from breaking out of their traditional roles as housewife and caregiver. Such indictment of the female characters, I argue, hampers the effect of the women's political activism and impedes spectators' potential identification with the female protagonists.

Chapters five and six consider how the most recent embodiments of the female labor activist in the films *Live Nude Girls Unite!* (2000), *Erin Brockovich* (2000), and *North Country* (2005), demonstrate the endurance of the book's previous findings and represent the current state of feminism, labor, and class issues at the turn of the century. I argue that, as these three films re-imagine the female labor heroine, the representations they feature provide an updated version reflective of the female activist in the wake of post-feminism and the decline of the American labor movement, and also extend the ideological trajectories established by their cinematic predecessors.

In chapter five I argue that *Live Nude Girls Unite!* shows how the gains made by the feminist movement have been incorporated into the culture more than thirty years later, as well as how the female labor activists in the film explicitly complicate aspects of second-wave feminism while they critique the cultural politics that continue to oppress women. The film ultimately offers an example of how third-wave feminists may fight to overcome such obstacles, and that the values of solidarity and collectivity still exist even in today's fragmented society.

In chapter six, I argue that *Erin Brockovich* and *North Country* represent the classical Hollywood notion of the female activist in post–Reagan America. I argue that Hollywood's depiction of the female labor activist has not evolved at all in the last half century, and that the heroines of this film represent the post-feminist media's perspective of feminism as a lifestyle that women can use on their behalf when necessary, but without the political or collective imperatives prevalent in the feminism of the second-wave.

Chapter seven provides a conclusion to the book by drawing out the tensions revealed through the analyses of the previous chapters to determine the range of representations of the female labor activist and their rhetorical implications.

CHAPTER ONE

Rising Up Against the Dominant
The Multiple Transgressions of Salt of the Earth

"Whose neck shall I stand on to make me feel superior? And what will I get out of it? I don't want anything lower than I am. I'm low enough already. I want to rise. And push everything up with me as I go."

— Esperanza Quintero, *Salt of the Earth*

In John Sayles's 1981 film *Return of the Secaucus 7*, a group of old friends reunite for a weekend in the country, where they reminisce about their days as student activists in the late 1960s. The group recalls the night they were all arrested in Secaucus, New Jersey on their way to a Washington march, and how they passed the time by re-enacting the jail house scene from a little-known film called *Salt of the Earth*. Herbert Biberman's *Salt of the Earth*, released in 1954, depicts the struggles of striking Mexican American zinc miners and their wives in Silver City, New Mexico. The women of the mining community in *Salt of the Earth*, with whom the members of the Secaucus 7 so strongly identified, were wrongly imprisoned for their activism. For the group of college students portrayed in Sayles's film, *Salt of the Earth*— an obscure, independent film made nearly twenty-five years earlier — reflected their political concerns regarding issues such as sexism, racism, and class inequalities. As a result, the *Salt* story became a rallying point for their own activism. Although these former student radicals and their anecdotal experience of *Salt of the Earth* are purely fictional, during the 1960s and early 1970s the film did find an audience in many real members of the student movement. The Student Nonviolent Coordinating Committee arranged for several New York showings of *Salt of the Earth* in 1965, and soon afterward the film reached a sort of cult status on college campuses, copies circulated through film schools and women's studies departments, and the film became a point of focus for those interested in Mexican American history, Cold War hysteria, or labor studies. The film experienced yet another resurrection in the 1980s through cable television broadcasts (sponsored by the AFL-CIO) and the making of the 1982 documentary *A Crime to Fit the Punishment*, which recounts the story of the film's production. More recently, *Salt* has been revived once again through an airing on the Turner Classic Movies network in 1997, as well as the 1999 release of a DVD version issued by the Library of Congress in their initiative to preserve U.S. films of cultural and historical significance.[1]

What is perhaps even more interesting than *Salt of the Earth*'s continued longevity is the mere fact of the film's creation during what many scholars have now come to regard as the compelling repressions of 1950s America, including the "paranoid" climate surrounding perceived Communist threat, the resistance to women's emancipation, and a rhetorical milieu that served to suppress most deviations from white, middle-class decorum.[2] A rare film with manifest themes of feminist, ethnic, and class consciousness, *Salt of the Earth* has been lauded in recent years by political and nonpolitical critics alike as one of the finest radical films ever made in the United States.[3] According to Tom Miller, "No movie before or since has attempted to reflect such honorable and progressive sensibilities while simultaneously attracting the venom of its own industry."[4] Indeed, those involved in the film's production faced numerous obstacles and overcame difficult challenges in order to express their left-leaning political views — views that not only were quite progressive during the 1950s but, in many ways, vastly unpopular.

The periodic revivals of *Salt of the Earth* over nearly forty years may be attributed to its bold and explicit handling of a variety of themes, which not only defied convention during the period in which the film was produced, but remain, in many ways, as poignant today as they were then. As "an eloquent cinematic statement of resistance to the predominant social, economic, and intellectual themes" of its time, *Salt of the Earth* is a rare example of a film that gives rhetorical expression to topics on society's margins, and a voice to those whose lives are affected by them.[5] This chapter examines the dynamic interplay of the various political, economic, aesthetic, and ideological processes that constituted the rhetorical function of *Salt of the Earth*, in particular the film's deft handling of socio-political issues at the intersection of racial, class, and gender politics often overlooked in films of that period. Through its transgression of a variety of dominant institutions and practices, *Salt of the Earth* constructs a unique vision that provokes spectators to consider a different way of thinking — one that values community over individualism and equality over domination. More specifically, *Salt*'s multiple transgressions allow for a

Salt of the Earth features the militancy of women's labor activism on behalf of their mine worker husbands, however, the more significant achievement of the women's determination and sacrifice on the picket line was the hard-won respect and movement toward greater gender equality in the home that they earned from their husbands. Here Esperanza Quintero (played by Rosaura Revueltas) is shown with her husband, Ramón (Juan Chacón), who by the conclusion of the film comes to thank her for her strength and dignity.

revolutionary portrayal of workers, and in particular one brave working-class heroine, on the margins of society. The film's narrative explicitly dramatizes the repression suffered by Mexican American members of the working class, and especially the working-class women of that community; however, it is primarily the main character, Esperanza Quintero, the female labor activist who gives voice to the power of the oppressed and represents the collective will of the people to rise up against the dominant. This important plot point also served as an allegory representative of the filmmakers' own resistance against the Hollywood "Red Scare" and the conservative politics that had come to define the film industry.

Cold War Hollywood and the Leftist Political Film

Salt of the Earth was an independent production in the golden age of the Hollywood studio when only a handful of major corporations ruled the industry, exerting onerous creative control and effectively insuring the hegemony of Hollywood product.[6] Consequently, a film like *Salt of the Earth* incited the wrath of many in the motion picture industry.[7] The inhospitable climate that existed for a film produced outside of the Hollywood system necessitated a significant level of innovation, devotion, and determination on the part of those who contributed to its making. Before filming had even finished, critics began lambasting *Salt* for its alleged Communist bent. *Salt of the Earth* was like no other film of its time, in part as a result of the "hard-won battles on the parts of mine union members, wives, and Hollywood filmmakers alike" to find a way for their vision to materialize, for their story to be told.[8] As a self-styled production arising out of the restrictive culture of the Hollywood film industry during the mid-twentieth century, *Salt of the Earth* would expose the limitations of American filmmaking and open up a new space in which the development of a reformist film of social and political magnitude could be achieved.

Salt of the Earth is a semi-documentary that recreates the events surrounding the strike of Local 890 of the International Union of Mine, Mill, and Smelter Workers in Bayard, New Mexico in 1950.[9] The strike began as a protest against the Empire Zinc Corporation over pay inequality and poor working conditions suffered by the miners, most of whom were Mexican Americans living in the company-owned village. In the film, an accidental explosion that severely injured a miner excavating a cave — an incident that happened far too frequently — incites a protest. Consequently, the union locals unanimously agree to a work stoppage and decide to strike for improved worker safety regulations. In conjunction with the miners, the miners' wives begin to evaluate their own working conditions and request that better sanitation and indoor plumbing in the company-provided housing be added to the union's strike demands. For the men, hot running water is a trivial concern compared to their own safety on the job, so the women's request is tabled. Within weeks, however, the men face a Taft-Hartley injunction that threatens the arrest of any miner found on a picket line obstructing outside workers (scabs) from entering the mines. In a highly contested discussion at a community meeting, the men reluctantly form a plan with the women: the women will take over the picket lines since the injunction prohibited only mine employees from striking. This turn of events not only allows the strike to continue, but brings on a surprising reversal of roles within the community. As the men are forced into the home, they realize the plight of the women and their domestic responsibilities, while the women on the picket lines realize a sense of their own identities as actors on a public stage, and as an integral part of the larger community and its survival.

A film such as *Salt of the Earth*, which addresses social issues with an eye toward change, was an unusual Hollywood production in 1954, but not unprecedented. After World War II, Hollywood producers, directors, and writers began to introduce increasing amounts of social content into their films. According to Dorothy Jones, this type of "adult" movie fare reached an all-time high in the last half of 1947 when twenty-eight percent of movies were devoted to exploring social themes, such as anti–Semitism, racism, and mental illness.[10] Yet, by 1954, the number of social problem films had declined sharply, accounting for only nine percent of all films that year. This shift was in part because of the increased production of war films and "escapist" fare, such as musicals, westerns, and adventure films. However, the primary cause of this major decline in socially-significant productions more than likely was the reaction of the motion picture industry to the political climate that had begun to dominate Hollywood during the late 1940s.[11]

In an attempt to assuage the accusations of subversive leftism that had begun to plague the motion picture industry, Hollywood quickly shifted production from social problem films to films with explicit anti–Communist messages. The Hollywood industry fell victim to the spread of Communist paranoia years before the larger American public began to feel its effects and, by 1946, "anticommunist rhetoric was ... the common currency of Hollywood politics."[12] As a result, the phenomenon of anti–Communist witch-hunting came to be associated in the public mind with Hollywood. By 1954, the year in which *Salt of the Earth* was produced, the industry had become unrecognizable to many of those who had entered it decades earlier. The growing concern over Communist sympathizers in the Hollywood industry began circulating as early as the late 1930s, reaching its apex in reactions to the Hollywood labor wars of 1945–1946.

For years, Hollywood workers had supported the mass labor movement, along with numerous other rank-and-file movements across the landscape of American industry. As a result, between 1929 and 1945, the motion picture industry became one hundred percent unionized, a percentage far ahead of national trends.[13] Such worker advances had created a number of large union organizations in Hollywood, to the dismay of many high-ranking industry officials. These groups included the International Alliance of Theatrical Stage Employees (IATSE), which organized already existing unions of skilled and semi-skilled manual laborers, such as painters, carpenters, and electricians, and the Conference of Studio Unions (CSU) formed in 1941 in order to give all craft unions the industry-wide unity IATSE had achieved. Such organizations arose out of workers' struggles to improve their professional situation, and their goals included higher wages, fewer hours, regularized hiring practices, standardized contracts, and effective arbitration.[14]

By 1945 the CSU had enrolled nearly ten thousand members and constituted a serious threat to both the production studios and IATSE — a situation that sparked the first instance of outright Communist allegations among Hollywood insiders. In March 1945, IATSE and CSU came to blows over which union would represent set decorators. This conflict resulted in a CSU-declared strike that caused many craft unions affiliated with IATSE to refuse to cross picket lines.[15] IATSE, under the leadership of Roy Brewer, already had a reputation in the industry as a somewhat corrupt organization more inclined to appease the needs of studio executives than to insure the well being of its workers, and its actions during

One. Rising Up Against the Dominant   21

the strike supported these allegations.[16] Brewer decided the best way to win the battle for union jurisdiction would be to accuse the CSU of Communist domination, an action that would ultimately threaten the careers of thousands of industry laborers. Brewer also colluded with the Motion Picture Alliance for the Preservation of American Ideals (MPA), a group considered to be anti-labor and created in 1944 for the sole purpose of fighting Communist influence in Hollywood and "turn[ing] off the faucets which dripped red water into film scripts."[17] During the eight month strike, the MPA, along with Brewer, fueled rumors of a Communist-led CSU and, by October 1945, had swayed several studio heads, including Jack L. Warner and Louis B. Meyer, to join their crusade against the CSU's belligerent Communism. With the additional support of major industry figures, such as Walt Disney and Gary Cooper, the MPA initiated a campaign for the expulsion of Communism from the motion picture business and brought national prominence to the problem of "Red" infiltration in the U.S. culture industry. According to Larry Ceplair and Steven Englund, "As a symbol of 'dangerous' radicalism, Hollywood was only the tip of an iceberg, but it was a flashing neon tip that captivated the nation's attention."[18]

Shortly after Winston Churchill warned that "the Communist parties ... [had] been raised to pre-eminence and power far beyond their numbers and [were] seeking everywhere to obtain totalitarian control" in his now famous "Iron Curtain" speech on March 5, 1946, Cold War paranoia began to invade Hollywood and soon Red-baiting became an explicit, industry-wide practice.[19] In April 1946, Eric Johnston, the newly elected head of the Motion Picture Producers' Association, wrote an article that appeared on the front page of the Screen Actor's Guild magazine and echoed Churchill's prophesy. In this piece, entitled "Utopia is Production," Johnston persuaded Hollywood leaders that they epitomized a new era in American history and, as such, should put aside their "class rhetoric" and embrace their role as protectors of the dream of "democratic capitalism" in the face of "Communist" threat.[20] Johnston's desire for a Communist-free movie industry would soon be actualized by members of the House Un-American Activities Committee (HUAC), the resulting Hollywood Red Scare, and the consequent discharge of alleged Communist sympathizers. These circumstances radically changed not only the landscape of the American motion picture industry, but the lives and careers of hundreds of industry members, including those who came to make the motion picture *Salt of the Earth* nearly a decade later.

In 1947, the MPA sent a barrage of letters to members of Congress regarding their suspicions of Communism in the movie industry, essentially beckoning HUAC to Hollywood. Consequently, hearings were scheduled for two weeks in October.[21] The House Committee labeled Hollywood a hotbed of un–Americanism, "seeing embodied in the industry all that was wrong with twentieth-century life — moral experimentation, cultural mixing, a militant class movement and middle-class activism."[22] Hollywood produced a number of "friendly" witnesses to corroborate this charge. Consequently, twenty-three well-known personalities, including Ronald Reagan, Robert Montgomery, and Robert Taylor, as well as IATSE's Roy Brewer, appeared during the first week of the hearings to provide testimony that indicted their colleagues. Thought to be the purveyors of these wrongs, nineteen "unfriendly" witnesses were initially subpoenaed by the committee, with eleven called to testify during the second week. Only one, Bertolt Brecht, a German playwright, answered the committee's questions and denied association with the Communist Party. Brecht returned to Europe shortly after the hearings. The remaining witnesses, the now legendary "Hollywood Ten," declined to answer what Committee Chairman J. Parnell Thomas called "The $64 Question": "Are you now or have you ever been a member of the Communist Party?"[23] Each pleaded the First Amendment in the hopes of making a political statement that would challenge the legality of the Committee's existence and defend the tradition of free speech in the United States.[24] All ten were cited for contempt of Congress, two were sentenced to six-month prison terms, the remaining eight served one year.

Film critic Richard Maltby describes the changes experienced by the industry in the wake of the hearings, arguing that Hollywood turned from "a dream factory" into a "paranoid fantasy"— a shift that significantly altered not only the ideological climate of the industry, but the content of Hollywood films.[25] On November 24, 1947 at a meeting of the Producer's Association at the Waldorf-Astoria Hotel in New York, Johnston initiated what became known as the Hollywood blacklist by stating: "We will not knowingly employ a Communist or a member of any party or group which advocates overthrow of the Government of the United States by force or by any illegal or unconstitutional method."[26] Guided by the tenets advocated by novelist Ayn Rand in her *Screen Guide for Americans*— of which the main precepts were "Don't Deify the Common Man," "Don't Glorify the Collective," and "Don't Smear Industrialists"— the industry vowed to stop producing social problem films and other movies considered "un-American."[27]

Unwilling to produce films bereft of political content in order to concede to the pressures of 1950s Hollywood, several committed filmmakers founded the Independent Productions Corporation (IPC), and *Salt of the Earth* became their first and only project. Notable among this group of Hollywood outsiders were IPC's principle officers, director Herbert Biberman and producer Adrian Scott, both members of the "Hollywood Ten." The two men formed IPC in September 1951 with a number of other blacklisted artists in order to have the freedom to make the kinds of films they felt Hollywood was restricting. According to producer Paul Jarrico, a founding member of IPC, "It wasn't until 1951, when we were good and dead professionally, that we could get involved in movies that packed a real social and political wallop."[28]

Believing film was the one truly democratic medium capable of reaching large numbers of diverse people, Biberman looked upon IPC as an opportunity to "take an appeal to the people of the country, in films."[29] Biberman, along with Jarrico and scriptwriter Michael Wilson, imagined *Salt of the Earth* as a platform to share their views, as active and principled radicals, with the public at large. All three men had been actively involved in the Communist Party and by the early 1950s had become respected party figures. All three also came from middle-class families and were drawn to political activism early in life and, according to James Lorence, their similar backgrounds united them as cultural workers in "a commitment to the production of engaged art that would grapple with important ideas as part of the advance toward a better society."[30] Although their company already had four projects under consideration, when the filmmakers heard about the Empire Zinc strike and the hardships of the Mexican American workers, they felt they had found a story worthy of the progressive enterprise they were striving to create.

Just as Biberman, Jarrico, and Wilson had been kicked out of Hollywood for their Communist associations, the International Union of Mine, Mill, and Smelter Workers (Mine-Mill), the organization that represented the workers at Empire Zinc and would eventually sponsor the production of *Salt*, had been kicked out of the Congress of Industrial Organizations (CIO) for alleged Communist ties. Another victim of the Cold War mentality, Mine-Mill was purged from the CIO because it was believed to be too radical and a threat to the CIO's merger with the American Federation of Labor (AFL). The story behind *Salt of the Earth*, then, was a result of the democratic collaboration between the Mine-Mill local in Bayard, the filmmakers whose own story paralleled that of the strikers: a universal morality play that allowed them to dramatize their own sense of injustice as "a crime to fit the punishment."[31]

For several months, Wilson visited the miners and their families in an effort to convey their tale through the film script in a manner as "true to life" as possible. During those visits, Wilson would allow the members of the mining community to read his drafts and suggest revisions, which resulted in a final script that met the satisfaction of both the filmmakers and nearly four hundred members of the community on which the film was based. Shooting on the film began on January 20, 1953, in Silver City, New Mexico. The film company had already faced the challenge of assembling a crew — a task made almost impossible because of Brewer's insistence that no member of his IATSE would work on a film made by Hollywood Communists. The next hurdle was casting, also made difficult by the Screen Actors Guild and its conservative president, former "friendly witness" Ronald Reagan, who guaranteed that any actor who wanted to keep working in Hollywood would not dare to sign on to a film produced by renegade leftists.[32] Deciding that it would be more authentic — and more consonant with the filmmakers' own commitments to socialist practices — to have the parts played by Latinos, the production staff hired Mexican actress Rosaura Revueltas for the main character and Juan Chacón, one of the miners and a member of Local 890, to take the male lead. The remainder of the cast also was made up of real-life miners and their wives, with the exception of Hollywood actor and fellow blacklistee Will Greer as the sheriff. The project seemed to be progressing forward at last until, in Biberman and Jarrico's words, "a storm of hysterical publicity burst over [the project]" in late February.[33]

The first press attack, which appeared on February 9, 1953, in *The Hollywood Reporter* gossip column, read:

> H'wood Reds are shooting a feature-length anti–American racial issue propaganda movie at Silver City, N.M. SAG Prexy Walter Pidgeon got the tip in

a letter from a schoolteacher fan in N.M. Pidge immediately alerted FBI, State Department, House Un-American Activities Committee, and Central Intelligence Agency.[34]

Over the next two weeks the industry papers, as well as the popular press, reported falsities about the activities in Silver City. It was reported that the shooting was taking place not far from the Los Alamos atomic proving ground and that the film included a sequence of mob violence against "Negroes" who were brought into the mining town in carloads. The most detrimental press followed an inflammatory speech given on the House floor by California Democratic Congressman Donald Jackson. Jackson reported: "Mr. Speaker, I have received reports of the sequences filmed to date.... This picture is deliberately designed to inflame racial hatreds.... [It] is a new weapon for Russia."[35] A *Newsweek* article that appeared the following week, entitled "Reds in the Desert," reported on Jackson's denunciation of the film and erroneously stated that the eight thousand residents of Silver City were "up in arms" over not only the film's content, but the Communist-tainted backgrounds of the creators behind it.[36]

Throughout the storm of public controversy IPC received notices from their various contractors that the service providers would be severing ties to the project: Pathé Laboratory decided to no longer process their film, the local theater refused to continue private projection of the dailies, their workman's compensation insurance policy was dropped, and IPC's accountants informed the group that they would no longer handle their business.[37] The most crushing defeat came when Immigration and Naturalization officials arrested Revueltas on the charge of an improperly stamped passport and, after hearings in Albuquerque, deported her back to Mexico. Soon after, the atmosphere on the set turned dangerous when vigilantes attempted to run the production crew out of town. A delegation was sent to the union hall, which was being used as a production studio, with the message, "Get out of town in twelve hours or go out in black boxes," and Clinton Jencks, the international representative for Mine-Mill, was physically assaulted in a parking lot and found his car shot through with bullet holes.[38] The film company was forced to end the shoot on March 6, yet the attempts to suppress the production of *Salt of the Earth* continued. The threats, industry boycotts, and negative publicity followed the film, and the filmmakers, through the post-production process.

Despite the hardships, *Salt of the Earth* was completed in 1954, but never achieved a general release. The film enjoyed an excellent initial showing at the Eighty-sixth Street Grande in New York City, where it completed a ten-week run and broke all previous attendance records. Almost immediately after the premiere, however, industry gatekeepers sprang into action and pressured theater owners to ban the film, or risk losing the opportunity to show major Hollywood productions. Even when some theater owners resisted the threats, the projectionists, most likely members of the projectionist union, refused to run the film. As a result, *Salt*'s subsequent showings were held in small movie houses in New York, Los Angeles, and San Francisco and the film disappeared from theaters less than three months after its release.[39]

Because of the hype over the film's production, a number of critics attended the initial showings ready to denounce the Red-tainted production. Several took this position in their critiques of the film, notably Pauline Kael in her extended review for *Sight and Sound*. Kael labeled the film "as clear a piece of Communist propaganda as we have had in many years," and concluded that "a film like *Salt of the Earth* seems so ridiculously and patently false that it requires something like determination to consider that those who made it believe in it."[40] In a similar vein, the *Newsweek* review summarized the film this way: "the film's final effect is wholly propagandistic — Red-tinged."[41] The majority of the reviews, however, were either mixed or quite positive. The *Time* reviewer offered that "within the propagandistic limits it sets, [the film] is a work of vigorous art," and the *Variety* reviewer noted that "it comes as something of a surprise to find [the film] a good, highly dramatic and emotion-charged piece of work that, in its pictorial values at least, tells its story straight."[42] That same reviewer also cautioned, "One would have to become quite analytical to read the alleged 'Red' line into this Paul Jarrico production," but added that, as a propaganda picture, *Salt* showings belonged in union halls rather than motion picture theaters where "audiences come for entertainment and not lectures couched in dramatics."[43] Bosley Crowther also noted his surprise in a review for *The New York Times*, writing that he found the film "in substance, simply a strong pro-labor film with a particularly sympathetic interest in the Mexican Americans with whom it deals." He went on to praise the script as "tautly muscled" and capable of developing "considerable personal drama, raw emotion, and power."[44]

As the majority of these reviewers' responses to the film demonstrate, the motion picture industry's focus on *Salt of the Earth* as a platform for Communist allegiances was largely the result of rumors and exaggerated accusations. Although *Salt* may not have lived up to its "subversive" label, it was a transgressive film that challenged the rhetoric of the "new American Way" that had begun to influence Hollywood projects of the period. Following the 1947 HUAC hearings, the Motion Picture Producers president Eric Johnston vowed, "We'll have no more *Grapes of Wrath*, we'll have no more *Tobacco Roads*. We'll have no more films that show the seamy side of American life. We'll have no pictures that deal with labor strikes"—and Hollywood productions over the next decade reflected that commitment.[45] As an independent production, Brian Neve attests, "*Salt of the Earth* was a rare effort to beat the system," and the end result was a product of the indignation of artists who felt abandoned by their industry.[46] The film these artists produced was a response to what they perceived as an oppressively conservative political climate prevalent in 1950s Hollywood. Indeed, one could argue that the film's production was a resistant act—an exigency born of the historical context of the film's creation and its creators' disgruntlement with the film industry, and expressed through the films' formal qualities.

Aesthetic Transgressions: Expressing Politics through Cinematic Form

Owing to the circumstances of its creation, including its independent status and troubled production history, *Salt of the Earth* presented a number of formal challenges for the filmmakers. Most significantly, however, they faced the especially difficult rhetorical task of finding a way to solicit spectators' identification with the film. Linda Dittmar notes the complexity of this challenge:

> Ultimately, [the film] had to move audiences to respect, not just pity, a denigrated community, to embrace a political position that contemporary national myths demonized as subversive, and to accept women as equal partners in defining society's political and economic as well as familial character.[47]

The radical nature of the film's message necessitated deviation from the classical Hollywood style. Although the film adhered to the situation-complication-resolution narrative model, its overarching theme of the interrelated struggles of workers, Mexican Americans, and women for dignity and equality warranted an innovation of form capable of rhetorically constructing such a vision. These aesthetic choices constituted another strategy of resistance on the part of the filmmakers and their production. These aesthetic qualities also set the project apart from the kinds of films being produced in the United States during the early 1950s.

The great majority of films coming out of Hollywood during the period of *Salt of the Earth*'s release included an array of film genres, including science-fiction films, such as the prototypical *Them* (1954) about an invasion of giant, mutant ants; westerns, notably *Broken Lance* (1954) and *Sitting Bull* (1954); and musicals, including *Seven Brides for Seven Brothers* (1954), *A Star is Born* (1954), and *Oklahoma* (1955). Beyond being fairly simplistic and highly formulaic, these films often upheld style over content in order to capitalize on audiences' increasingly heightened appetite for spectacle. As far as Hollywood executives were concerned, the purpose of film in the 1950s was to offer audiences seeking amusement the kind of big-budget productions they could not find on their television sets. In the midst of the "that's entertainment" ideology that dominated the motion picture industry in 1954, *Salt of the Earth* presented audiences with an authentic portrayal of the immigrant working poor and the harsh realism of their lives in an American mining town.

Salt of the Earth differed from other films of its time primarily because of its blend of Hollywood convention and the creative risks of an independent production, which distinguished the film as progressive, yet allowed more accessibility to diverse audiences than an avant-garde or experimental production.[48] On the whole, *Salt* contains a traditional, organized plot that winds its way to a relatively uncomplicated dénouement; employs elements of melodrama that create simplistic archetypes of the "good" laborers versus the "evil" establishment and the characteristic happy ending; and uses resources such as framing, camera angles, editing, and sound track to underline its themes rather than complicate them — all conventions to which an average audience could relate.[49] Yet, the film also employs a stark visual style and an honest portrait of labor in the American Southwest that captures the poignancy of cultural struggle localized within a particular New Mexico mining community's saga. Although the film focuses primarily on two main characters, husband and wife

Ramón and Esperanza Quintero, the adversity faced by these characters represents the hardships that confront the entire community of Mexican Americans living and working in the Grant County mining village, and signifies the broader social/historical situation of working-class people throughout the United States.

Committed to documenting the stark socialist realism of working-class lives in American society, Jarrico and Biberman looked for ways to avoid the pitfalls of naturalism, or a mere surface record of actual events. Rather, the filmmakers aspired to create a work of art that attempted to "blend the social authenticity of documentary form with the personal authenticity of dramatic form."[50] That is, they believed that the film should express the social and economic hardships historically faced by members of the working class in terms that could be accessible to the people thus represented. In order to meet these objectives, the filmmakers decided to fictionalize the story of the miners' strike through the "personal" story of Esperanza Quintero, the female protagonist, and borrowed a style that had recently become popularized in Italian cinema, Neorealism.

NEOREALISM AND THE POLITICS OF THE EVERYDAY

Beginning with the opening credit sequence, *Salt of the Earth* invites the spectator to witness the struggle of working-class people, which the film portrays as an existence tainted by drudgery and banality. The first visuals, which appear behind the credits, consist of a medium shot of a woman mechanically attending to her daily chores. Only the woman's legs, arms, and torso are visible in the frame as she drives an axe through pieces of plywood against a large tree stump. The remainder of the sequence reveals the woman, shot from behind, undertaking a variety of tasks: chopping and hauling wood, building a fire, boiling a large tub of water for the day's laundry, and hand-scrubbing the clothes in a steel tub. By chronicling the subject's actions with her back to the camera, the group of shots creates an image of a faceless woman who could easily be any woman, anywhere. This scene of an anonymous woman laboring systematically through her domestic duties, which opens the film, highlights the ordinariness of working-class people and their everyday existence. Although perhaps somewhat simplistic and condescending in its depiction of the woman's toil, this brief montage renders textually the film's representation of working-class reality in its historical concreteness. The central character presented in the opening sequences functions as both an individual and a type expressive of this larger social group.[51]

Over the last shot of the opening sequence a caption reads: "Our scene is New Mexico, land of the free Americans who inspired this film, home of the brave Americans who played most of its roles." The screen then fades to black and brightens again onto a shot of the desert landscape dotted with mine shafts, which is followed by a series of quick dissolves that orient the spectator to the New Mexico scene in which the story will unfold. The second shot in the series reveals the natural beauty of the desert and mountains, creating a juxtaposition with the first shot and emphasizing how the mining industry and its heavy equipment have marred the once pristine environment. These first two scenes, as well as the remainder of the film, function rhetorically as a result of the film's employment of Neorealism, a formal film style invented by Italian filmmakers with a social conscious working between 1945 and 1952 that both dramatizes a Marxist critique of society and acts as a means of consciousness-raising between the spectator and the film.[52]

The term Neorealism began as a literary designation, coined in 1930, to describe a style that arose in reaction to autobiographical lyricism and, according to filmmaker Arnaldo Bocelli, offered instead a "strenuously analytic, crude, dramatic representation of a human condition tormented between will and inclination by the anguish of the senses, the conventions of bourgeois life, [and] the emptiness and boredom of existence."[53] Following World War II, Mussolini's overthrow, and the Nazi expulsion, a number of Italian filmmakers used film techniques to dramatize the kinds of stories that they now possessed the freedom to tell, including the oppression of Italian workers and the peasant class. For example, Gerald Mast and Bruce Kawin note that directors such as Roberto Rossellini, Vittorio De Sica, and Luchino Visconti strived to make films that would allow them to

> show things as they are, not as they seem, nor as the bourgeois world would have them appear; to write fictions about the human side of representative social, political, and economic conditions; ... to capture and reflect reality with little or no compromise; to reveal the everyday rather than the exception; and to show a person's relationship to the social environment.[54]

This movement toward such a style of filmmaking represented its makers' partisan hopes for social justice and, as a reflection of such a leftist world view, the films these men produced functioned morally, politically, and epistemologically.[55]

Many of the innovations that defined this style, however, were derived less from the filmmakers' philosophical motivations and more from the difficult economic conditions they faced — a circumstance shared by the creators of *Salt*. Raw film stock was scarce in Italy after the war, as was money to construct sets and hire professional actors, which made the polish of controlled lighting and studio filming impossible. The results of working under such circumstances were frequent long takes, the use of natural lighting, unobtrusive editing, gritty environments, and a vernacular dialogue suitable for untrained actors — all of which was in stark contrast to the glitz and glamour coming out of Hollywood. Yet, despite the nontraditional characteristics of this film style, Neorealism's formal techniques ultimately initiated a popular film movement that generated a variety of innovations and influenced politically-committed filmmakers, especially in Europe.[56] The legacies of this revolutionary style are clearly evident in *Salt of the Earth*, the first — and perhaps the only — American film to participate in the Neorealist movement.[57]

The remainder of *Salt of the Earth* builds upon the film's first scenes; the woman shown in the opening sequence, Esperanza Quintero, tells the story of the New Mexico mining community of which she is a part. Several overlapping themes make up this story: the relationship between Esperanza and her husband Ramón, the labor struggles of the Mexican Americans working in the mining industry, the community's endeavor to overcome their exploitation at the hands of the Anglo mine owners, and the emergence of the community's women, which insured that they, too, would achieve greater respect. Incorporating these themes, the film's plot charts the progress of the mining village's members from despondent individuals into an enlightened community united through their common fight for human dignity. The film's structural elements, such as plot devices and thematic content, function simultaneously with the stylistic elements of Neorealism to collapse the immediate political and moral aspects of these men and women's circumstances into a "new synthesis of life and art."[58]

Even before Esperanza Quintero's face is fully revealed in *Salt of the Earth*, the spectator hears her voice. Immediately after the opening credits, a woman's voice is heard over the image on the screen: "How shall I begin my story that has no beginning?" As a sequence of shots unfolds detailing the scenes where the story will take place, this woman explains in voice-over the significance of the landscape for the people of her village, and how her family's roots go "deep in this place, deeper than the pines, deeper than the mine shafts." She explains how the "Anglos" changed the landscape, and renamed her home "Zinc Town," when they laid claim to the land and the minerals it produced. As the shot of the Quintero family home dissolves, the next shot reveals her face for the first time in a close-up as she hangs out the laundry. In a voice-over narration, she informs the audience, "My name is Esperanza. Esperanza Quintero. I am a miner's wife."

The next scenes show the two main characters, Esperanza and her husband Ramón Quintero, in relation to each other and to their social environment. While Esperanza, who is pregnant, tries to take care of the ironing, tend to her young daughter, and console her son when he returns from school with a black eye from fighting with the "Anglos," Ramón tries to handle the pressures of his job at the mine, which includes nearly being caught in an explosion caused by a faulty fuse. Throughout the film such parallels occur; for example, in an early scene Esperanza speaks with a group of other wives about the difficulties of completing domestic chores without indoor plumbing while Ramón and the miners voice their complaints about safety conditions to the management. By crosscutting scenes that illustrate the daily demands on both Esperanza and Ramón, the film emphasizes how the circumstances of this couple's lives have taken a toll on them both as individuals and on their marriage. The focus on Esperanza and Ramón's relationship also adds an emotional dimension to the larger story of the labor struggle in the mining community. This technique is used frequently in *Salt of the Earth* and follows a tradition in Marxist thought that also became prominent in Neorealist films, repeatedly showing how "unjust and perverted social structures threaten to warp and pervert the essential and internal human values."[59]

One of the most poignant scenes of the film again uses the crosscutting technique to show the extent of the pain and suffering that the strike has brought to the couple, and the depths of their bond with one another. About a third of the way through the film, the men have established a picket line and the women have formed a ladies' auxiliary to serve the men coffee and tacos out of a small shed. At one point, the Quinteros' son, Luís, yells to his father from over the hill: "Papa! We've seen 'em! Two scabs! Over there!" Ramón runs down the hill and confronts one of the scabs, a former co-worker from the mine, while Esperanza realizes she has gone into labor. In a rapid succession of shots Ramón is handcuffed by the sheriffs as Esperanza cries: "Luís, the baby! Get the women! Quick!" As the percussion-heavy music swells in the background, the sheriff takes Ramón into the patrol car and begins pistol-whipping him while the strikers scramble to find help for Esperanza. Close-ups of Esperanza crying in pain and begging God to let her child be born are rapidly crosscut with close-ups of Ramón crying out in pain as the sheriff and his deputy punch him in the stomach. The scene ends with a close-up of Esperanza crying out "Ramón!" and a dissolve into a close-up of Ramón, now bleeding, crying out "Esperanza!" During this scene, Esperanza and Ramón are visually linked; their identities merge through the dissolve, and their love for each other overrides all of the differences between them. The formal style of this sequence captures the physical and emotional pain that comes from both their present circumstances and their larger social situation. The scene not only underscores the strength of the Quintero's relationship, it also foreshadows the unity between men and women that will come to define the community as a whole—and allow the strike to be won.

The relationships between the miners and their wives constitute a major theme of the film, a division that creates a running tension in the film and a desire on the part of the spectator for the community to eventually resolve their differences and unify in order to overcome their collective struggles. A number of scenes early in the film function both formally and thematically to accentuate the division between the men and the women in the community along gender lines. The film visually illustrates this separation when the women first address the issue of sanitation as a labor demand of their own. For example, in one of the film's pivotal scenes, a loud siren alerts the community that there has been an accident at the mine. The women, many of whom were outside already completing their daily chores, run down to the mine to see what happened. In the meantime, the miners demand that the supervisor listen to their safety concerns. When he refuses, the miners decide to shut down the operation. The scene concludes with several parallel shots of the men standing uniformly in a large group, which signifies their solidarity against the mine management who stands opposite them. These shots of the men are juxtaposed against a shot of the women also grouped together on the hill.

Complete silence emphasizes the dramatic moment while a group shot of the men looking collectively upward rapidly cuts to a shot of the women gathered on the hill above, symbolizing the similarity between their situation and the men's. One woman slowly raises a crude sign that reads: We Want Sanitation Not Discrimination. The shot cuts back to the men, who look at the women with wide-eyed expressions of surprise. The final two parallel shots show the large group of men shot from above and the large group of women on the hill shot from below, which functions to dramatize the distance that separates the two groups — both physically and politically. From this moment, it becomes clear that the women's demands, and subsequent activism, will become a major crisis that the community must overcome.

The visual and symbolic gender war between the community's men and women continues over the course of the film as they battle for their separate demands. As the men struggle against the mine bosses, the women are forced to plead their case and fight their end of the battle on two fronts: in the face of both the mining company and their own husbands. Depictions similar to the scene with the women on the hill occur throughout the film and serve to catalogue the gendered segregation within the community. This segregation becomes most evident when the men form the initial picket line during the strike and the women are relegated to duties in the ladies' auxiliary. Halfway through the film, however, these positions become inverted: when a Taft-Hartley injunction prohibits the men from picketing, the women take over the strike duties while the men watch from the sidelines. Yet, the divisions between the sexes remain — only their gendered roles become reversed. While the women gather together in Esperanza's living room to discuss the strategy for their activism, the men bond at the bar by lamenting their double emasculation — partially due to their inability to win the strike and partially due to their wives effectiveness in doing so. Scenes such as these also dramatize how each group distinguishes its own priorities in the labor strike independently of one another. During much of the film, *Salt of the Earth* upholds the idea of community over individualism, however, in the first two-thirds of the film, the communities formed by the miners and their wives are for the most part separated by gender. Although the women are clearly willing to enter into a community with the men (as made evident through their eager participation on the picket line, for example), the men are reluctant to recognize the women as their equal partners.

It is not until the men are forced into the roles and responsibilities traditionally undertaken by the women that they come to realize that their wives' working conditions are as deplorable as their own, and that the women deserve the same kind of labor equality as the men working in the mines. In a scene near the end of the film, for example, Ramón is shown outside hanging laundry with Antonio while the women are being held in the county jail for obstruction of justice on the picket line. The scene replicates an earlier one in which Esperanza is outside hanging clothes with Luz (Antonio's wife). Once again, the film's Neorealist style explicitly illustrates the collective hardships of working-class men and women and the shared labor practices necessary to fulfill their basic human needs. Through this scene, the film explicitly raises the issue of sexual politics as the reversal of gender roles caused by the women's absence exposes the everyday drudgery of housework, which the men now discover. The scene opens with a close-up of Ramón hanging a sheet on a clothesline and wiping sweat from his brow. While he yells at the children to stop playing in the laundry baskets, the tone of his voice betrays his frustration. Antonio calls to Ramón over the fence in Spanish: "Como va?" (How goes it?) Ramón responds with irritation, "Esto no tiene fin." (It never ends.)[60] After just a few days of standing in their wives' shoes, the men have been converted to the women's cause. Ramón confirms Esperanza's earlier complaints, lamenting in English: "Three hours just to heat enough water to wash this stuff! I'm telling you something—if this strike is ever settled—which I doubt—I'll never go back to work for that company unless they install hot running water for us. It should have been a union demand from the beginning." "You're telling me," Antonio replies. Within the film's narrative, the men quickly discover the toil of domestic labor and come to respect their wives' diligent perseverance. The revelation becomes an impetus for the men to begin questioning the gendered roles traditional to their culture.

Although the men now clearly empathize with the women's plight, they remain reluctant to accept the women's desire to break out of their domestic prison and find expanded opportunities for work within the public sphere. Antonio laments to Ramón the seemingly inevitable consequences of delving too deeply into "the woman question." He explains: "[Charley Vidal] says give 'em equality. Equality in jobs, equality in the home. Also sex equality.... He's some organizer, that Charley. He can organize a wife right out of your home." The remaining scenes of the film emphasize the community's onerous adjustment to the newly inverted social structure. While the men find solace together in the bar, and later on through a group hunting trip, the women forge their own bonds on the picket line and commiserate about the men's resistance to their wives' newfound independence. Commenting on the men's desertion of their posts on the stand-by squad (which served as a secondary form of resistance against the strike breakers), Teresa, the picket captain muses: "So they had a little taste of what it's like to be a woman and they run away. These changes come with pain." Scenes such as these focus on the personal dimension of political and economic struggle, as well as the difficult consequences of social change. Through both its visual style and narrative content, *Salt of the Earth* dramatizes the power of a community initially divided due to its sexism (but eventually united through their interlocking struggles against racism and class inequalities). According to Deborah Silverton Rosenfelt, the film's force "as a narrative structure comes largely from its acknowledgment and use of that pattern of conflict and convergence, of division and unity."[61] In the vein of Neorealist filmmaking, *Salt* not only portrays the world of the humbled and the injured, but also adopts a certain perspective on it.

Salt of the Earth emphasizes the community's initial divisions across gender lines, and their eventual alliance and victory over domination, as a didactic rumination on the ability of oppressed people to assert their dignity despite the misery surrounding them. Their convergence in light of their common quest for fairness and decency emphasizes the potential power of collective action. The story takes on an even more radical dimension, however, through the inclusion of a strong feminist theme that anticipated the feminist movement by more than a decade. The issue of women's emancipation occupies a central position in *Salt of the Earth*, and is most decisively expressed through the story of the main protagonist, Esperanza, whose own feminist emergence symbolizes the collective transformation of the community's women.

Voicing Esperanza's Story: Narrative Subjectivity and Female Emergence

Writing on *Salt of the Earth*, Margo Kasdan argues that the film traces the transformation of the community through one of its members, the film's female protagonist, Esperanza. Kasdan writes: "It is through her eyes and her voice that the viewer apprehends the events of the story.... At the outset, triply oppressed as a woman, Mexican American, and worker's wife, Esperanza becomes by the end, strong, active, and dignified."[62] Similarly, Lillian Robinson asserts, "the story of Esperanza is deliberately typified, almost archetypal. It is the social, the collective situation that matters, and that is realized through embodiment in the experience of a particular individual who we come to care about."[63] Both dramatic and recuperative, Esperanza's transformation represents the progress of the entire community, men and women, toward a new way of life based on mutual understanding, greater equality, and respect. The film reveals Esperanza's development in a series of stages, however. The juxtaposition between the strong, confident woman who narrates the story in voice-over and the woman portrayed visually in the film's plot creates an expectation, from the first lines of the film, that her eventual emergence will occur by the film's close. This formal structure — the employment of a female protagonist and the use of her first-person narration throughout the film — represents another way that the film broke new ground. According to Robinson, the character of Esperanza functions to "record ... the dynamic quality that women are bringing to our social scene."[64] Acting as both an individual heroine and a representative of a broader social type, Esperanza embodies the struggles of one woman and of an entire community, while also showing their — and her own — potential for resistance.

Directly after the film's opening sequence, a scene begins in which Esperanza completes her ironing in the cramped kitchen of the small house. In voice-over, Esperanza, the narrator, orients spectators to the starting point of the story they are about to experience:

> Who can say where it began, my story? I do not know. But this day I remember as the beginning of an end. It was my Saint's Day. I was thirty-five years old. A day of celebration. And I was seven months gone with my third child.

This statement immediately distinguishes the "new" Esperanza who narrates the story from the "old" Esperanza shown in the recreation of the story's main acts. The Esperanza we hear embodies a sense of agency missing in the Esperanza we see. The narrator demarcates with assurance the point when things began to change for her and for her community, and assertively justifies her claim to be the only person who can tell this story. In contrast, the Esperanza on screen appears passive and unsure of herself as she acts out the events comprising the first third of the film. Esperanza's voice-over functions rhetorically by not only pointing out this incongruity between her image on the screen and her active role as narrator, but it also creates an expectation that her transformation will be rendered over the course of the film.

In one of the film's early scenes, Esperanza timidly approaches her husband after dinner, saying softly, "I don't like to bother you," and goes on to inform him that they are a payment behind on their newly purchased radio and that the store is threatening repossession. The expression on her face — a vacant stare with parted lips — reveals her uneasiness and humiliation at having to make this request of her husband. Ramón replies angrily that it is Esperanza's fault for wanting the radio in the first place. "'No money down. Easy term payments.' I tell you something: this installment plan, it's the curse of the working man," he yells as he slams his coffee cup on the console. Esperanza rushes to polish the spot where he struck the radio. As Ramón goes into the kitchen to wash his face before he heads to the union to discuss the strike, Esperanza follows him. Ramón clearly has forgotten Esperanza's birthday, and she quickly hides the cake in the cupboard. With tears in her eyes and a pained look of rejection on her face, Esperanza says in despair: "Alright. Have your strike. I'll have my baby. But no hospital will take me, because I'll be a striker's wife. The store will cut off our credit, and the kids will go hungry. And we'll get behind on the payments again, and they'll come and take away the radio —" Ramón interrupts, "Is that all you care about? The radio? Can't you think of anything except yourself?" to which Esperanza responds, in tears, "If I think of myself it's because you never think of me. Never. Never." "Stop it! The children are watching!" Ramón scolds her.

While this scene shows how the harsh political and economic conditions of the mining industry have begun to strain the Quintero's marriage, it also illustrates Esperanza's status in that union. Ramón, unable to see his wife's struggle beyond his own, chastises her for wanting the radio. Yelling, "But you had to have it, didn't you? It was so nice to listen to," Ramón simultaneously mocks and scolds his wife while he readily denies her even the simple pleasure she so enjoys. As the film unfolds, however, Esperanza begins to take responsibility for herself and her own happiness and the spectator witnesses this change both through her actions and her narrative retelling of the events leading up to the strike. Although the change happens slowly, the laborious nature of her emergence conveys the difficulty women face in giving up an identity they have inhabited for so long, and the challenge women must confront when they attempt to overturn centuries of thought regarding their place in the social hierarchy.

During the first half of the film, Esperanza maintains her submissiveness, sitting quietly at the union meeting, tolerating Ramón's dominance, and taking his orders. The turning point in Esperanza's emergence takes place about halfway through the film during a town meeting to discuss the court injunction. The strike has been going on for eight months, and the men are hesitant to abandon their fight after so much sacrifice. One of the wives stands and suggests that the women could take over the strike, and the men in the room erupt in laughter. Ramón voices his concern that having women on the line will not only be dangerous for the women, but humiliating for the men. When the union president calls for a vote on whether women should join the strike, Esperanza slowly stands to speak to the crowd. As Ramón turns in surprise, she begins, hesitantly, "I don't know anything [pause] about these questions of parliament. But, um, you men are voting on something the *women* are to do, or not to do. So I think it's only fair that the women be allowed to vote—" As she pauses, it appears she may not have the courage to voice the last words, but she breathlessly concludes, "especially if they have to do the job." Looking as if she may faint, she sits down quickly, while the women around her reach out to her in support, and smile at her in gratitude. The women begin to applaud loudly. This scene clearly demonstrates Esperanza's struggle between choosing to stay in her place, as dictated by Ramón, or take on a new, bolder role. Her uncertainty is made evident through her voice—a voice that will continue to become stronger throughout her imminent transformation in the remainder of the film.

As a result of Esperanza's suggestion, the women are allowed to vote in the community meeting, and it is decided that the women will take over the picketing. Esperanza describes the scene of the next morning in voice-over: "And so they came, the women. They rose before dawn and they came—wives, daughters, grandmothers. By sun-up there were a hundred on the line. And they kept coming—women we had never seen before, women who had nothing to do with the strike." She continues, "But not all the women went to the picket line. Some were forbidden by their husbands." As Esperanza narrates, the camera pans over the group of marching women, and then tracks to the hill where a group of men stand, watching the picketers. She pauses, as if ashamed of her past subordination, and slowly confesses, "I was one of them." The use of Esperanza's voice-over recollection of this course of events serves as a means of expressing her subjective feelings about her former subordination and elicits a sense of understanding and identification from the spectator.[65] The shot jumps to a close-up of Esperanza who, in a voice stronger than we have heard previously (except in her extra-diegetic narration of events), confronts Ramón: "It's not fair. I should be there with them. After all, I'm the one who got the women the vote." As her eyes dart quickly back and forth, her anxiety is apparent, as is her desire to join the women in solidarity. As Esperanza accuses Ramón of undermining the democracy of the vote, he replies arrogantly, "The union don't run my house."

While Esperanza stands watching from the hill with longing, the other women fulfill their duty as strikers until the sheriff, his deputies, and a convoy of scabs attempt to drive through the picket line. When the women gather to block the cars, a fender catches one of the women, pulling her to the ground. Chaos breaks out and soon half the women are fighting off the deputies, and the other half are holding back their husbands. In the midst of the scuffle, Esperanza hands the baby to Ramón and runs down to help the women. As one of the deputies pulls a revolver from his holster, Esperanza quickly removes her shoe and knocks the pistol out of his hands. A medium shot reveals her holding up her shoe in victory, with a broad smile. Afterward, the women reconvene in the line, with Esperanza now a part of their ranks. When she returns home later that night, her face aglow with the excitement of the day, her posture reveals her changing identity — she now stands tall with her head raised high. As she hugs the children and charges from room to room with a new-found authority, Ramón remarks: "I guess you got enough today to last a lifetime, huh?" "I'm going back tomorrow," Esperanza states matter-of-factly.

The final turning point for Esperanza comes near the end of the film. She has spent weeks marching with the women, organizing the pickets, and holding strategy meetings at the house. Ramón, however, still has not grown accustomed to her independence; in fact, he outwardly resents it. Realizing that she cannot continue to fight for the miners' equality while being denied the same respect in her own home, Esperanza confronts Ramón:

> ESPERANZA: Have you learned nothing from this strike? Why are you afraid to have me at your side? Do you still think you can have dignity only if I have none?
> RAMÓN: You talk of dignity? After what you've been doing?
> ESPERANZA: Yes. I talk of dignity. The Anglo bosses look down on you, and you hate them for it. "Stay in your place, you dirty Mexican"—that's what they tell you. But why must you say to me, "Stay in *your* place"? Do you feel better having someone lower than you?
> RAMÓN: Shut up, you're talking crazy.

At this point, Esperanza's expression makes evident the hurt and indignation she feels. As the shot frames her in extreme close-up, her eyes narrow and her jaw tightens. Then, after a moment, her voice begins to get louder and, as Ramón stands, she steps forward within the shot and looks directly into his eyes. Her eyes now blazing with passion, she confronts him once again:

> ESPERANZA: Whose neck shall I stand on to make me feel superior? And what will I get out of it? I don't want anything lower than I am. I'm low enough already. I want to rise. And push everything up with me as I go—
> RAMÓN: Will you be still?
> ESPERANZA: And if you can't understand this you're a fool—because you can't win this strike without me! You can't win *anything* without me!

In this scene, Esperanza visually and verbally confirms how the strike has transformed her into a strong, assertive woman with her own voice and her own identity, apart from her husband and family. Robinson notes the mastery of this speech because of its ability to accomplish two different and difficult things at the same time: make a theoretical political position concrete (working-class men's tendency to pass on their oppression) and create a moving piece of individual characterization.[66] According to Robinson, by having Esperanza voice these oppressions, the film asserts the leftist ideology that "the most oppressive aspects of sexist domination within the Chicano family ... come from the power structure of society."[67]

In the conclusion of this scene, the film also raises the issue of domestic violence as an all too frequent consequence of women's domestic oppression. By the end of the argument, Esperanza begins shouting at Ramón, imploring him to hear her for the first time. He immediately responds to her apparent indignation by raising his hand to slap her. She quickly admonishes him: "That would be the old way." Then she warns him, "Never try it on me again — never." This new Esperanza makes it clear that the strike has changed more than the material conditions of the mining community; the dynamics within the Quintero's relationship also have shifted. Esperanza now has found the strength and assertiveness to appropriate the resistance she learned from the strike to fight off the domination she experiences in her own home.

In *Salt of the Earth*'s concluding scenes, the mining company issues an eviction order for the Quintero home in an effort to intimidate the strikers. In light of the crisis, the entire community of men and women gather on the Quintero's front yard as the sheriff and his deputies remove the furniture and belongings from their house. Realizing that the eviction is an act of desperation on the part of the company, and that the disgruntled workers far outnumber the deputies, Ramón signals for some of the watching women to carry the furniture back into the house through the side door. Ramón's actions signify a pivotal moment in the film when the community actualizes its power as a collective. The sheriff, with a helpless look, orders Ramón to discipline the women in order to keep them from obstructing justice. Ramón replies with a laugh, "I can't do nothing, Sheriff. You know how it is — they won't listen to a man anymore." Soon, the company representatives step in and call back the sheriff and the deputies. Declaring victory, Ramón mounts the front steps of his now re-claimed home and offers a humble gesture of gratitude to the large crowd: "Thanks sisters and brothers. Esperanza, thank you for your dignity. You were right. Together we can push everything up with us as we go." In the film's final scene, the men and women finally unite through their mutual understanding of discrimination, exploitation, and disrespect, and through their common quest for greater human dignity.

By the film's conclusion, Esperanza's transformation is realized not only by spectators, who have been alerted to her growth by her voice-over recollection of the story, but also by Ramón within the film's narrative. Ramón's gracious tribute to the women affirms Esperanza's hard-won ascension into respectability within her marriage, as well as the women's progressive transformation within the community. As the music swells in the background, the camera focuses in close on Esperanza, whose beaming face and sparkling eyes reveal her elation at finally being recognized as an integral part of the community. Her final voice-over confirms the power of the true victory — the working-class community's achievement in overcoming its own divisions: "Then I knew we had won something they could never take away — something I could leave to my children — and they, the salt of the earth, would inherit it." According to Annette Kuhn, "Esperanza's final voice-over suggests that the broader struggles of history will go on, and be worked through, in the lives of her children."[68]

By emphasizing Esperanza's empowerment through both the development of her voice within the narrative and the articulate and compelling authority of her retrospective voice-over, *Salt of the Earth* imparts its female protagonist with a tradition usually reserved for men. In this way the film integrates a social critique "into the life and consciousness of a single individual" by offering Esperanza's narrative evolution as a trope for the complexity of gender relations at the intersection of issues of racism and domination by the ruling class, and as an invitation for spectators to embrace Esperanza's and the film's ideal of equality.[69]

Ideological Discourses of Resistance and Feminist Emergence

Salt of the Earth's resistance was not limited to its status as a renegade production or even its textual violation of Hollywood's formal conventions. Indeed, *Salt*'s greatest contribution may be its transgression of certain cultural expectations during the 1950s and its efforts to challenge dominant ideologies. Consideration of these social discourses allows for a better understanding of how working-class conditions and militant labor activism were constructed through this film and how these representations may have functioned rhetorically for *Salt of the Earth*'s spectators, both those who saw the film in the 1950s and those who might be exposed to its messages today. According to Christine Gledhill, the value of considering a film's social discourses is

> that it avoids the humanist reduction of textual productivity to character or image and cuts across the division between text and society, thus permitting reference to social life outside the text without falling into the trap of reflec-

tionism. A film, in constructing a recognizable fictional world, draws discourses circulating in society and in other cultural forms into the fabric of the film.[70]

Salt of the Earth drew on discourses related to three overlapping groups: the working poor, Mexican Americans, and women. By documenting these groups' struggle for equality and self-respect, as well as their cooperative and interdependent realization of their actualization through collectivity, the film calls into question traditional stereotypes regarding laborers, ethnic groups, and women by emphasizing the strength and power of these marginalized groups.[71]

The film's most obvious effort to trouble dominant ideologies was through its depiction of a working-class, Mexican American woman as its main protagonist. Rosenfelt comments on the boldness of such a choice, especially during the period of the film's creation: "the outspoken feminism of *Salt of the Earth* is rare in films of any era, particularly rare in the fifties when the feminine mystique exerted so powerful a hold."[72] Most portrayals of women in film during this time consisted of mainly young, attractive female characters motivated by romance. According to Stephen Powers, David Rothman, and Stanley Rothman, many films during this period were "lighthearted comedies following the classic injunction to end with marriage" with "the women characters' goals usually [involved with] getting the men they care about to behave the way a 'good' father or husband should."[73] Within these conventions, the social discourses central to *Salt of the Earth*, such as the critique of domestic slavery and women's liberation, would have functioned as a radical reversal of the societal consensus on what constituted "women's issues."

Noting that trends of the 1950s represented a symbolic "reigning in" of the forties wartime heroine, Marjorie Rosen writes, "One of the few constants during the decade was the direction women were heading: backward. Not since Grandma starched her bustles had the strains of Mendelssohn been so universally revered, or women so pressured out of the employment market and into conjugal bliss."[74] This shift in women's social status — in which Rosie the Riveter was sent packing when the boys came home from war — was reflected in both the larger society and in the many films of the era. As the culture recoiled from the strides women had made during the war years, the mass media served as a rhetorical device for reminding women of their proper place in society. Within such a context, *Salt of the Earth*'s construction of a strong female labor heroine likely would have impacted spectators due to its sheer opposition to other films of the day. As an obscure independent film with a severely limited release, however, very few members of the film-going public would have had the opportunity to see such a progressive representation.

Although Esperanza Quintero does not represent the prototypical "working woman" so frequent in films of the 1940s, her emergence into the public sphere in the fight for equitable labor practices would have stood in contrast to the domestic portrayals of women in the widely popular melodramas of the 1950s. While most of these films, even those with a social-problem focus, relegated women (especially ethnic minority women) to the private or domestic realm (to maintain the integrity of the family), *Salt* daringly emphasized women's role as problem-solver through her capacity for public activism.[75] Although the women's occupation of the public realm is not guaranteed after the strike (and, in fact, the real women on whom the film was based did return to the private domain), even the momentary resistance demonstrated by the women functions as a potent critique of the cultural politics that subjugated them. In this way, the film effaces the passivity typically associated with female characters of the period, instead providing Esperanza Quintero as "a truly complex and evolving female character who, in her activity and strength, becomes an unusual and worthy model for the female viewer."[76] Further, because the part of Esperanza was portrayed in such a self-effacing manner (and by a relatively unknown actress), spectators could more easily identify with such a role model.

As a result of its creative risks, formal inventiveness, and ideological contestations, *Salt of the Earth* remains significant today as an account of racial, classed, and gendered resistance that continues to offers contemporary spectators one of the most potent and complex representations of female labor activism on film. Gary Keller asserts that even today, *Salt* "serves as the paradigm that helps define the limits of the Hollywood social problem film and the consequences for filmmakers who would seek to overreach the boundaries of the Hollywood formula."[77] The film ultimately serves as an example of the kind of revolutionary film that challenges the status quo and expands ideologies of race, class, and gender and community activism, which could only be created with the courage that accompanies an artistic freedom exercised despite the homogenizing forces of an industry characterized by paranoia, control, and individualist enterprise. However, if Esperanza Quintero represents an example of the kind of female labor activist that could be created with the benefits of artistic freedom, *The Pajama Game*'s Babe Williams represents the Hollywood establishment's view of a union activist more appropriate for mainstream consumption.

CHAPTER TWO

Working-Class Women, Protofeminist Performance, and Resistant Ruptures in the Movie Musical *The Pajama Game*

> "[Y]ou've got to listen to me. I don't know why the union is so important to me, but it is. I guess you've just got to be on a team. So, that's why, no matter what's with us, Sid, I'm going to be fighting for my side and fighting hard."
>
> — Babe Williams, *The Pajama Game*

During the 1950s, certain ideologies constitutive of the American social fabric began to shift as well-established institutions were called into question. American women began entering the workplace, no longer in response to the war effort, but of their own volition. According to Brandon French, the postwar economy provided women opportunities to re-enter the workforce in response to production demands, yet at the same time they increasingly married and fostered the baby boom, balancing their roles as wives and mothers with their "double life" as career women.[1] Jackie Byars argues that during this period, "change was imminent but not yet explicitly acknowledged," however, "with the clarity of hindsight, we can see this upheaval in progress in the cultural documents of the period."[2]

The seeds of women's changing status already were being projected onto the nation's movie screens throughout the beginning of the previous decade. The women's films of the 1940s "often juggled and balanced feminine interests with marvelous dexterity," according to Marjorie Rosen, in which "individualistic heroines dignified good-natured plots; their exquisite humanity, humor, and intelligence giving added dimension to the image of woman in film and in life."[3] Films starring strong personalities such as Bette Davis, Rosalind Russell, and Joan Crawford found ample audiences in the first half of the decade due to the large number of women attending the movies alone while the men were fighting overseas. Yet, by the end of the 1940s, women already were being pushed back into their gilded cage. Rosen notes that "as the men returned home from the war, box-office — and social — demands changed. Slowly heroines moved into the background, becoming less aggressive or incapable of working out their own fates."[4] Molly Haskell assesses that "for the most part, the superwoman, with her angular personality and acute, even abrasive, intelligence, begins to disappear in the fifties."[5]

According to Byars, during the post-war years, "most women and men were not yet actively questioning their own traditional attitudes about their 'place,' but they were being bombarded from all sides by contradictory positions ... in advertisements, popular novels, songs, television shows, and films."[6] While the surplus of ambitious women that populated forties films certainly waned in the following decade, and the Woman of the Year turned into the post-war pin-up, not all female characters in film surrendered unconditionally to traditional feminine roles. French notes that a significant number of 1950s films simultaneously reflected the untenably narrow boundaries of the female role by producing a "double text" — depicting women who openly assert their equality, but who do not, in the end, challenge their destiny as wives and mothers.[7] Similarly, Haskell observes, "if fictional heroines wound up following the traditional line on what women should do — settle down and become compliant wives — they nevertheless offered enough subversive resistance along the way to indicate that all was not peaceful and placid in the supposedly natural order of things."[8] This duality functioned to document "the practical, sexual, and emotional transition women were undergoing beneath the threshold of the contemporary audience's conscious awareness."[9]

It was in the context of this cultural milieu that Hollywood marketed a decidedly mainstream story of love and labor in the Warner Bros.–produced musical comedy *The Pajama Game* (1957).[10] Adapted from Richard Bissell's novel *7½ Cents*, and the subsequent Broadway musical, *The Pajama Game* features disgruntled workers at a Junction City, Iowa pajama factory who, through song-and-dance numbers, express their solidarity and air their labor grievances. The workers are aided in their struggle by the smart and dedicated head of the union grievance committee, Catherine "Babe" Williams, and by the reluctant, but fair, factory superintendent (and Babe's lover), Sid Sorokin. The Hollywood musical, one of the decade's most popular film genres, served as a perfect vehicle for such a mixture of progressive and reactionary elements.

As an exemplar of the 1950s musical comedy, *The Pajama Game* represents the outer limit of the kinds of stories and characters that could be produced within the conservative constraints of the Hollywood industry during the final years in which major studios reigned and stars were signed to long-term, single-studio contracts. That is, the resistant ruptures made possible by the *The Pajama Game*'s aesthetics — a classical narrative form punctuated by the spectacle of musical numbers — enable the expression of a working-class woman's agency through her participation in the dual plot lines of the labor story and the love story, as well as her intermittent role as an active agent of the spectacle during her musical performances. While *The Pajama Game* often emphasizes Day's character as the embodiment of the quintessential fifties woman looking for Mr. Right and domestic bliss, it also reveals a subtle foreshadowing of women's changing status during that time by both confirming and resisting the cultural ideal of 1950s femininity. Through Babe's performance of a revised notion of traditional womanhood, in which she could temper her assertive commitment to respect and dignity for those on the margins (women and the working-class) with a nurturing and feminine side, this movie musical offers a vision of women's growing independence more than a decade before such demands for liberation would be voiced in the feminist movement. Although she does not, in the end, undergo the transformative emergence of *Salt of the Earth*'s Esperanza, or even transgress conventional Hollywood notions of femininity, Babe does demonstrate a certain resistance to the feminine destiny — a resistance evidenced through aspects of Babe's character within the narrative and her participation in various musical numbers. These contradictions are not only depicted through Babe's actions within the film, however; they also are a function of Doris Day's star persona and proto-feminist identity as it had developed, not only on the screen, but through her public image crafted over the course of her extensive acting career.

In this chapter, I demonstrate that the musical's form effectively allowed for the cinematic expression of women's ambitions simmering below the surface of mid-century mores. Within the musical, female actors/characters and the stars that perform within them simultaneously identify as both visual spectacle and active agents, representing both the old conventions and the new alternatives that exist for such transitional women in this particular period. This construction, I argue, allows for the meeting of both text (the narrative representation of "woman" in story) and performance (expressed both through musical numbers and star personae), which produces various tensions in the spectators' understandings of gender roles and relations, as well as the appropriate behavior dictated by them. In what follows, I perform a critical re-evaluation of Doris Day as the traditional 1950s "girl next door" through a consideration of her complex rhetorical construction of both femininity and a nascent feminism in this role, which I argue fuses her star personae and her performance in a way that invited spectators to imagine a new space for progressive women in such a conformist climate. I illustrate that the film's portrayal of Babe as a tenacious union activist willing to postpone love and wedded bliss for the benefit of the workers she represents, combined with the paradoxical star persona of Doris Day, opens a space for contradiction within *The Pajama Game* that imbues the film with a nascent form of feminist awareness. By tapping into evolving cultural discourses that contrasted traditional images of American women in the mid-twentieth century with a feisty and independent female performance, I conclude that *The Pajama Game* illustrates the productive, albeit tenuous, possibilities for transgression through a feminist and class conscious narrative within the context of the 1950s Hollywood establishment.

Beyond Babe: The Star Persona of Doris Day

Since the publication of Richard Dyer's groundbreaking study *Stars* in 1979, consideration of the "star text" has emerged as a productive analytical tool for film scholars, performance scholars, and rhetorical scholars alike. According to Christine Gledhill, Dyer's work expanded the study of film stars from more narrow emphases on fandom and sociology to a broader consideration of the star as "text." By expanding the study of film stars from a narrow emphasis on fandom and sociology to a broader view that considers both what the star image is and how it functions in society, Dyer raised star studies to a critical endeavor that accounts for issues related to "the social production and creation of meaning, linking industry and texts, film and society."[11] Dyer uses Marilyn Monroe as an example of a star whose image can only be understood within the social and cultural fabric of her time, and thus "she seemed to 'be' the very tensions that ran through the ideological life of 50s America ... historically living out the tensions or painfully exposing them."[12]

Building on Dyer's studies, Richard de Cordova's work has investigated the history of the American star system and argues that the central paradox of stardom is that stars are seen as both institution and individual. Along these lines, de Cordova notes that it is not only to the character in the film that a spectator responds, but also to the actual actor/star who performs the role and that "the pleasure and process of the American film has in fact been dependent on the assumption that actors hold a productive, transitive relation to their images on the screen."[13] More recent explorations of the star image have expanded on Dyer's emphasis on performativity and subjectivity, as well as the relationship between the film, the context, and the audience. Pam Cook focuses on the contradictions at work in films that "render its ideological closure problematic," which she sees as arising from a number of factors, including the historical place of film in the industry, the contradictory nature of the image of woman in contemporary ideology, and "the film's uneasy relationship between its female star and her place in its ideological project (in other words the power of the visual codes connoting 'stardom' to overcome narrative closure)."[14] Adrienne McLean also examines such contradictory forces at work in the star image of Rita Hayworth by considering how she may have "employed fictive aspects of her identity in strategic ways." McLean argues that because Hayworth was both constrained by patriarchy and resistant to it, the material effects of her performances in the social world were conflicted, ambivalent, and unexpected, while also "participating in the formation of a feminist consciousness rather than only keeping patriarchy in place."[15] I argue that, although she played a very different role on screen than Hayworth, Day's persona was similarly complex.

In the case of *The Pajama Game*, film spectators in 1957 who were familiar with Doris Day's star persona (as cultivated through her many previous films) undoubtedly would have brought certain expectations to their viewing experience, as would spectators today who are familiar with Day's film legacy. In particular, the rhetorical construction of a female labor activist in *The Pajama Game*, who both complements and challenges traditional feminine identities, is comprised by more than the mere textual interpretation of the character within the narrative. As Andrew Klevan notes, more concerted attention to the various dimensions of film performance

> brings out the relationship between appreciating a performance and understanding a film's meaning as it *develops*— the unfolding of and interpretation — undermining our inclination to condense and compress meanings in films, often to the point of banality. Established understandings may then be substantially deepened — or unseated.[16]

The contradictory character of Babe Williams also is constituted by the star whose performance created her — and the complicated meanings about American women that Doris Day represents for film spectators.

Given the significance of this transitional time in American culture, a consideration of the contemporary context in which Day's star persona emerged allows for a more nuanced understanding of her influence. Within the context of changing sexual mores and shifting roles for men and women, Day in many ways symbolized the very tensions that were constitutive of cultural ideology in that particular historical moment. In one respect, Day was recognized as the "American woman incarnate" and became a venerated symbol of ideal femininity for the post–World War II generation.[17] In the musical comedies in which she starred, however, Day also epitomized the self-sufficient woman with a "driving, single-minded ambition," a strength she often used as a weapon to temper her femininity.[18]

Contemporary descriptions of Day abound with sentiments that articulate the paradox of her public image. For example, Hollis Alpert wrote of Day in the *Saturday Review* in 1956: "She's authentic. She's the girl every guy should marry. Marilyn Monroe, Elizabeth Taylor, Kim Novak? They'd all be trouble. Doris Day would be true blue, understanding, direct, honest, and even a little sexy. You can trust her in any situation."[19] Cameron Shipp, however, after interviewing Day for *Cosmopolitan* the same year, commented on the vulnerability evident beneath what critics like Alpert saw as Day's stalwart appeal. Shipp wrote:

Throughout *The Pajama Game*, Doris Day as Babe Williams, both transgresses and confirms traditional gender roles with regard to 1950s womanhood. In this duet with co-star John Raitt (who plays Sid Sorokin in the film), Day's performance of womanhood is a mixture of femininity and female power as indicated by her feminine costume (pedal pushers and blouse tied at the waist) contrasted with her tough and assertive posture as she sings "There Once Was a Man."

But she leaves you with the distinct impression — and not an unhappy one, either — that the indecisiveness which marked her start, and which still shows in many small things, will remain with her. The girl-next-door has grown up for a fact, but, like most girls-next-door, Doris Day doesn't yet feel quite sure of herself and her new high heels.[20]

More recently, critics able to evaluate Day's image with the distance of time have identified Day's incongruous appeal in even clearer terms. Rosen, for example, has commented on Day's agility in combining "a quite modern ability to express her anger at men and a certain élan in taking care of herself with a comfortingly old-fashioned attitude toward love and marriage."[21] For many, Day is remembered for these distinctive attributes, characteristics that have defined her now iconic status. Ethan Mordden's descriptions of Day attempt to explain why she stood out from other contemporary film stars, such as Debbie Reynolds. He writes, "Day isn't a charmer, though she has charm, nor a romancer, though she's a fine-looking woman. What she is is candid."[22] *L.A. Times* critic Kenneth Turan's memory of Day as "feisty, forthright, and fearless" prompts him to celebrate her as the female equivalent of a John Wayne or Clint Eastwood.[23] Over the course of a career that spanned more than twenty years and produced nearly forty films, Day's complex traits were part of what made her a lasting star, and she imbued her film characters with those same intriguing qualities.

Often the embodiment of ideological contradictions gives rise to the star's sense of charisma. According to Dyer, the star's popularity with audiences may be traced to the condensation of values within the star persona felt to be under threat or in flux at a particular moment in time.[24] Part of Day's appeal was, and remains, clearly her wholesome image, which confirmed social norms regarding the idealistic vision of "woman." Day's image was partly based on her "sunny" personality, but mostly focused on her body — she visually represented how the ideal American woman *should* appear. In his book *On Movies*, Dwight Macdonald describes Day as the archetypal American beauty: "She has the healthy, antiseptic Good Looks and the Good Sport personality that the American middle class — that is, practically everybody — admires as a matter of duty. Especially the females."[25] Haskell writes of the contradiction in Day's cinematic image: on the one hand, Day "was like a hundred-watt reminder of the excessively bright and eager-to-please feminine masquerade of the fifties"; on the other, she was a symbol of "proto-feminist boldness" who seemed able to "combine romantic desirability with some kind of spunky resistance."[26] Such a combination was symptomatic of the classical Hollywood style. Films of the 1950s often were ambivalent in their depictions of the independent woman. By keeping a constant tension between "the spirited single girl and the whimpering bride, between the 'star' and the 'stereotype,'" Hollywood producers could ensure that their films would remain interesting to audiences made up of both men and women without necessarily subverting society's accepted gender-based role definitions.[27] The movie musical proved to be a productive venue for Day to perform that balance of being both the feminine mystique and the defiant diva.

The Musical's Emergence as a Mainstay of American Leisure Culture

Although the film-going public's preferences shifted direction from time to time during the film industry's first few decades, they consistently returned to the movie musical as an ideal forum for guaranteed entertainment between the years of 1929 and 1958.[28] According to Gerald Mast, the "clarity of [the] musical's conventions, constructions, and compact with audiences" allowed the cinema's skilled artisans to improve on the popularly accepted form by incorporating their own innovations of style.[29] By the beginning of the 1950s, Hollywood had produced well over a thousand musicals and continued to release new musical productions at a rate of nearly one per week, leading contemporary scholars to characterize this period as the heyday of the Hollywood musical.[30] The products of this era were distinguished by a commitment to the most professional scripts, designs, choreography, and cinematography, as well as an emphasis on adaptations of Broadway shows. The films, however, served an even greater function, according to Fehr and Vogel, as "beacons of Americans' aspirations" and as a bulwark against the growing cynicism of American culture in the 1950s.[31]

By the time *The Pajama Game* reached the screen, the story of pajama factory workers' demand for a 7½ cent pay raise had already achieved popular success through Richard Bissell's novel and a long-running Broadway show.[32] Warner Bros. acquired the rights to the musical in 1956 and tapped their gifted director of movie musicals, Stanley Donen, to oversee *The Pajama Game*'s translation into film. Donen, who had formerly directed *Seven Brides for Seven Brothers*, *Funny Face*, and *Singin' in the Rain* for various studios, collaborated with George Abbott and Richard Bissell to develop a screenplay. Donen also replicated the entire creative team from the Broadway version, making just one significant change from the original cast: the substitution of Doris Day for the film's lead.

With Day as the box-office attraction, *The Pajama Game* was released in theaters in August 1957. Like the stage production before it, the film, according to a *Time* magazine review, portrays the "silly, seamy saga of life and capitalistic strife" in a garment factory, and lost none of the musical's "fresh and idiosyncratic" qualities in its transference into film's visual narrative.[33] The classic "boy-meets-girl/boy-loses-girl/boy-gets-girl" story line constitutes the structure of the musical's primary plot. The film opens with the arrival of Sid Sorokin (John Raitt) as the new superintendent at the SleepTite Pajama Factory. Sid unwittingly becomes the new sparring partner for Local 343 of the Amalgamated Shirt and Pajama Workers. When the union committee realizes that Local 343 is the only one in the trade not to have received a 7½ cent raise they cause a production slowdown and, briefly, a work stoppage initiated by Babe Williams (Doris Day). After Sid fires Babe over the incident, the union calls a strike and a rift occurs between the lovers. Sid saves the day in the film's final scenes by blackmailing the factory president into granting the workers the pay raise for which they have been fighting. In the end, Sid demonstrates his admiration and respect for the factory workers—thus mending the strife between management and labor—and he gets the girl, too.

Rick Altman describes the musical as "Hollywood's rhetorical masterwork" since audiences would pay money to have their desires predetermined and come away convinced that life is rosy, that they belonged to a worldwide community of music lovers, and that love conquers all when people of good will get together and put on a show.[34] Similarly, Fehr and Vogel argue, for post-war audiences, the musical represented a return to faith, hope, and frivolous escape into a fictional world based on cardinal virtues, such as self-reliance and forbearance, and "the belief that better days would soon displace the distressing present."[35] According to Andrew Dowdy, movie musicals, especially those of the 1950s, employed "a deeply centrist form, dependent for consistent popular success on widely shared sentiments no less than sizable budgets.³⁶ Indeed, many film musicals produced during this time, such as *Singin' in the Rain, Damn Yankees,* and *Oklahoma* invite a "consensus mentality" that rarely delves very deeply into issues of social unrest. In an attempt to reach audiences seeking amusement rather than enlightenment, many of these films did not explicitly try to fight philosophical battles, advocate social causes, or sponsor a cultural revolution.³⁷

The Pajama Game epitomized the frivolity that film scholar Robert Matthew-Walker describes as characteristic of movie musicals in 1957: the story "immediately puts the audience in a pleasant frame of mind — for whatever happens during the course of the [movie], they are not going to be emotionally challenged."³⁸ *The Pajama Game* was praised by film reviewers for its value as sheer amusement; film critic Philip K. Scheuer of the *Los Angeles Times* wrote that the film's entertainment qualities were "diverse and spirited enough to insure its success with almost any kind of pleasure seeker."³⁹ Rick Altman argues, however, that to dismiss the musical as mere diversion rather than message is to overlook the musical's rhetorical power as a narrative of redemption, as well as the subsequent ideological function musicals serve through their recovery of "lost values."⁴⁰ Similarly, Jane Feuer notes that, as the quintessential Hollywood genre, the musical often has been wrongly regarded by critics as an innocuous medium, devoid of social meaning or ideology.⁴¹ As the following analysis of *The Pajama Game* shows, the form and style of the musical is structured in such a manner that it has the potential to both rhetorically inscribe a conservative social position (acting as warning against liberal advances that threaten to destroy the status quo) while at the same time endearing audiences to the socially progressive and proto-feminist impulses of its main protagonist as performed by Doris Day.

Resistance in the Musical Comedy: Narrative Conformity and Performative Disruption

The Pajama Game, like most musicals, consists of a number of dualities, including two plot lines, the dual registers of narrative scenes and musical numbers, and the parallel development of the male and female protagonists who inevitably couple by the film's conclusion. According to

David Bordwell, the standard conventions of classical Hollywood narrative follows the arrangement of a double plot line — one involving heterosexual romance (boy/girl, husband/wife) with the other involving another sphere (often related to work, war, a mission or quest).[42] *The Pajama Game* follows this paradigm by including a romantic plot line that involves the relationship between Babe and Sid, and a plot that consists of the sphere of work, namely the conflict between the factory's management and the labor union. Throughout the film, the unfolding plotlines are interspersed with musical numbers, which both provide commentary on the narrative action and momentarily create a pause in, or distraction from, the action because of their spectacular nature.[43] From its very beginning, the film establishes a parallel relationship between Babe and Sid, which develops through similar settings, shots, and musical performances. These multiple dualities constitute the defining style of the musical comedy by producing narratives that ultimately reify societal norms.

Scholars such as Feuer have noted that, in addition to these conventional elements, an underlying paradox exists in the musical comedy: although culturally conservative in its themes and narratives, the musical also employs bold forms similar to those of deconstructionist modernist art.[44] Innovative cinematic performance techniques definitive of the musical comedy, such as the employment of direct address (characters speaking directly to the camera), the creation of multiple levels of reality (including that of the film's narrative and the theatricality of the musical numbers), and the development of oppositional characters, often function as a challenge to the dominant cinema and the cultural status quo, even if only momentarily. Further, as Stacy Wolf notes in her study of queer appropriations of female performances in musicals, "just as the image of the homogeneous postwar era belies the complexities of that time, the idea of the musical as simplistically conservative underestimates its ability to produce a range of meanings."[45] In *The Pajama Game*, while the culmination of the musical's dual narratives conform to commonly-held societal values, such as heterosexual marriage and individualism, the narrative interruption of the musical numbers and the cultural oppositions as performed by Day (and further refracted through her complex star persona) exposes, as well as at times transgresses, the dominant values that drive the film's narrative structures.

Babe makes her entrance in *The Pajama Game* during the film's sixth scene. By this point, spectators have already been introduced to Sid Sorokin, who has just come to town as the new superintendent of the factory. The scene just prior to Babe's arrival announces her entrance. After Sid shoves a worker for not pulling his weight on the job, the worker yells, "I'll fix you, I'm gettin' the Grievance Committee." After the worker leaves, another worker assisting Sid warns, "That Grievance Committee can start quite a rhubarb!" Before Babe arrives on the scene, the film already accords her a sense of authority and power as the representative for the Grievance Committee. She soon substantiates the warnings by marching confidently into the room, followed by an entourage of union representatives. Wearing a long, blue smock and a fifties-style pompadour hairdo, Babe approaches Sid and looks him square in the face. Sid observes condescendingly, "So this is the Grievance Committee." Babe responds, "That's right, Mr. Sorokin. This *is* the Committee." Sid proceeds to look Babe over from head to toe before commenting, "Charlie, this Grievance Committee *is* different." "Never mind the snow job," Babe replies as she crosses her arms across her chest. As the two discuss the previous incident, and the rules that govern interactions between workers and management, Babe clearly controls the situation. Babe's subtle nonverbal movements—a shrug of her shoulders and slightly exaggerated blink of her eye—suggest that she does not tolerate the kind of behavior Sid enacts. Because Babe speaks with authority and refuses to respond to Sid's attempts at humor, the film initially portrays her as a serious professional committed to her role as head of the Grievance Committee.

Several scenes later, Babe and Sid meet again when he calls her into his office and she informs him, "The Committee decided just to drop the matter." Sid replies, "For a while there I thought that you and I'd have to fight a duel," which foreshadows the course their relationship will take as they do battle from their opposing sides of the labor negotiations while embarking on a romance amidst the growing tensions between factory management and its workers. Before the meeting ends, Sid abruptly asks Babe, "How about going to dinner some night?" After a few short exchanges, Babe informs him, "It really wouldn't work, not at all," as she gets up from the chair. "It's nothing personal," she explains, "But, you see, you're the superintendent and I'm the Grievance Committee," before she exits the room. Early scenes such as this one continue to emphasize Babe's feistiness and independence in the public world of work and company politics — at the union picnic she even volunteers to let a co-worker throw knives at her in an effort to demonstrate her fierce courage and unpredictable character. As the romantic plot line unfolds, however, the film reveals Babe's recourse to more traditional values and predictable impulses toward more domestic roles in the private sphere of home and family.

The picnic scene fades into the scene of Babe and Sid's first date. In contrast to the bright technicolor of the picnic that highlight Day's vibrant performance and unity with her fellow workers, this scene begins on Babe's front porch where it is dark and raining, and Sid sits with Babe's father. When Babe comes onto the porch, she wears a sleek black dress with a black-and-white polka dot scarf around her neck. The sleeveless dress shows off her svelte figure. Shortly, Babe's father leaves for his night shift as a railroad engineer, and Sid follows Babe into the kitchen. Once inside, Babe immediately dons an apron over her sexy dress and Sid, sitting in a chair, sighs, "I feel good, Babe. I feel like home." Babe, standing behind him with her hands in his hair asks aloud, "I wonder if we've got any onions" and then offers to make Sid an omelet. The scene, in which Babe and Sid easily slip into their new identities as lovers, appears to provide a glimpse into the couple's future when Babe will assume the duties of wife and homemaker, while Sid carries on with his management job at the plant. Sid declines Babe's offer to cook for him, and later of coffee, since he has other activities in mind. He begins to sing, "I don't want to talk small talk" and proceeds into a duet with Babe in which he expresses his desire to engage in sexual relations, while she quickly reverts to "small talk" in order to distract him.

After the musical number, at the end of which the couple kisses and Sid confesses his love for Babe, she turns to him very seriously and admits, "I think you're wonderful and I love you. But we're in for a lot of trouble.... Because something's going to come between us." "Who?" Sid asks. "Not any who," she responds, "Seven and a half cents." Babe quickly stands and turns to face Sid, replicating the earlier scene of their first meeting. Once again, the film accentuates the obstacle that separates them, and clarifies their staunch positions regarding the labor struggle. "That contract, lover — that's important. Maybe we ought to face that before ..." Sid pulls her to him, and dismisses her concerns by saying, "Don't talk such nonsense!" "Sid, you mustn't treat me like a baby!" Babe angrily retorts. "I'm not, darling," Sid replies hurt. "Well, you've got to listen to me," Babe explains, "I don't know why the union is so important to me, but it is. I guess you've just got to be on a team. So, that's why, no matter what's with us Sid, I'm going to be fighting for my side and fighting hard." In an effort to resolve the conflict, Sid asks, "If we both feel the same way about each other isn't that enough?" "Oh, you don't know me," Babe replies, indicating that her commitment to the union and the impending strike will not — can not — be compromised, even if she is now also part of a romantic union as the superintendent's girlfriend. This statement also echoes an earlier remark Babe makes to Sid at the Union picnic. She informs Sid, "Miss Williams is a very cold, hard-boiled doll. He [Sid] wouldn't like her at all if he got to know her." These comments indicate that Babe regards herself as more than just the woman Sid sees, that there is another component to her identity that remains hidden from him — an identity of which he may not approve.

This scene and several others reveal the dichotomous nature of Babe's character. Babe does not fit neatly into either the stereotype of the 1950s feminine ideal, a passive, oppressed, and objectified plaything of men, or into the identity of the independent and self-sufficient career girl. Instead, Babe inhabits both categories to some extent. Even her name, "Babe," reflects this duality. On the one hand, the name "Babe" denotes an inferior status; a shorthand for "baby," the term positions the label's recipient in a subordinate role. The negative aspect of the name "Babe" recalls its common usage as a male catcall — a derogatory term that serves to objectify women. On the other hand, the name "Babe" may be an affectionate nickname given to her by her colleagues, a positive appropriation of the term more indicative of her no-nonsense attitude and "tough babe" character. Throughout the film, Babe's character both confirms and transgresses women's traditional role. Babe represents the working woman in a position of power, an archetypal role that had become a more common feature in films of the 1940s and 1950s. According to Haskell, such a position allowed characters, such as Babe, to slip "cunningly through the cracks of a patriarchal world order."[46] However, her participation in the film's love story functions in a way that confirms what Patricia Mellencamp has described as a prominent feature of the musical comedy: the reenactment of "the ritual of re-creation/pro-creation of the privileged heterosexual couple, the nucleus of patriarchal society."[47] Such a feature is, as Wolf explains, "a choice that producers likely don't even see as a choice — hence the power of dominant ideology. But this most innocent of cultural forms is distinctly and powerfully political."[48] Thus, *The Pajama Game*'s romantic narrative serves to contain both Babe, as a character, Day's boldly suggestive performance of women's self-determination, and any other cultural threat to the sanctity of marriage and family.

Another way that the paradoxical nature of Babe's character becomes evident in the film is through her scenes that occur within the public narrative. As the plot line develops, Babe challenges the convention of the traditional female narrative role through her strong and determined actions, which reflect her belief in autonomy for both women and workers. About halfway through the film, the president of the union and several of its members meet with the plant supervisor, Mr. Hassler, to discuss the 7½ cent raise. They quickly realize that the negotiations are going nowhere and that Hassler has not been taking their requests seriously. They decide to resort to a work slowdown and spread the word to the other workers on the floor. In an exaggerated song-and-dance number the cast laboriously acts out their duties in super-slow motion. Soon, the factory efficiency expert enters and alerts the crew that he is going to inform the superintendent about the slowdown. Seconds later, Sid appears and threatens to fire anyone caught slacking. As work resumes at a normal pace, Babe looks around with an expression of disbelief. She then commits an act of militant rebellion by stuffing a piece of material into the gears of her sewing machine, which blows the circuit breaker and effectively shuts down the whole line of production. "Who did that?" Sid yells. Babe stands, and once again the two meet in face-to-face confrontation. "I did," she replies with confidence. "You're fired," Sid informs her with a snarl. "I am?" she asks incredulously. "Yes," Sid states. "Well, that's just fine," Babe replies with an indignant smile, "I haven't had a vacation in three years. I need one." Yelling, "So long girls," Babe runs out of the factory. In this scene, Babe not only demonstrates her conviction and courage in taking a stand for her cause (and sacrificing her job), she also flaunts her independence from Sid by defying his orders outright (and sacrificing their relationship).

The scene of Babe's firing once again positions Babe and Sid in opposition. The film characterizes Sid as the strong, conservative man of authority, while Babe, by questioning that authority, functions as the voice of the exploited workers who forces him to recognize that even those lower on the hierarchy of power deserve consideration and respect. These two roles are most explicitly expressed in a scene three days after Babe's firing where Sid comes to her house demanding to know why the labor negotiations must affect their romantic relationship. "What kind of a queen are you?" he asks her. "Haven't you heard?" she replies, "I'm the sweetheart of Local 343 Associated Garment Workers of North America. My gosh, Sid, I warned you, I told you. You knew all about how I felt. I happen to think there are certain things a person has to stand for in this life. You seem to have forgotten all about that." In this scene, Babe once again stakes out her position as a representative of the workers who must side against Sid, the representative for the factory's management. Their interaction ends with Babe resisting Sid's advances by admonishing him, "Watch those hands, tycoon." Once again, Babe chooses labor over love and her aggressive commitment to her career and the union's cause demonstrates her resistance to the notion that women should passively concede to male (or managerial) authority.

While Babe's participation in the public narrative presents one form of resistance in the film, her participation in several musical numbers provides another opportunity for her character to demonstrate a strong sense of autonomy. In musicals, Feuer argues, the two main plots follow the pattern of traditional Hollywood narrative in which the film audience looks onto the story from a position outside it, while during the musical interludes the audience experiences a much closer type of identification with the character/performer.[49] According to Jim Collins, this second type of identification often occurs through the performers' employment of direct address strategies that recognize the presence of the spectator through a look or glance at the camera or through the use of pronouns in lyrics that openly acknowledge the audience.[50] Such instances allow for the musical's stars to acquire a greater sense of agency by providing an opportunity for the performer to interact directly with the film's spectators, rather than only with other characters within the film's diegesis. Wolf uses the term "performative spectatorship" to describe the literally embodied participation (tapping of feet, humming along with the tune) and visceral experience of the audience while interacting with such a musical performance.[51] Further, these sequences most effectively unite the star persona with the cinematic performance. Lea Jacobs and Richard de Cordova explain that "star and camera, moving in concert, serve to enact or elaborate a space directed to us — often literally the space of a stage or screen" and that performance of such a discourse through spectacle frequently "involves a shift from the situation of the character to the position of the star."[52] For female stars, such as Doris Day in this film, this shift allows them to control the spectatorial gaze through their ability to halt the narrative (and their frequent objectification within it) by addressing and gazing back at the spectator during the musical performance. These resistant ruptures afford the audience an opportunity to engage with Babe/Day as a woman testing the limits of her recuperative feminine destiny (within the narrative) and to identify with her expanded sense of gendered identities through her control of the musical performance.

The Pajama Game contains several instances in which Babe/Day breaks through the narrative by enacting the spectacle of the musical performance. For example, in the second musical number of the film, which occurs after Babe's confrontation with Sid, Babe informs the audience, as well as the girls in the factory, that she is not in love with Sid. Looking directly into the camera, Babe begins by singing to the spectator, explaining, "All you gotta do is say hello to a man/And they've got you whispering in his ear/All you gotta do is be polite with him/And they've got you spending the night with him/ If there's a guy you merely have a beer with/ They've got you setting the wedding date." These first lines, as well as Babe's direct gaze into the camera, function to invite the spectator into the performance. As Babe walks forward and points her finger out at the film viewers, it is as if she is confiding her problems to them directly. Although her co-workers surround her, Babe walks away from the group and leans forward, clearly addressing her complaints to an audience beyond the room in which the scene takes place. Within the scene, Babe is framed in such a way that every look, that of the camera, the characters within the film, and the spectator, is funneled to the performer as "star."[53]

At the same time, throughout this scene Babe/Day gazes outward, directly at the camera/spectator in such a way that she no longer signifies a sense of, in Laura Mulvey's terms "to-be-looked-at-ness," in which the "cinema builds the way she is to be looked at into the spectacle itself," but rather she controls the gaze and the way in which she is gazed upon.[54] Such formal codes "create movement between the narrative and spectacle, shifting the position of the spectator from the 'once upon a time' of the fictive narrative to the 'here and now' of the performed spectacle."[55] In addition, Babe's denial of her feelings for Sid in this number signal her early sense of herself as a self-sufficient woman not easily swayed by a man's charms ("You may be sold/But I'm not buyin'"), but the reality of Babe's interest in Sid underlies those sentiments. Her stubborn denial of attraction for Sid continues through the rest of the song, in which Babe insists that she's "not at all in love/Not a pin, not a crumb/Not a snit, not a bite." Despite her protests, however, she clearly is intrigued by him, and as the film unfolds this tension becomes a theme of every musical number in which Babe stars.

The most interesting musical number that illustrates the tension between Babe's attractions for Sid and her desire to retain her independence occurs after their second date, but before he fires her from the factory. The musical number exemplifies what Altman labels the challenge song, in which the two singers echo each other in a non-stop bickering fashion, until the final duet when they sing together in unison. Altman refers to the Fred Astaire and Ginger Rogers films as the most famous examples of this style, and notes that the progression of their films depends on "the simultaneous growth of their quarreling and of their love."[56] Babe and Sid's relationship follows the same pattern in *The Pajama Game*, and the couple's duet to "There Once Was a Man" explicitly reveals this contradiction. The number begins when Babe screams at Sid, "Tell me!" and he yells back, "I love you!" The song then proceeds as a contest between who loves who more, with each taking a turn at describing how much ("I love you more than all the heroes in all the history books in the world"). During the duet, the performers' movements and gestures are very dramatic and exaggerated, and at one point their lyrical bickering escalates into simulated battery. As Babe sings, "I just can't tell you how it feels!/I only know there once was a woman who loved a man/Loved him enough to cause the Trojan War," she grabs Sid by the ear then hauls off and punches him in the stomach. Then, after turning to the camera briefly, with her hands defiantly on her waist, she sings "They say nobody ever loved as much as she-ee" while she slaps Sid across the face and knocks him over the porch railing before she finishes, "But me-ee I love you more." The song ends with both singing directly to the camera/spectator and proclaiming their love, "but me-ee I love you more." Throughout the number, however, the words of the songs are juxtaposed with the couple's aggressive gestures, including clenched fists and fake punches, which suggest the ambiguities in their relationship.

These scenes featuring Sid and/or Babe in musical numbers also allow Babe, through her performances, to project an image of woman as both vulnerable and tough, both committed to a man and determined to maintain some of her own identity. Her conflicted position reaches its full actualization during her only solo number, which parallels Sid's solo from earlier in the film. Both sing a song entitled "Hey There," but with slightly different lyrics. In Sid's earlier scene (which takes place in the public site of his office), after Babe turns him down for a date he sings into his Dictaphone "Hey there! You with the stars in your eyes/Love never made a fool of you/You used to be so wise!" Babe's number parallels Sid's by beginning with the same verse. While Sid's version goes on to berate Babe for declining his proposal for a date ("Better forget her/Her with her nose in the air"), Babe chastises herself for becoming smitten. The scene occurs in the very private setting of Babe's bedroom after she has told Sid that she cannot abandon the labor union. Her room is decorated in pastel colors with frilly curtains, and in such a context she appears girlish and, for the first time, very unsure of herself. She sings into the mirror, which reflects her image as a direct gaze toward the spectator, "Get on the ball, girl/Just take it all in your stride/Don't let him make you fall apart/You've always had such pride." Yet, Babe's actions belie such strong advice, and she drops onto the bed unable to finish the song because she is sobbing so hard.

The scene of Babe singing "Hey There" in her bedroom reveals a more traditional view of her character. She is a woman-in-love who knows she must abandon her beliefs, and the fight for her cause, if she is to keep her man.[57] In the previous scene, she appeared to already have made her choice, to stick by the union, but this scene immediately following reveals how great the pull is for her to continue to pursue her romantic relationship instead. The spectator now has reason to doubt whether Babe will stand tough and give up love for labor. In the end, though, Babe does not have to make such an agonizing decision because Hollywood convention insures that she will be saved by her, and the union's, new hero, Sid. Although Babe performs with the union president in a musical number called "I Figured It Out" at the strike rally, it really takes Sid to figure out how to get the boss to give in and provide the workers with their desired pay raise.

Not only does Sid save the day in the end, he also reaffirms the status quo, assuring that both narrative plots (the public and the private) are resolved in such a way that capitalism and patriarchy remain firmly in place. After Sid does some detective work and finds that Hassler had budgeted in the 7½ cent raise six months ago, Sid blackmails the boss with that information and then drives him over to the rally in order to settle the strike by granting the workers their wage increase. Babe exclaims, "Oh, Sid. I could kiss you, you've been wonderful!" and collapses into his arms. Because part of the deal Hassler offers to the workers is that they will forgo their claims to retroactive pay and settle for the raise only, Sid's efforts help both the company and the workers win through "compromise" and, as a result, the union loses some of its credibility in the eyes of the film's spectators. Labor scholar Ken Margolies notes with interest that this ending deviates from Bissell's novel. In *7½ Cents*, Margolies explains, the union is efficient and wins the raise through its own efforts, whereas "the film presents a union that is likeable enough, [but] it is not the kind of organization a worker could trust to get much done." *The Pajama Game* essentially portrays the union as "ineffectual," and, even worse, "someone in management brings home the bacon for the workers."[58] Further, Hassler gives a rousing speech to the crowd of factory workers urging them to put the strike behind them. "And I say to you again," he shouts, "in this hour of decision, that your responsibility to the garment industry ring like a battle cry through the land. Production must increase, cost must go down." With this call to community, the film insures that capitalism still triumphs and that the threat of unions is contained, at least for the moment.

The final scene of the film reconciles professional goals and personal affairs in the form of a SleepTite pajama party designed to celebrate both the symbolic re-marriage between management and laborers, and the actual marriage of Sid and Babe. Martin Sutton comments on the accommodating resolution of musicals when he writes, "The musical finally turns its wayward dreamers into conformists. The plot overtakes the numbers, and the protagonists achieve only an apparent victory. They get their partner, or even the break they have been looking for, but they are also absorbed into society and its norms via some established group."[59] The characters' victories are achieved through means that work to assure that the social order remains in tact. In *The Pajama Game*, the happily-ever-after ending emphasizes the triumph of the capitalist boss (Hassler praises the SleepTite spirit of solidarity) and the conquest of a heterosexual union that ends in marriage (Sid remarks: "Married life is lots of fun," while Babe concludes, "Two can sleep as cheap as one"). In the finale, the resolution of Babe's character is rendered visually—she wears the top half of a pair of heart-print pajamas while Sid wears the bottoms (indicating also that he "wears the pants" in the relationship). The scene is particularly powerful given Babe's past struggle over her relationship with Sid, and her concerted efforts to retain her own identity as a representative of the workers. By the closing scenes, however, it becomes clear that she no longer retains a separate identity, but instead she has merged completely into the romantic couple, giving up part of herself (along with the bottom half of her pajamas) for the benefit of the relationship. Babe's struggle has been resolved—she comes to accept patriarchal society's definition of herself—she gives up her authority as a union leader in order to become the super's girl.[60]

In a symbolic re-marriage between the labor union and management, and in celebration of the actual marriage of Babe (Doris Day) and Sid (John Raitt), the factory workers celebrate with a pajama party. Here, the previously transformative and proto-feminist figure of Babe concedes to a more conventional role for the 1950s woman by, literally, letting her new husband wear the (pajama) pants.

Musical Resolution and the 1950s Working Girl

By the film's conclusion, the classical Hollywood musical has it both ways: *The Pajama Game* successfully creates a free-thinking, energetic female lead that expands traditional views of womanhood, as well as a narrative structure designed to surround her, which ultimately places her in a more conventionally feminine role, choosing marriage over career and professional community over labor strife. Wolf explains the material effects of such resolutions: "The entire cast reassembles at the end of the musical to celebrate the uniting of the couple, which serves as a synecdoche for the unification of the community, of the world at large. The celebration that attends the finale of musicals symbolically resolves U.S. social conflicts of class and labor."[61] Yet, I argue that in this case, the diversions from the social values conventional to the classical form are particularly evident through the character of the *female* protagonist whose loyalties to the union are consistently negotiated with her own personal desires. While, for the most part, the romantic (private) narrative positions Babe in the traditional domestic role of the woman-in-love, seemingly content to assume her place in the private sphere that represents "woman's domain," her role as a labor activist in the public narrative and her performance in various musical numbers allow her to break out of such traditional stereotypes by revealing her intrepid, forthright, and confident nature as a principled working woman. As McLean has asserted, musical numbers starring talented and competent women offer ideological criticism through performance that the conventionally romantic narratives in which they are embedded often cannot, allowing these performing women to be both "'seen and heard.'"[62] Along these lines, the musical showcases Babe's greatest agency and independence when both musical and narrative sequences intersect in sequences in which Babe struggles between her romance with Sid and her dedication to the labor union.

In such moments, during which these distinct but interdependent plot lines overlap, the cultural opposition between Babe and Sid becomes clear: Sid represents capitalist authority and tows the line as the company boss, thereby upholding the status quo, while Babe represents a more broadly progressive position in which she identifies with the subordinate, and more socialist-oriented, perspective of the workers. For the majority of the film, Babe maintains her identity as a labor activist despite her growing involvement with Sid. When Babe's singular act of protest threatens to destroy her relationship, however, Babe's resolve begins to weaken. Subsequently, by the end of the film, even though Sid steps in to "rescue" both Babe and the labor union, and she concedes to a marital union followed, presumably, by "domestic" bliss, the spectator cannot easily label her as either a revolutionary heroine or a victim of patriarchy. Rather, the film demonstrates that women have *choices*: they may have to temper their personal desires in order to succeed in the public sphere (or vice versa), but they no longer necessarily have to subvert their identity to a predetermined patriarchal ideal.

In *The Pajama Game*, as in most musical comedies of that time, an understanding of the film's ideological function arises out of an identification of the constitutive dualities that comprise the film's form.[63] In order to fully account for the rhetorical impact of such a socially unconventional female protagonist, however, I argue that it also is necessary to explore aspects of that representation that go beyond the formal qualities of the film itself. According to Shari Roberts, the musical offers a rich field in which to investigate issues of feminine representation and spectatorship because of its specific resistance to typical Hollywood narrative positioning.[64] The previous analysis of *The Pajama Game* confirms this observation by offering an exploration of not only the musical's use of spectacle or the feminine image constructed through the film, but also the complex dynamics of the star text—the integration of both character and performer—within the musical.

In many of her films, Day portrays the upholder of virtue with the girlish image, the consummate virgin who still longs for a little adventure. She also plays the leading lady who, if hard-to-get in the beginning, usually winds up donning a husband, an apron, and a frying pan by film's end.[65] Although her characters frequently acted as a purveyor of the status quo by the conclusion of her films, nearly all of Day's early roles also offered an early insight into the progressive possibilities for women. This double duty image was the result of her portrayals of "working girls" in twenty-six of her films. Because Day usually played "some variation on the aggressive, attractive woman who has to make it on her own in the real world before she can find happiness," she provided spectators with an image of a real woman with whom they could relate, who also had a little something more.⁶⁶ In this way, Day reinforced the dual relationship that Pam Cook describes as the function of the star "as both similar to ordinary people and different from them, special"—the combination of identification (participation) and distance (separation) that film spectators so enjoy.⁶⁷ Although some of her films emphasized her roles as perfect wife and mother (such as *The Man Who Knew Too Much*), many of Day's early star turns, such as her role as Babe in *The Pajama Game*, offered her the opportunity to rupture the narrative surface with the performance of a strong, intellectual, and self-sufficient woman who embodied a sense of feminist acuity that would not be fully actualized by women for more than a decade. Day's star text—comprised of her many film roles and her own identity as one of the hardest-working actresses in show business—ultimately was that of an ordinary and extraordinary woman, "one of that handful of great stars who were able to be both ideal and real at the same time."⁶⁸

Such intertextuality and contradictions in Day's star image functioned to open up the possibility for divergent or oppositional readings of her film performances by different audiences. As a result, even if a Day character, such as the female heroine Babe Williams, chooses domestic happiness in the end, her strong image displayed through her early independence and acts of worker rebellion lingers in the spectator's mind. In this way, Day's charismatic persona reinforced for spectators that "even if the story made sure that the strong heroine got her comeuppance, her dazzling image lingered ... overriding the knowledge of her punitive destiny."⁶⁹ Due to the portrayal of tough boundary crossing females over the course of numerous films, the potentiality for a spectator's more oppositional reading of a "feminist" character in a single film may have been strengthened as the result of the spectator's intertextual training in what to expect from Day as a leading lady. Such a cumulative interpretation of Day through the amalgamation of her textual roles is significant to spectator's response to Day as Babe in *The Pajama Game*. As Philip Auslander argues, "The way that audiences participate in this process is not limited to simple identification with a performer with whom they share some crucial identity trait. Rather, an audience actively *constructs* the performer's identity in ways that speak to what it wants and needs that performer to be."⁷⁰ Spectators familiar with Day likely would have acquired a set of reading practices that would have allowed them to retain images of her intelligence, personal style, and ambition rather than her compromises and narrative resolutions. As a result, and despite the ending forced on Babe, fans of Doris Day who viewed *The Pajama Game* likely would have remembered her intermediate achievements for gender politics, rather than her ultimate subjugation to gendered roles — resurrecting Day/Babe as an immanent feminist victor ahead of her time rather than the inevitable victim of Hollywood patriarchy.

CHAPTER THREE

Recovering Women Activists' Voices
Union Maids, With Babies and Banners, *and the Feminist Historical Documentary*

"Women who have to work for a living in the factories, in homes, or in offices have a whole different concept of life and what is needed and required."

— Stella Nowicki, *Union Maids*

"The red beret woman became a symbol of a different, new type of woman, ready to sacrifice her life, as the men felt they were, in the victories we had finally won from the world's largest industrial corporation."

— Genora Johnson, *With Babies and Banners*

As the women's movement began to gain momentum in the early 1970s, a number of women turned to independent filmmaking, and specifically to the medium of the documentary film, as a means to illustrate and advocate a feminist politics. According to Patricia Erens, "These women saw film as a tool for raising consciousness and implementing social change; they had a message and a wish to treat subjects of importance to women that male filmmakers had so far ignored."[1] In addition to exploring themes of importance to women, these emerging filmmakers also were committed to making women themselves the important subjects of their films. In an effort to reject stereotypical images of women — and to offer an alternative to the versions of femininity projected through classical Hollywood cinema — a number of feminist filmmakers began creating documentary films that presented women as subjects by providing a forum for them to share their lived experiences with audiences. Through the act of telling their own stories, the women subjects of these films become active agents through both their representation in the film and through the role they play in the restoration of a previously untold history.

Lyn Goldfarb, a producer of feminist documentaries, has described the broader socio-political goals of such a project: "we felt we had to give working women back their history. Union women see this and say they've been given their roots and now they'll continue the struggle."[2] For these filmmakers, the creation of archive-based films offered more than just a correction to the historical record; they also were a means of feminist expression that fostered a critical consciousness in the public by filling "the still-gigantic gaps in public awareness of women's past."[3] One form of these early feminist documentaries featured groups of women who explicitly conveyed, in Julia Lesage's words, "their frustrated but sometimes successful attempts to enter and deal with the public world of work and power."[4] Two films in particular were intended to recover the history of women's participation in the widespread American labor movement of the 1930s. *Union Maids*, released in 1976 and directed by Julia Reichert, James Klein, and Miles Mogulescu, features three women who were union organizers in various factories in and around Chicago between the two World Wars.[5] *With Babies and Banners*, directed by Lorraine Gray and released in 1978, recalls the United Auto Worker's (UAW) 1937 sitdown strike in Flint, Michigan and features the stories of the Women's Emergency Brigade members who were integral to the strikers' eventual victory.[6]

To construct these films, the directors employed a simple format, including interviews with the women, collections of still photographs and newspaper clips, and snippets from contemporary newsreel footage. This combination of film forms functions as a rhetorical device to both capture a dramatic sense of the past and emphasize the significance of these women's contributions within the context of a critical historical moment. By raising issues that a number of women faced in their lives and careers nearly four decades earlier (such as sexual harassment in the workplace, women's burden of the "double shift," and the obstacles women had to overcome in order to enter the public realm of union organizing), these films also spoke to the political arguments for women's rights that were circulating in the culture during the period of their production.

Upon their release, the films functioned rhetorically as a form of consciousness-raising, a popular feminist strategy that brought together groups of women to express their feelings and experiences in the name of creating greater awareness of women's oppression.[7] Yet, the rhetorical work of these feminist historical documentaries continues to endure almost three decades later because they function as a counterhistory of the 1930s labor movement — a history spoken from the margins that acts as both a documentation of oppression and a revisionist perspective on women's standing and potential power. Paula Rabinowitz notes that what is at stake in the political projects of radical documentaries is "the status, meaning, interpretation, and perhaps even control of history and its narratives."[8]

This chapter analyzes how *Union Maids* and *With Babies and Banners* rhetorically employ the representational strategies of realism and the documentary form to put forward a correction to the historical record that counters established versions of events. By visually constructing an oral history consisting of women's memories from the 1930s, these films challenge ideology in the 1970s within the context of second-wave feminism through an act of historical revisionism. For contemporary audiences, however, I argue that the film's production of a counterhistory of women's labor reform activities also clearly demonstrates women's capacity, as early as the 1930s, to transgress the gender politics that often constrain and oppress them, all in the service of greater social and political consciousness. I also discuss how this film invites twenty-first-century spectators, who through their viewing experience become part of this revised history, to better understand and embrace feminist ideas about women's worth, accomplishments, and potential. Such rhetorical work also has the ability to call a contemporary audience into being who now, with a more inclusive view of their historical past, has the equipment necessary to continue these women's legacy. As such, the sacrifices and achievements demonstrated through these women's shared past becomes a historical foundation on which to build women's collective potential and future feminist action.

A New Medium for a Growing Movement

By the mid– to late–1960s, documentary film had become the chosen medium for a number of groups trying to advocate social change. Although at the time the second-wave feminist movement was divided into three distinct groups based on varying ideas about the most effective form of political action, each of them also was acutely aware of the media's potential for cultural influence. From its beginning, members of the women's movement were, according to Jan Rosenberg, "preoccupied with the role the mass media play in shaping social values, institutions, and attitudes."[9] The different approaches these women adopted in their social criticism of the media varied greatly, however, depending on the particular perspectives and agendas associated with the branch of the movement to which members were aligned.[10] Each of these branches of the movement formed from distinct origins, which accounted for their differences in membership, ideology, organizational structure, reform agenda, and political style.

The reformists, also known as the "older" women's rights branch, represented the typically mainstream members of the movement, notably those feminists associated with the National Organization for Women (NOW). Tending to draw their membership from white, middle- and upper-class, upwardly mobile women, this arm of the movement reflected the professional and personal allegiances of its leaders, many of whom came from labor, government, and the communications industry. They viewed their political mission as "the integration of women into the existing system as the equals of men," and generally focused their energy on "bread-and-butter" issues, such as women's work, the legal system, religion, and women's educational opportunities.[11] This group also typically directed their media reform efforts at changes within the dominant institutions, with a particular focus on the images of women in mainstream television and film and the status of working women in these media outlets.

A second category, women's liberationists (often referred to as radical feminists), were smaller in number and emerged out of various protest movements, such as the Civil Rights, New Left, and Anti-War movements. Often considered the "younger" branch of the women's movement, these activists received their political socialization and training in the sixties counter-culture where they acquired a contempt for "mainstream" politics.[12] These feminists viewed the oppression of women "as primary but far from exclusive in a system that also exploits the poor, minority groups, gay people, and children."[13] As a result, these radicals saw no merit in reforming the system of mass culture from within (in the vein of the reformists). Rather they tried to create alternative forms of media in order to challenge or replace the negative images found in mainstream publications, television, and films. According to Rosenberg, "While the rights group exerted political pressure on dominant cultural institutions, the liberationists built alternative cultural institutions in order to enhance and provide outlets for their creativity."[14] These outlets often included "underground" communications networks, such as alternative newspapers, magazines, and abstract art.

The third grouping of women within the larger movement was closely related to the liberationists, but viewed women's oppression from a Marxist perspective. Considered the "politicos" of the movement, these activists emphasized the largely structural determinants of women's oppression. This focus distinguished the Marxists from the radical feminists' concentration on the psychological aspects of women's oppression, namely issues of identity and interpersonal relationships. Marxist feminists instead focused their critique on economic structures and believed that the woman question was inseparable from class oppression and the exploitative capitalist system. Working from a largely socialist framework, these women viewed alternative media as a way to critique a system in which rich nations dominate poor countries, bosses exploit workers, and patriarchal fathers rule over families.[15] Part of the solution, according to these cultural workers, was to move in the direction of a more collective society — without hierarchies or competition — and to use the media to show how the people have shaped history and how ordinary citizens can use their power to progressively change the present society.

Through their common commitment to establishing alternative communication networks, the liberationists and Marxist feminists were jointly responsible for establishing what would become known as the feminist film movement. These women sought out opportunities to make feminist-oriented films that would "diffuse new knowledge and values among movement adherents and serve as recruitment nets to those not yet in the ideological fold."[16] In an effort to overturn the status quo, these emerging filmmakers embraced film as a way to reach broad audiences through an accepted and accessible "entertainment" medium. These independent artistic endeavors also would offer a feminist alternative to the representational practices prevalent in the dominant commercial cinema by employing a form capable of representing the reality of women's lives: the documentary film.

The rise of the feminist film movement coincided with the upsurge of documentary filmmaking within the film industry, and especially in film schools, during the 1960s. Beginning in the late 1950s, technological advances allowed for the production of lightweight, handheld motion picture cameras and compact tape recorders powered by small batteries, which made the synchronous recording of images and dialogue possible at a low cost. The new equipment offered greater flexibility and mobility, and provided the opportunity for filmmakers to enter naturally into the event they intended to record. According to Lewis Jacobs, "The result was a strong feeling of intimacy and involvement that transmitted to an audience a keen sense of participation."[17] These developments also made the possibility of film production accessible to growing numbers of female film students who had little technical experience, and even less capital, but an urgent desire to document issues previously not addressed on film.

Many feminist documentaries began production between 1969 and 1970, and by 1971 an outpouring of new films was being screened around the country for various women's groups and on college campuses. By 1976, more than 200 women had joined the feminist film movement and had produced over 250 independent films.[18] The large numbers of female filmmakers who entered the independent film industry during this time "made a remarkable breakthrough in a genre dominated by men for more than half a century," according to Jacobs, and constituted a conspicuous development in documentary filmmaking during the 1970s.[19] Inspired by the potential to make women's films with socio-political rather than aesthetic agendas, women both within and outside of the film industry began to look for new ways to replace the negative images of women offered by Hollywood with politically-conscious stories about how women actually live and work. Independent documentary filmmaking also offered these emerging filmmakers a number of creative advantages that would have been unavailable to them in the traditional film industry. First, the women were able to exert creative control over their films from conception to production. Second, feminist filmmakers could choose to work individually, occupying multiple positions such as cinematographer, editor, and director, or they could challenge the artistic "imperative" of individual creative control by bringing other women on board as partners in cooperative production.[20] Finally, filmmakers were attracted to the potential of the documentary form to function as a "disturbing presence," capable of giving a voice to those on society's margins and bringing public attention to their cause.[21]

The documentaries produced through the feminist film movement consisted of several subgenres, each differentiated in form and content as dictated in part by the film's purpose and its intended audience.[22] Many of the early feminist works were issue films created primarily to address topics of importance to women and to provide information on a variety of subjects such as women's health, rape, and abortion. The filmmakers hoped that the social problems raised through these films would promote further discussion in women's groups. As the feminist film movement continued to develop, however, greater numbers of women began producing portrait films of a personal, biographical, or autobiographical nature. Film portraits sought to offer a reconstruction of women's social history through their inclusion of variable film modes, such as interviews and historical film footage. These films fulfilled several goals toward that end: they created new and affirmative images of women, highlighted women's accomplishments, offered women positive role models, and presented reinterpretations of the past from a feminist perspective.[23] Eventually, as the movement continued to grow, younger filmmakers joined the movement and began to create experimental documentaries and avant-garde films designed to critique the medium itself by challenging the formal qualities of film that serve to exclude or objectify women.[24]

Although feminist documentaries differed from one another in both style and substance, the overall goal for most feminist film projects was largely the same: consciousness-raising about the condition of woman in society and the struggle to improve her situation. According to Lesage, feminist documentary filmmakers used the film medium "to convey a new and heightened sense of what *woman* means or can mean in our society—this new sense of female identity being expressed through both the subject's story and through the tangible details of the subject's milieu."[25] Many films, particularly the early issue films and biographical portraits, allowed their female participants to speak in their own voices and validate their personal experiences. As precursory ruminations on the "personal is political" slogan that would later motivate much feminist thought and writing in the 1970s, these films subjected the once "trivial" aspects of women's daily lives to feminist scrutiny. The films thus helped to expose the privatization of women's lives, and challenge their segregation from the public sphere, through the public forum of documentary film. According to Lesage, "Women's personal explorations establish a structure for social and psychological change and are filmed specifically to combat patriarchy. The filmmaker's and her subject's intent is political."[26] The films, then, upon their release functioned rhetorically as a mode through which women could communicate their personal experiences and establish political views. Through these shared experiences women also established their own subculture, which then could be activated as a means through which greater political change could be effected at present and in the future.[27]

By documenting and presenting women as a growing political collectivity during the 1970s, feminist films were one means of mobilizing movement members. Often shown at feminist gatherings, the films functioned to further promote solidarity within the women's movement and to motivate established members toward organized political action. Filmmakers soon began looking for ways to move their films into public circulation, however, so they also could be used to mediate between the movement and the public in order to recruit new members.[28] Because feminist films appealed to distinct audiences, the filmmakers faced the problem of limited distribution through existing marketing patterns and, as a result, a number of pioneer filmmakers had to invent new ways to market their films. According to Annette Kuhn, "Independent distribution ... offer[s] film makers a degree of control over their work: first by actually providing an outlet for that work, and then in that, in working through a distributor a film maker may direct her or his work towards particular audiences and may even be able to maintain some direct contact with those audiences."[29] One of the ways feminist filmmakers accomplished greater marketability for their films was through the establishment of distribution companies and film collectives for the sole purpose of financing feminist film projects.

A number of feminist media organizations were established in the early 1970s to enhance the distribution of feminist-oriented films, including Women Make Movies, Herstory, and the Women's Film Project. These collectives were designed to provide filmmakers with an opportunity for egalitarian cooperation, as well as a place where women could learn filmmaking skills and distribute their films and videotapes.[30] According to Claire Johnston, collectives such as these "represent a challenge to male privilege in that they seek to disseminate skills which have been denied to women by the film industry." Through these organizations women were able, as a minority group, to challenge male privilege "from the shop floor."[31]

One of the first collectives to make an impact on the film industry was New Day Films, which was founded in 1971 by two American filmmakers, James Klein and Julia Reichert. Klein and Reichert were soon joined by filmmakers Liane Brandon and Amalie Rothschild and, as a result, New Day became a co-operative developed to distribute films made by its members. New Day began with the production of independent films that demonstrated "a feminist consciousness in one way or another," while "at the same time having a sufficiently wide appeal to be successful also with audiences outside the women's movement."[32] Over the next decade the membership of New Day continued to expand and, by the early 1980s, the co-operative had released more than twenty films, many of which were chosen to run at prominent film festivals and often received critical acclaim.

Union Maids, distributed by New Day, was the third film produced by filmmaking partners Reichert and Klein (along with Miles Mogulescu). The film was nominated for Best Documentary Feature at the 1977 Academy Awards. The inspiration for *Union Maids* came from Alice and Staughton Lynd's book *Rank and File: Personal Histories of Working-Class Organizers*, a collection of first-hand accounts by the people involved in the industrial organizing drive of the 1930s.[33] Made up of the stories of rank-and-file workers (people actually on the job rather than paid union leaders), the book offered an insight into the movement for labor democracy by showing how thousands of committed persons worked for years to bring unions into being, resist bureaucratization, and better the lives of others, not just themselves.[34] The filmmakers chose three of the trade unionists featured in the Lynd's book — Stella Nowicki, Sylvia Woods, and Christine (Kate) Ellis — and constructed the film around the telling of the women workers' stories in an effort to convey both the worth of cooperative social action and, especially, the strength and possibility of women's activism.[35] According to Reichert and Klein, the film was intended to speak to three audiences — unions, unorganized working people, and the women's movement in the United States — and "to raise the question of women as potential leaders in unions today as they were then."[36]

With Babies and Banners, also distributed by New Day Films, was produced by the Women's Labor History Project and nominated for a Best Documentary Feature Academy Award in 1979. Originally slated to be part of a longer film project on women workers since 1930, the short forty-five minute film took more than five years to complete. Lyn Goldfarb, a social historian, and Lorraine Gray, a former photojournalist and the film's director, spent three years researching the activities of the UAW and the Women's Emergency Brigade before they could even begin preparing the screen treatment.[37] Although the project was funded through twenty-five grants, from agencies such as the American Film Institute, the National Endowment for the Arts, and the Ford Foundation, the filmmakers still incurred a $30,000 debt in order to finish the film. According to Gray, the filmmakers took on the project because they believed it was "important to explore and recognize the lives of working-class women, through film. They have been the backbone of the economy, both at home and alongside men at the workplace. Yet, their story is never told in history books."[38]

Both films received positive critical reviews upon their release, as well as showings in major cities and independent film festivals, such as the Women's Film Festival and the prestigious New York Film Festival. The *Variety* review of *With Babies and Banners* called the film "not only a fine documentary, but a touching story of real people who fought for and achieved a goal that, to some, changed the direction of this country."[39] Linda Gordon praised *Union Maids* as "an important, compelling, and happy new film; product of a new class-conscious social movement that is emerging out of the strengths of both the New and Old Lefts."[40] Despite the laudatory comments by such film critics early on, the films were deemed problematic just a few years later when feminist critics began to evaluate women's progress in independent cinema. As representative examples of the realist cinema of the early feminist film movement, *Union Maids* and *With Babies and Banners* quickly became the targets of criticism by feminist film scholars who accused the films' producers of so-called "naïve" attempts to use documentaries to capture and project realistic representations of women. Having established a foothold in film schools and film studies departments during the late 1970s and early 1980s, feminist film theorists began to debate the power and productivity of issues such as realism, politics, and representation in feminist films.[41] At its root, the feminist debate surrounding the realist tradition is about how cinematic forms, in this case documentary film, function to produce representations of women — and the politics and possibilities of finding a cinematic form capable of expressing the complexities of female identity without at the same time encouraging female objectification.

Recovering Women's Historical Past through a Contested Form: Realism, Representation, and Feminist Politics

The filmmakers who were part of the early feminist film movement emulated the documentary style of an earlier time, and envisioned a cinema that would be accessible, immediate, and capable of communicating with a now-identifiable audience of women who shared the same concerns. The realist tradition of the American cinema began during the First and Second World Wars with the growing desire of directors to capture on film the experiences of ordinary people. According to E. Ann Kaplan, this was done through a variety of strategies, including using working-class people and the issues that concern them as film subjects (with the assumption that the concerns of this class was somehow more "real" than those of the middle class); basing films on real-life events instead of fictional stories; using on-location shooting instead of artificial sets; and employing the techniques of Italian Neorealism, such as the long take and unobtrusive editing.[42] Feminist filmmakers were attracted to the realist form of the documentary primarily because it allowed them to employ the resources of film as a powerful organizing tool, rather than out of a desire to produce a new cinematic aesthetic. Realist cinema allowed feminist documentary filmmakers to achieve these ends by conveying to spectators the coherence of public space, and in the case of women's documentaries, the form was put to use "precisely to *create* public space" for women that did not formerly exist on film.[43]

Union Maids and *With Babies and Banners* applied the tenets of realism in an effort to open up a space in the public sphere for the recollections of female labor activists and their experiences in the labor movements of the 1930s. The films are relatively brief (less than an hour each) and are organized primarily around the oral history of women's early contributions to the industrial unionization campaign that their subjects provide. The major portion of these films, then, consists of women speaking (to each other in *With Babies* and to the camera in *Union Maids*) regarding their memories of the role they played in the labor activism of the period, as well as their struggle to participate with the men in the union campaign. These discourses related to gender and class shape the thematic content of the film. In this way, the films offer feminist-oriented perspectives on issues such as the restrictions of conventional gender roles and the strength of women's collective organization. The rhetorical meaning of these films, however, may be best understood as a complex combination of their status as a political tool of the feminist movement in the late 1970s, their employment of the realist style, and their position as a central point of contention within the feminist debates over realism in the following two decades.

According to documentary filmmaker and feminist film scholar Alexandra Juhasz, the realist form that has become the center of these feminist debates may be defined as "any of a number of always-changing conventions that signify for the maker and/or the spectator a condition, experience, or issue found in the 'real world' or in the 'real experience' of a person or group of people within the world."[44] The apparent "naturalness" that these conventions effect is often produced by the employment of certain cinematic codes, including grainy monochromatic images, shaky hand-held cameras, extended long-takes that required little editing, and subjects' direct address to the camera. These features allow for an appearance of transparency that, according to Kuhn, non–dominant film practices (such as social realism and feminist documentary) draw on "in order to appeal to as wide an audience as possible, and also with the assumption that a politically oppositional message will come across more clearly to the extent that it is not complicated by 'noise' from the foregrounded textual operations."[45]

Because of the feminist cinema's link to an evolving political movement, and the desire of feminist filmmakers to reach large audiences, strategies of realism were employed almost exclusively in independent feminist documentaries during the early 1970s. During this same period, however, theories deriving from French poststructuralism, semiology, and psychoanalysis were becoming more prominent in the U.S. academy, and feminist film scholars began using these theories to interrogate the brief history of feminist film.[46] These elaborate and complex theories of signification and subjectivity led feminist film theorists to challenge the assumptions behind a cinematic language of representation that claimed to reflect an outward "reality," and initiated a long feminist theoretical debate over both the dangers and the possible merits of a representational cinema.

The feminist critique of representation was an idea borrowed from semiology, which denies that there is any knowable reality outside of discourse or signifying practices. Taking this view, film functions as a systematic network of binary oppositions, organized metaphorically, if not literally, like language.[47] According to Kaplan, such theorists believed that "documentary filmmakers were misguided in returning to the eighteenth-century notion of art as capable of simply imitating life, as if through transparent glass, and in believing that representation could affect behavior directly."[48] Influenced by such theories, Eileen McGarry takes up a similar argument in her essay "Documentary, Realism, and Women's Cinema." McGarry argues that filmmakers, even those in the non–fiction tradition, are not dealing with reality but with a "pro-filmic event," or that which happens in front of the camera and mediates reality into the finished film. She writes, "To ignore the manner in which the dominant ideology and cinematic traditions encode the pro-filmic event is to hide the fact that reality is selected and altered by the presence of the film workers and the demands of the equipment."[49] According to theorists such a McGarry, the "documentary idea" of revealing truth is inherently duplicitous because there could be no neutral, recording camera; any film event would always be an arranged, edited, and manufactured intervention between audience and reality.

Building on the foundations of cinema semiology, feminist theorists arguing from a structuralist perspective soon joined the debate and criticized realist films for merely reflecting the dominant ideology, which preserves rather than challenges the status quo. These theorists believed that all representation is tied to cultural codes and, therefore, function to construct and maintain sexual difference along patriarchal lines. In order to combat this danger, theorists such as Claire Johnston argued that feminist cinema must develop a revolutionary strategy to "challenge the depiction of reality."[50] According to Johnston, the "truth" of women's oppression "cannot be 'captured' on celluloid with the 'innocence' of the camera: it has to be constructed/manufactured."[51] Johnston and other feminist theorists have argued for a deconstructionist approach that would use the master's tools against the master by interrogating the language of the cinema and its depiction of reality so that "a break between ideology and text is effected."[52] In essence, the type of avant-garde cinema Johnston and others advocated would more explicitly challenge issues of representation, language, voyeurism, desire, and the image of woman — and would begin to more accurately mirror the concerns of the emerging group of academic feminists to which these theorists belonged.[53]

Not all feminist theorists agreed that the realist documentary needed to be discarded and replaced by an avant-garde cinema, however. For example, Christine Gledhill questions the validity of equating all varieties of realist practice with the goal of naturalism and the practice of bourgeois ideology when different audiences come to different films with dissimilar expectations and reading practices.[54] Further, Kaplan argues that "the debate about realism is in some sense a false debate" premised on a theory of knowledge that is "inadequate when applied to practice in the sense of bringing about concrete change in the daily lives of women."[55] According to these scholars, what the feminist critique of realism failed to consider was that this cinematic style can function on a variety of levels. Although in the dominant cinema the "reality" reflected often serves to confirm and perpetuate a bourgeois, patriarchal view of the world, as employed by feminist documentarists the realist style provides a politicized, opinionated version of reality that functions as a view alternative, marginal, or subversive to that of patriarchal ideology.[56]

Counter to the feminist deconstructionist critique, I argue that *With Babies and Banners* and *Union Maids* effectively utilize the strategies of documentary realism to provide a perspective on women's political contributions to the labor movement as a correction to the lack of women's inclusion in the narrative of American labor history. Both films record and share the story of various women's emerging involvement in the American labor movement. By combining multiple film styles and realist conventions, the films document the women's struggles and visually capture a sense of the cultural conventions these women strived to overturn.[57] Rosenberg argues that, by taking such an analytical approach to history, films such as these exploit the popularity of the portrait film form while they simultaneously develop political themes that transcend personal issues.[58] The compilation structure these films use — an incorporation of interviews, newsreels, and photographs — also creates a layered approach that functions to construct a historical, social, and feminist perspective through a reexamination of the historical record that reconstructs events from a woman's view of history. Lesage comments that this layered realist approach also "immediately established and valorized a new order of cinematic iconography, connotations, and range of subject matter in the portrayal of women's lives."[59]

The foundation of the realist style used in both films emerges from the employment of the "talking head" interview technique. Consisting of multiple subjects speaking to an off-screen interviewer (which masks the interviewer's presence and creates the effect of the subject's direct address to the camera), this technique often has been disparaged by film critics as visually dull. In *Union Maids* and *With Babies and Banners*, these interviews bring various accounts of women's union activities together into a single story, and recovers women's inclusion in the events of labor history. The accumulation of these women's memories recorded on film functions to compile an oral history of the American labor movement and to articulate these individual experiences into a coherent social history. Bill Nichols writes, "Like oral histories that are recorded and written up to serve as one type of primary source material ... the articulateness and emotional directness of those who speak gives films of testimony a compelling quality."[60] Further, the inclusion of the interviews foregrounds the voices of *women* in these films, and enters those women's opinions, subjectivities, and identities — previously unrecognized — into the public discourse of the labor movement.

Union Maids is structured almost entirely around this straightforward interview format. The film alternates between interviews of three women in their mid– to late-sixties, each filmed individually. The interviews take place separately in the women's homes, which provide an authentic atmosphere replete with coffee cups, family photographs, and 70s-style décor. The film weaves the autobiographical discourse provided by the three women together to provide the structuring principle of the film. The "plot" is derived through the linear chronology of the women's narratives.[61] Although the women tell their stories separately, the film edits these stories together into a seamless version of events. For example, the film begins with the three women describing their childhood and how a family member influenced them from a young age toward a socialist view of life. Sylvia tells of her father, a skilled roofer, union man, and Garveyite, who told her as a girl, "Any union is better than none, and if there isn't one, help organize it." Stella remembers an odd phrase her father used to say often, "You don't work, you don't eat," which friends later explained to her was an old socialist position. Kate recalls her grandmother who, after marriage, chose to go out and work with the men in the fields rather than make breakfast for the members of the household and keep up the domestic duties. "I hope I've inherited some of my grandmother's fighting spirit," Kate remarks.

Union Maids continues as the three women chronicle how they all left their homes to find jobs in "the big city of Chicago." Silvia worked in a laundry, Kate in a garment factory, and Stella in a stockyard. They discuss the conditions they faced in the industries in which they labored, including long hours, exhausting speed, and low pay. "But you needed to eat," Sylvia explains, "so people took whatever work they could get." Each woman also discusses the pivotal moment that led her to activism. For Stella it was when a woman lost two fingers in a hotdog-cutting machine because it lacked a safety guard. Kate describes the verbal abuse she was subjected to daily by the company foreman. Sylvia addresses the issue of race and her disgust, as an African American worker, when the laundry brought in a white woman with no factory experience to serve as the forelady. The women then discuss in detail their individual experiences in organizing workers, finding innovative ways to fight off a hostile management, and, finally, in unionizing their industry. The film concludes with each woman reflecting on her involvement in the American labor movement and how it changed her life for the better.

With Babies and Banners structures the story of the UAW's Women's Emergency Brigade's activities around the event of the fortieth anniversary of the Flint, Michigan sit-down strike. The film opens with Genora Johnson standing at a podium and speaking to a large audience gathered in an auditorium. Johnson tells the crowd:

> The Women's Emergency Brigade of Flint, Michigan made American history. We are the foremothers of today's young women — and we are proud of it, because it was there that I learned of the great stamina, and the great courage, and the intelligence, and the foresight, and the daring of women when they are put under fire. I think that you men saw that, too, and it was one of the greatest experiences I have ever had.

Johnson's remarks, which occur before the title of the film, serve as an epigraph for the story to come. The film's chronology then reverses briefly, and the story begins again, this time from "the day before the 40th anniversary" (indicated by a subtitle).

The film next chronicles Johnson's reunions with many of the women who participated in the strike forty years earlier. The spectator watches as Johnson walks up to the first house, and views Johnston from a position inside the house as she opens the door to the closed-in porch. The positioning of the camera provides the feeling that the spectator already has been invited inside to join the women's reunion. A small group of women meet her there and they embrace. The film then cuts to the living room where the women gather around a tattered scrapbook full of old newspaper clippings and photos and recall how they became involved in the strike, and why. For example, one woman comments, "no sick benefits, there was no health and welfare programs, there was no social security, there was no unemployment or anything like that. All of that has been built since we founded the UAW." Johnson later meets another group of women at a second home that sits right behind the General Motors plant, and there the women discuss how the workers began to organize with the help of the Congress of Industrial Organizations (CIO).

Beyond functioning as a structuring device and oral history, these interviews also imbue the film with the feminist views upheld by the filmmakers. The interviews are designed in such a way that they allow the female union activists to be presented as acting subjects in the film on several levels. Sonya Michel notes that the soundtrack full of women's voices heard — and seen — in these films allows the women to "constitute themselves not only as subjects — as actors in their own lives — but simultaneously as actors in history and in feminist politics, *and* as subject/actors in cinema."[62] The interviews function for these women as empowering devices through which they have the opportunity to express themselves and their political perspectives — a position that stands in stark contrast to the way women generally are objectified, eroticized, and discounted in the dominant media.[63] The use of interviews also offers a sense of validation for the women's politicized conversation and, as Lesage writes, the "act of telling one's story as a woman in a politicized yet personal way gives the older tool of women's subcultural resistance, conversation, a new social force as a tool for liberation."[64]

In these two films, the women interviewed address a number of topics that initiate a critique of the patriarchal culture that consistently attempted to derail the women's efforts. For example, in *With Babies and Banners*, Genora Johnson comments on the double bind that the women who volunteered to join the striking workers found themselves in: "she couldn't be too masculine, she couldn't be too feminine, you couldn't be too intellectual or men resented this more than anything in the world. She was in a damn, damn never-never land!" Another woman comments on the sexual harassment perspectives in the plant, remembering, "If you were the kind of girl that would let a boss pat you anywhere he felt like pattin' you or would go out with him after work or something like that you was pretty well assured of a job." Similarly, in *Union Maids*, Sylvia explains: "There was a real sexist attitude then by society generally and by the radicals themselves. It was sort of preordained that men would have all the leading roles — and the few women who aspired to be leaders, if you want to put it that way, didn't come by it easy." Through the many interviews offered by the various women activists, these films present a collective of brave, smart, political and articulate women giving witness to the obstacles society has laid down before them, and serving as role models because of the manner in which they overcame those barriers. According to Juhasz, who analyzed similar strategies used in the 1972 documentary *It Happens to Us*, the power of such a film "is not in its conventional realist function of confirming these women's realities or identities as fixed or complete — in inspiring identification with individual women — but in its documentation of the reality of a collective, gendered oppression."[65]

Another way that these films validate the voices of these women is by allowing the women to serve as the sole narrators of the films. The films explicitly avoid the voice-over narration associated with the older tradition of filmmaking because of its detached and authoritarian connotations.[66] According to Nichols, films that privilege the interview style

> give the impression that the argument is the witnesses' and that the filmmaker merely acts to present and illustrate it.... The difference is quite significant, but the important point here is the shift of emphasis from an author-centered voice of authority to a witness-centered voice of testimony.[67]

The lack of outside narrator frees a space for the women's perspectives to remain the only arguments put forward through the film. The power of these women's statements and views are reinforced in the film through the frequent use of close-ups of the women talking, which functions to focus all attention on their words rather than distracting visual effects. The films highlight the material authenticity of these interviews as an alternative record of the truth, adding "another dimension of physical reality."[68] Further, because the interviews provide the overriding structure of the film, spectators are given the opportunity to interpret the women's testimony and make meaning for themselves, since the all-knowing voice of the narrator is not available to offer an interpretation for them.

Although the films lack an outside narrator, they do offer several means of aural and visual support to complement the stories told by the women. The films use a combination of still photographs, film footage, newspaper clippings, and music to further connect the women's stories and to visually dramatize the narratives they provide. As the films intercut the women's interviews with historical images, those visuals serve to verify not only the "truth" of the women's spoken discourse, but a challenge and exception to the dominant view that, previously, only authority figures could speak.[69]

The historical film sequences, in particular, provide "a sense of the texture of the period," situating the spectator in the context of these women's memories.[70] Additionally, the large groups of people that appear in the moving footage evidence the great masses of workers that were involved in these campaigns, a movement much greater than that represented by the few women included in the film. These sequences also show the diversity of women who entered the workforce during those years, and the large variety of industries that relied on women workers. In *Union Maids*, there is footage of women working in textile factories, as phone operators, and in a meat processing plant. Further, the newsreels reveal the poor conditions at the factories, including the long lines of men and women running the machines and manning the assembly lines, and the almost inhuman speed at which they were forced to execute their work. According to Susan Reverby, a film such as *With Babies and Banners* "blends past and present and historical fact and cinemagraphic imagination, appealing to our intellect and our emotions. The film sets the record straight on the critical importance of women in a key 1930s strike in the male bastion of auto production."[71]

Old photos of the films' principle subjects also add to the historicity of the films by showing these now aged women as formerly young, beautiful, and vibrant—a juxtaposition that makes their militant activities appear even more extraordinary. The inclusion of these personal photos

In *With Babies and Banners*, the use of historical photos and footage from the General Motors Sit-Down strike are included to add authority and authenticity to the women's recollections of their strike activities. This photograph shows a children's picket organized by the wives of the striking workers, a brilliant publicity event that garnered the union and the labor dispute featured coverage in many regional and national newspapers.

also creates parallels between the women being interviewed. At the beginning of *Union Maids*, for example, still photos provide a sense of each woman's childhood and family life, alluding to the sources that shaped their later views on socialism and labor. Further, the photos reveal the solidarity the women shared; for example in *With Babies and Banners*, the photos show the women marching together wearing matching berets and armbands, holding picket signs, bringing food to the men in the factories, and organizing a children's picket. Other photos show women taking an active role in situations that would be considered perilous for workers of either gender, which acts to heighten the sense of drama and spectacle associated with the activism of this time. For example, both films include newspaper clippings with headlines such as "Thousands Out as Strikes Spread East and West" and "Strikers Clash with Police at Auto Plant." The newsreels of such confrontations, including the Bull Run battle in which the Flint Police Department sent in to dispel the revolution drew their pistols and opened fire into the crowd, confirm the real danger that these men and women faced. Quickly edited scenes and jarring camera movement add to the frenzied feel of these scenes of shootouts between workers and police, mob riots, and tear gas explosions, as well as injured workers being loaded into ambulances. In *Union Maids*, for example, footage shows the police chasing and beating the men and women before loading them into paddy wagons as Kate explains, "The police were usually vicious. Believe me they fought us, with police clubs, with black jacks, with brass knuckles, and dried banana stalks because they showed less bruises, they used everything." Newly recorded union songs, such as "Solidarity Forever" and "We Shall Not Be Moved" are used to enhance the spectacular effect of these scenes, as well as to add an aural sense of the period's music.[72] Reverby comments, "The footage and the sound ... combine to capture the despair, the fear, and the exhilaration inherent in this Depression struggle."[73] The cumulative effect of these strategies, then, functions to direct spectators' attention in a way that invites them to share in the militant experiences of these women.

These various strategies, by providing a visual record of the people, places, and activities that comprised the movement of which these women played a part, accentuate the women's stories with a sense of authenticity and authority of experience. However, they also show that memories can be reconstructed. By using these newsreels and newspaper clippings alongside the voices of the marginal actors in this historical drama, the films reorganize rather than simply repeat a popular memory — that is, the films propose a new perspective on memory by reconstructing a view not represented in the popular memories of the official culture.[74] These strategic acts of realism have a significant impact on the spectator in that they invite him or her, in Michel's words, "to play an active role not only in interpreting the film but in constituting its very meaning by piecing together disparate, incomplete, incongruous, or contradictory images and sounds."[75]

Indeed, these films' capacity to both move spectators to thought and action, while also providing a form of entertainment, may be the most significant function of *Union Maids* and *With Babies and Banners* employment of the realist form.

Spectatorship and the Feminist Realist Documentary: From Consciousness-Raising to Collective Action

One of the most interesting rhetorical aspects of the feminist historical documentaries produced by the feminist film movement are the way the films function as invitations to viewers, or how the films construct certain spectatorship positions and identities. Of course, this was a key concern as well among feminist film theorists who were debating the productivity of the realist style and its employment in feminist independent films. Feminist film theorists who adhered to the tenets of deconstructionism were not only concerned about realism as a cinematic form as discussed earlier, but also about the relationship between the realist cinema and the spectator. A common argument from these scholars was that "realism as a style is unable to change consciousness because it does not depart from the forms that embody the old consciousness," namely the realist codes of the camera, lighting, sound, editing, and mise-en-scène.[76] The dangerous consequence of such a style, some feminists have argued, is that it invites a passive and gullible public to swallow the false promises of bourgeois illusionism unquestioned. Similar to Johnston's call for a counter-cinema, these deconstructionists argued that the prevailing realist codes must be abandoned and the cinematic apparatus used in a new way that would challenge audiences' assumptions and expectations.[77] Yet, Juhasz points out that these concerns, when applied to feminist documentaries, obscure "the distinctions allowed by the always unique extratextual conditions that define the production, reception, and form of non-industrial film and video, especially when film and video is motivated primarily by political urgency."[78] That is, deconstructionist theories often do not attend to how the filmmakers' political intentionality, the spectators' viewing context, and the strategies of identification when watching a documentary differ from those same dynamics in the case of Hollywood fiction films. Most significantly, while Hollywood films project for women identities that are harmful and oppressive, feminist documentaries attempt the strategic reconstruction of a feminist identity that is positive and liberating.[79]

According to Kuhn, in feminist realist documentaries, "identifications may take place more directly with what is represented in the image, so that, for example, a film about a woman's life and her work as a mother and housewife may bring about forms of recognition in female spectators of themselves and their own everyday lives."[80] It is this aspect of feminist documentaries that separates them from the counter-cinema advocated by theorists, such as Johnston, and taken up in the films of the feminist avant-garde. While experimental films suffer from problems of accessibility and audience response due to their efforts to create distance between the spectator and the image, documentaries such as *With Babies and Banners* and *Union Maids* invite a response from the spectator that, according to Kaplan, "has the potential to challenge assumptions about what we expect from cinema and [adds] to what we know about the world."[81]

Another problem with the avant-garde films privileged by some feminist scholars that distinguishes them from other forms of feminist cinema is that their political function is limited because of their inherent relativism; that is, films that demand of the spectator a sophisticated level of knowledge about the cinema, philosophy, psychology, linguistics, and Marxist theory are constrained in their ability to reach only those already committed to their values.[82] Further, this limitation speaks to the double bind inherent in the very basis of poststructuralist feminist film theory: these theorists' more radical approach to the cinema would fail to engage a mainstream public conditioned to expect certain cinematic forms. As a result, the deconstructionist focus on the discursive effects of feminist films neglects a concern with the audience to whom their film discourse is directed. In order to achieve any sort of praxis, films, as a form of effective political discourse, "must articulate the experience of its audience even as it seeks to mobilize them."[83]

Early feminist documentaries grounded in the realist form (such as *Union Maids* and *With Babies and Banners*), on the other hand, are much more productive for the feminist cause than experimental cinema because of their ability to draw a variety of spectators into the film-viewing experience based on their straightforward and accessible structure. By recreating the condition of the consciousness-raising group — the most fundamental structure of the women's movement — these films accomplish several objectives: they construct a collective identity for women through their representation of the realities of women's political struggle; they create inroads toward a blurring of the private and public spheres, and simultaneously offer a critique of women's traditional roles and limitations; and they effectively recover and record women's past acts of feminist resistance. Further, these films embody the power to mobilize spectators to ponder their own potential for collective action. Juhasz describes these functions as the political efficacy of realism, which she argues is "the power to convince, document, move to anger and action and the ability to take control of identity and identification within systems of representation so as to move toward personal and collective action."[84]

Most notably, feminist documentary films utilize the realist structure and the oral history format to cinematically re-create the feeling of the consciousness-raising group by capturing women's testimony on film and encouraging female spectators, especially, to find meaning in those experiences that will help them to better understand their own circumstances. The consciousness-raising group came to prominence during the second-wave feminist movement as a forum for women to collectively share their personal experiences and feelings, and as an opportunity to analyze and build on the knowledge they found there in order to find strength in unity and action. According to Barbara Susan, for women

> consciousness raising is a way of forming a political analysis on information we can trust is true. That information is our experience. It is difficult to understand how our oppression is political (organized) unless we first remove it from the area of personal problems. Unless we talk to each other about our so called personal problems and see how many of our problems are shared by other people, we won't be able to see how these problems are rooted in politics.[85]

The films' formal style creates an environment similar to the consciousness-raising group by using familiar settings, such as a kitchen or living room, and by using camera work to provide a view of each woman in close-up as she tells her story. As they watch these women, spectators are invited to experience the film as if they were sitting in a circle listening to these women along with other members of a larger, unified group. Although viewers of the films are not afforded the opportunity to physically participate in the discussion, the spectator's interaction with the film mimics the principle of the consciousness-raising group that depends on the "invited member" realizing the power of shared experiences.

The film's subjects reinforce this sense of collective identity, and the unified strength of a political "we" made up of women and the working class, through comments they make in the film. For example, in *With Babies and Banners*, one of the women comments that the members of the Women's Emergency Brigade involved in the Flint strike "understood the dynamics of power more so than the workers did — through unity there is strength." Also, at the conclusion of *Union Maids*, Stella states optimistically: "There's some tremendous potential in people, in labor people, in working people, in union people. I think they're very democratic, you know, and I think there's tremendous militancy that's sometimes below the surface and it'll rise and come. I don't think the working people are going to let down this country."

Another way that the films attempt to unify women is by speaking to their collective experiences of oppression. The films provide a critique of women's traditional roles and reveal the slippery boundaries between the public and the private by demonstrating how these activist women worked to traverse those boundaries in their own lives. Reverby notes that the primary concern of *With Babies and Banners* "was to show the process by which 'ordinary' women, locked up in their homes with the wash and the kids, become militant activists." Yet, the films do more than just demonstrate these women's ability to move between the private and public spheres, they also raise issues that challenge notions of power and gender politics, thus advocating women's inherent *right* to transcend the boundaries imposed on them. This sentiment is expressed powerfully by Genora Johnson, who comments in *With Babies and Banners*, "The red beret woman became a symbol of a different, new type of woman, ready to sacrifice her life, as the men felt they were, in the victories we had finally won from the world's largest industrial corporation." Similarly, Kate in *Union Maids*, comments on the change in women's situation due to their participation in the union campaign: "I wasn't about to do housework or anything else, because now I was convinced and I became a dedicated radical, you know, working with these friends who I liked very much and who made a lot of sense."

With Babies and Banners goes a step beyond *Union Maids* by incorporating the critique of women's narrow role prescriptions into the organizing structure of the film. By beginning and ending the film at the Fortieth Anniversary commemoration of the Flint sit-down strike, the film provides "a sense of the enormous struggle necessary to overcome sexism and the extent to which militancy, no matter how courageous or crucial to a victory, cannot alone bring about permanent change."[86] In the final scene of the film, the story ends where it began, with Genora Johnson at the anniversary gathering. However, now we see the events that took place before Johnson stepped up to the podium. In a voice-over, Johnson describes the men's response to the women when the strike was finally over: "What happened, in effect, if you can imagine this, from the international on down, everybody in it said, 'Thank you ladies, you have done a wonderful job and we appreciate it. But now the laundry's piled, the dishes are piled up, and the kids need attention.'"

This closing scene opens in the convention hall, with shots of numerous young women holding signs with slogans such as "Women are history past *and* present." In the background these women can be heard chanting, "Let the women speak" and a lone woman in the audience yells, "There isn't one woman up there!" As Johnson petitions the organizing committee from her seat, begging them to fulfill her earlier request for female representation at the ceremony, the chant turns to "UAW needs an ERA." An offer is made from someone off-screen to allow "whatever spokesmen" the women want to approach the podium before the floor is closed. Johnson runs to the podium for her chance to finally, forty years later, address the men's dismissal of the Emergency Brigade women after the strike. She tells the crowd: "The women, I feel, need a greater representation in this union." She goes on to ask the union to take up the issue of nursery schools on behalf of working women because "women have not been able to participate on a full-time basis in the shop because she has to go home and get the supper, buy the groceries, take care of the kids, and do the washing and ironing and cleaning on the weekend — you know this!" Johnson's speech reminds women — her former colleagues from the Brigade, the young women now sitting in the audience, spectators of the film during the late 1970s, as well as those who have discovered the film decades later — that women's work will not be done until their labor, both in the home and outside the home, truly receives the level of recognition equal to that of men.

The Rebel Girls and Their Cinematic Legacy

For Reichert and Klein, capturing the experience of multiple women sharing their stories was important when making *Union Maids*. Reichert explains the filmmakers' desire to have the compilation of the women's stories serve a greater purpose: "we cut their stories so that one blends in with another so that you get a sense that there is a collectiveness and it's not just isolated people who are written up in history books and credited with having created history."[87] These are unique films that expose an oppositional social culture and recover their great legacy for those still working from the margins and future generations of activists to come. This film allows us to not only remember a great moment in labor history, but also to rehabilitate the contributions and counterhistories of those not always recognized in mainstream accounts. Both *Union Maids* and *With Babies and Banners* effectively convey the sense that these are not great women in history, but ordinary women who accomplished something historical. The subjects of these films are the kind of women with whom common people identify — these activist women describe the events of their lives without pretense, but with a strong sense of conviction and self-determination. According to B. Ruby Rich, when these female subjects enter into history, spectators are able to see reflections of themselves on screen, which leads "to identification with and understanding of social movements past and present" through spectators' act of witnessing the film protagonists' experiences and potentially realizing similarities to their own.[88]

By framing the film with the women's struggle for representation at the anniversary meeting, forty years after the women's participation in the strikes, *With Babies and Banners* shows that there is still much work to be done. *Union Maids* concludes on a similar note as the filmmakers ask Stella how she feels about the women's movement. Stella remarks that she thought the movement was great and long overdue, and that she became a part of it, but that she "lost patience with the young women who couldn't relate to the working-class women." In her view, the movement still had a long way to go. Given these comments, both films function, finally, as an act of public memory about women's social past and a call to action to ensure women a better future. Gary Crowdus, in his review of *With Babies and Banners*, writes: "This is not a radical history safely and romantically sealed off into the past, but one with a vital connection to the present. Not only can the Women's Emergency Brigade serve as role models for young women, but their history and their struggle is something we can all learn from today."[89] That may be these films' greatest legacy. These films perform a valuable cultural function of returning the control of the historical narrative chronicling the early organizing efforts within the American labor movement to the women who took part in its very creation, but whose perspectives had previously gone unrepresented. Maybe even more significantly, however, they are a reminder to women of today that the work of the "rebel girls" is not to be forgotten because, in many ways, it has only just begun. However, two films produced during the same period in Hollywood, *Norma Rae* and *Silkwood*, reveal that the mainstream industry had not only forgotten the radical activism of women in the 1930s, but also had not yet reconciled with the changes wrought by second-wave feminism.

CHAPTER FOUR

Hollywood's Working-Class Heroines
Norma Rae, Silkwood, *and* The Politics of the Docudrama

"You're right, I've got a big mouth. You know cotton mill workers are known as trash to some. I know the union's the only way we're going to get our own voice — make ourselves any better. I guess that's why I push."
— Norma Rae Webster, *Norma Rae*

"There's a moral imperative here."
— Karen Gay Silkwood, *Silkwood*

By the late 1970s and early 1980s, the momentum of the women's movement had all but come to a halt. The movement's politicization of feminist issues, however, had made enough inroads for Hollywood to begin to take notice of women's changing status in American culture. Yet, as Winifred Wandersee points out, the new image of womanhood that emerged through the American media during this period was "one that reflected some aspect of women's liberation but too often defined the successful woman in terms characteristic of an intensely consumer-oriented, individualistic, and competitive society that almost completely negated the true meaning and intent of feminism."[1] During this time, and within this cultural milieu, two films emerged that exemplified the contradictions of a Hollywood brand of feminism: *Norma Rae* (1979), the story of a cotton mill worker turned union organizer, and *Silkwood* (1983), the story of whistle-blower and nuclear activist Karen Silkwood.[2] Although these films invoke a feminist and liberal sentiment in their focus on a female working-class heroine, the progressive meanings initially invited by the films are largely negated by their conclusions. Rather, the films present a rhetorical problem for feminism, in particular, by portraying the female labor activist as a tainted heroine and outsider who, because of her insistence on liberation for herself and social justice for the working class, ultimately faces either defeat or some form of acquiescence to the status quo. These negative or politically unfulfilling outcomes become the result of the women's feminist and political ambitions. Such contradictory constructions are symptomatic of the "conflicting visions" that marked this period of American filmmaking. According to Peter Lev, such films are the result of the remarkable pluralism, and heterogeneity, of American filmmaking during this historical moment, during which a number of compelling visions reflected conflicting ideological currents, constituted the debate on what America is and what it should be, and competed for the attention of a large and diverse cinema audience.[3]

Norma Rae and *Silkwood* reflect the desire on the part of those involved in the production of these films — all self-stated liberals and feminists — to impart a social and political consciousness emblematic of the 1960s, the period that had come to define a generation of artists. Yet, the films also embody a nostalgic sense for what had once been, before those turbulent years of corrupt politicians, lost wars, and feminist radicals. Despite the films' subtle feminism and ruminations on working-class life, both consist of plot lines and characterizations, especially of the female labor activist, that in many ways represent a superficial liberalism that fails to delve beyond melodramatic stereotypes. In both films, the female protagonist is characterized as the prodigal daughter and the labor organizer is upheld as the politically-evolved Svengali, without whom she would not have begun her journey toward salvation (or martyrdom). In part because of the context of their production during the early corporatization of Hollywood, and partially because of the formulaic Hollywood classicism inherent in the genre of the docudrama, *Norma Rae* and *Silkwood* fail to impart a strong social message regarding either the heroine's social-political actions or her feminist enlightenment. Rather, by imposing a familiar narrative structure and compressing the circumstances of the protagonists' lives and labor activism, these films temper the women's socialist and feminist impulses with the more politically-correct, legally safe, and primarily individualistic story of a woman who comes of age by discovering meaning in something larger than herself.

The structures of *Norma Rae* and *Silkwood* are nearly identical. Both films gloss over the larger history of their subjects' activism and focus instead on two separate tensions in the film: the woman's personal development (in which she transforms almost overnight from an ignorant proletarian to an impassioned labor organizer) and her complex relationships with the men in her life, especially the union leader who offers her political enlightenment. Subsequently, the societal norms that oppress women and members of the lower classes are reinforced through the ideological biases coded into the films' traditional myths about femininity and masculinity, working-class culture, and socially-conscious heroism. As a result of this construction, the personal growth achieved by the working-class heroines Norma Rae Webster and Karen Silkwood does not, in the end, seem to provide enough ammunition for a continued struggle against the very public structures, both social and ideological, that exist to oppress women, especially working-class women. Within these films, rather, the women's private struggles overwhelm their public successes and result in contradictory representations of the female labor heroine: she is portrayed as an activist subject who strives to transcend the constraints of her social position and, at the same time, as the unfortunate victim of such a Sisyphean struggle.

The "New Hollywood" and the Problem of the Liberal Cinema

Some have nostalgically labeled the early years of the 1970s the period of Hollywood's "true" golden age.[4] According to film critic Diane Jacobs, the "frenetic activity of the previous decade" had generated "a period of cinematic 'rebirth'" in the industry during the first half of the 1970s.[5] Those years are now recognized by many as "the new Hollywood," the result of significant alterations in the industry that changed the business of filmmaking in ways that would impact those involved at every level. According to Geoff Gilmore, "The economics of the film industry underwent an extreme paradigmatic shift ... that created a different set of exigencies."[6] The movie studios, unable to retain their independence in the face of a shrinking market for film productions, were bought out by larger, diversified corporations or individuals. According to Robert Kolker, however, these new owners were not concerned with making films of artistic merit, but rather with "amassing media outlets for various ideological reasons, the most important of which is the production of profit from the dissemination of news and fiction."[7] The shift toward greater commodification of films brought on by changes in the Hollywood corporate structure also led to drastic modifications in the marketing and distribution patterns for films.

Mass marketed ad campaigns became more common for films during the 1970s. Often the advertising concepts were developed before the film was completed. Steven Spielberg's 1975 blockbuster *Jaws* became the benchmark for such tactics. Advertising for the film saturated the television market for three days before the film's opening and a few weeks later the production broke all previous box-office records.[8] As a result, the corporate executives, accountants, and talent brokers who now ruled the development of Hollywood film projects began to privilege the notion of "high concept" films that would be commercially successful in a nation-wide distribution, which also led to homogeneity of both production and product throughout the industry.[9] The desire for an easily marketable film project also was driven by the expanded income streams provided by several new technologies (such as cable–TV and VCRs) that brought post-release Hollywood product directly into people's homes. The overriding consequence of all of these industry developments was an even greater profit motive than that experienced by the big studios. In fact, within the realm of the corporate conglomerate, movie-making became, according to film historian Robert Sklar, "an all-or-nothing gamble: a flop meant total failure, a loss of millions and no second chance."[10] These shifts in the process of project development and film production had their most profound impact on those trying to maintain the creative force behind the filmmaking endeavor: the film directors.

For a brief moment during this period of rapidly changing filmmaking practices, the status and autonomy of film directors reached an all-time high. By 1970, a generational transformation had occurred in Hollywood as the great figures of the studio era retired from the scene.[11] According to Sklar, the retrospective recognition attributed to directors such as Frank Capra, John Ford, and Howard Hawks during the early 1970s "conferred enhanced status on the director's role in filmmaking," which resulted in a shifting emphasis "away from studios and producers toward individualistic directors whose vision or style could capture public and critical attention."[12] After the old studio system fell in the mid–1960s, a number of emerging filmmakers found that a Hollywood culture dominated by directors afforded them the independence and artistic freedom to make the kinds of films they wanted to produce. Owing to this newfound autonomy, these filmmakers found they also had greater latitude over who would join them on their film projects. These "package deals," consisting of independent directors, writers, actors, agents, and producers, would then be offered to the studios, who now acted as investors or distributors.

The effect of this period of transition, according to Kolker, was a "certain freedom of inquiry, which, no matter how compromised, continues to leave a small mark" on the artistic endeavors of filmmakers who were developing their craft during the late 1960s and early 1970s.[13] These new directors had varying backgrounds, including film criticism, the theater, and acting, and felt less bound by the institutionalized conventions of the film industry that had characterized the big studio era. According to Robert Ray, these directors began their careers "as obsessive movie buffs who learned about filmmaking from going to the movies" and "having seen most of Hollywood's Studio Years product, they were now prepared, if not to disassemble it, at least to show its paradigms less respect."[14] The films of this period reflected the complex relationships among a disorderly film industry transferring ownership and control from one form (the major Hollywood studio) to another (corporate conglomerates); a group of critical, self-conscious filmmakers, and a culture seeking solutions to the social problems that had been raised in the politically-conscious decade of the 1960s.

Two directors gained prominence during this time because of their ability to find their own niche within this complex intersection of economic, social, and political factors in filmmaking. In the turbulence of this critical historical moment, filmmakers Martin Ritt and Mike Nichols sought project opportunities that would allow them to inflect their art with a critical and social consciousness, while also allowing them to garner enough mainstream appeal to become commercial successes. Nichols had made his mark with the breakthrough film of the 1960s, *The Graduate* (1967). Having begun his career in the theater, where he developed his directing style through works such as Neil Simon's *Barefoot in the Park*, Nichols was, from the beginning, attracted to the humanistic aspects of drama, including the universal juxtaposition of the comic and the tragic. According to biographer H. Wayne Schuth, Nichol's productions, including his large body of film work, generally focus upon a certain subculture and offer "an honest look at the grimness and tragedy of the human condition, with a tentative, resolving note of hope and nobility."[15] Similarly, Martin Ritt had made his early mark as a theater director, and also had enjoyed a successful career in television before he began directing films in 1957. However, while Nichols concentrated on the profound meaning of the human condition, Ritt's work remained more focused on the problems of modernization and industrialism on human society. In his biography of Ritt, Gabriel Miller writes that the director's work "exposes the deleterious effects of a modern, industrialized world yet allows the protagonist to triumph over conditions that militate against growth and achievement."[16]

Ritt and Nichols built long and successful careers by making committed films, and by maintaining as much control as possible over their productions. Because both Ritt and Nichols had established themselves in the film industry before the political-economic changes of the 1970s took place, their iconoclasm often clashed with the transformed industry's inherent conservatism. This conflict, Ray notes, "determined and reproduced the period's simultaneous impulses toward irony and nostalgia" as these old-school directors attempted to find means to make their films of conscience in a manner that would be acceptable to both the new studios and to a mass market.[17] *Norma Rae*, directed by Ritt, and *Silkwood*, directed by Nichols, represent this emerging trend. Both films were disparaged by critics as oversimplifications of a bygone era that romanticized the notion of labor activism. For example, Penelope Gilliatt, in her review for *The New Yorker*, comments that *Norma Rae* "has an innocence that almost seems to go back to the thirties," and David Ansen in his review for *Newsweek* accuses the film of confirming for spectators "that Hollywood is still capable of making condescending paeans to the 'little people' with all the phoniness of yesteryear."[18] Similarly, Jack Kroll, reviewing *Silkwood* for *Newsweek*, stated that the screenplay "reminds you of the clear, honorable simplifications of the 1930s 'social consciousness films.'"[19] Perhaps owing to this inclination toward sentimentalism, *Norma Rae* and *Silkwood* also share a similar narrative structure and production history.

Norma Rae tells the story of a female cotton mill worker from the South who, as a single, widowed mother of two children, lives with her parents who are also mill workers. Already unhappy about the working conditions at the mill, Norma (Sally Field) becomes an easy recruit for Reuben Warshovsky (Ron Liebman), a Jewish labor organizer from New York. The two meet very early in the film when Norma Rae gets thrown out of a motel room after her adulterous acquaintance bloodies her nose. Reuben, who is staying in the next room, comes to her aid and their friendship begins. When the management at the mill begins to suspect that Norma Rae might become a problem because of her association with Reuben, they promote her to quality control checker. After a few weeks of pushing her friends, and even her own parents, to speed up production and work beyond their human limits, Norma steps down from her management position. From that point on, Reuben begins to direct Norma Rae's restless energy into working for the unionization of the mill. Simultaneously, Norma develops a relationship with a co-worker, Sonny Webster (Beau Bridges), which quickly leads to marriage. The remainder of the film plays up the tension between Reuben's efforts to enlighten Norma by encouraging her free thought and independence and Sonny's disgruntlement at the changes in his wife (although her relationship with Reuben receives considerably more screen time). By the final third of the film, Norma Rae is working night and day at her grass-roots organizing of the mill workers and, in the film's climactic moment, she makes her final stand on a table in the middle of the factory with a hand-scrawled sign that reads: UNION. The film ends with the union winning by a modest vote after which Reuben returns to New York and Norma Rae is left with the memory of their success.

The idea for *Norma Rae* originated with two female film producers, Tamara Asseyeu and Alex Rose, who came across an article in the *New York Times Magazine* about Crystal Lee Jordan. Jordan was a cotton mill worker from Roanoke Rapids, North Carolina who had played a significant role in winning union representation from the notoriously labor-hostile J.P. Stevens Company. The article soon was extended into a book-length study by Henry P. Liefermann, which was released in 1975 as *Crystal Lee: A Woman of Inheritance*.[20] Asseyeu and Rose bought the rights to the book and, interested in making a woman's film with a contribution to feminist thinking, the producers chose liberal-minded filmmaker Martin Ritt to

In this now iconic image of Sally Field as Norma Rae, the embattled mill worker takes a public stand after spending months organizing a grassroots movement for unionization within the factory. Although *Norma Rae* presents a problematic portrayal of the female protagonists' public work undermined by her personal circumstances, the power of this image has become synonymous in our collective history with the heroism of labor activism.

direct the film.[21] Ritt agreed on the condition that he could choose his own writers for the screenplay, at which time husband-and-wife writing team Irving Ravetch and Harriet Frank Jr. were added to the production crew. Ritt had collaborated with Ravetch and Frank on a number of earlier films, including *The Long Hot Summer* (1958) and *Hud* (1963). The next problem faced by the self-assembled development team was finding a studio to finance the production. Columbia Pictures, Warner Bros., and United Artists all rejected the idea because of the proposed film's prounion subject matter. The production team finally approached Twentieth Century–Fox, who had recently enjoyed unprecedented financial success with the release of *Star Wars* (1977) and critical and popular success with the low-budget, working-class hero-themed *Rocky* (1976). The team convinced the studio that *Norma Rae* was indeed a story about "a female Rocky," another "determined underdog, except in this case the film could prove particularly appealing to women."[22]

The filmmakers took their script to many noted actors during that time who had found recent success playing strong, female characters. Acclaimed actors, such as Faye Dunaway, Diane Keaton, Meryl Streep, and Jane Fonda, all declined the invitation to play the lead role in the film. Ritt finally decided to take a gamble on Sally Field who, although well-known for her work in television sitcoms (including *Gidget* and *The Flying Nun*) was not thought to be a sophisticated actor capable of handling a dramatic role. The choice turned out to be a wise one as the film became the Cinderella story of the awards circuit, beginning with the Best Picture prize at the Cannes Film Festival, where, according to Ritt, "they were delirious about Sally Field."[23] *Norma Rae* also received Golden Globes for Best Drama and Best Actress, Best Actress honors at the American Movie Awards and, after receiving five Academy Award nominations, won for both Best Actress and Best Original Song. The film, however, was not an overwhelming box office success and grossed just a little more than twelve million dollars.[24]

Silkwood received similar acclaim and did considerably better at the box office than *Norma Rae*. The film remained in the top ten for eighteen weeks and ended its theatrical run by grossing thirty-seven million dollars. The film also garnered five Academy Award nominations, although it lost in all categories. *Silkwood* shares a similar plot with *Norma Rae* as it portrays Karen Gay Silkwood (Meryl Streep), a fuel-rod technician for the Kerr-McGee Cimarron plutonium plant in Oklahoma City, and her efforts to unionize the plant workers in order to promote greater safety conditions. Like Norma Rae, Karen is also a single mother, but her three children live with her ex-common-law-husband in Texas. Karen, who shares a house with her boyfriend, Drew Stevens (Kurt Russell), and friend, Dolly Pelliker (Cher), gradually awakens to the dangers facing the plant workers, as well as the questionable safety inspection practices employed by the plant in the name of greater (and faster) production. The pivotal moment in Karen's transformation comes after an elderly friend and co-worker is contaminated at the plant. A few weeks later Karen finds herself contaminated also, at which point she joins the effort to fight the corporation's decertification of the union. During a trip with several co-workers to Washington, D.C.,

Karen meets Paul Stone (Ron Silver), a national representative for the Oil, Chemical, and Atomic Workers Union, who enlightens her to the political import of the situation, and convinces her to fight the corporation on the basis of its violations of government health and safety regulations. Paul persuades Karen to secretly gather evidence for a *New York Times* reporter that would prove Kerr-McGee's safety violations. The remainder of the film chronicles Karen's ongoing documentation of plant activities (and her alienation of her co-workers), as well as her continued contamination. The film concludes with her mysterious death in a car accident on her way to deliver materials to the *New York Times* journalist.

The executive producers of the film, Buzz Hirsch and Larry Cano, became intrigued with Silkwood's story shortly after her death when they were both graduate students in UCLA's film school. Within a year, Hirsch and Cano began working with the Silkwood estate and compiled a wealth of information about Karen's life and work at Kerr-McGee. While working on the project, Hirsch was subpoenaed to appear as a witness in the federal suit filed by the Silkwood estate against Kerr-McGee. When he refused to turn over the information he had obtained to Kerr-McGee, he was threatened with a jail sentence. A variety of organizations associated with the Hollywood community came to his defense, including the Motion Picture Association, the Writer's Guild, and the Reporters' Committee for Freedom of the Press. Eventually, the U.S. Court of Appeals in Denver ruled in Hirsch's favor. The court handed down a landmark decision that granted filmmakers the same first-amendment protection afforded print journalists.[25] Nora Ephron, a well-known feminist novelist and playwright, and Alice Arlen eventually were asked to draft a screenplay, and the producers convinced Mike Nichols to emerge from an eight-year hiatus to direct the film.

Because the foundation of both *Silkwood* and *Norma Rae* rests on their visual dramatization of the true stories of real-life characters, each project became immersed in controversy at some stage of its production. *Norma Rae* ran into problems when Crystal Lee Jordan refused to sign a release to allow the film to portray her likeness on screen (as stipulated by North Carolina law) unless Ritt guaranteed script control to her, Eli Zivkovich (the real labor organizer from New York), and her husband Larry "Cookie" Jordan.[26] Ritt, who valued his artistic control as director above all else, refused to give script control to anyone, including the film studio and Crystal Jordan.[27] According to Ritt, his fictionalized version of "Norma Rae" arose out of his desire to "home in on this woman and on her growth" and, although he later called *Norma Rae* "probably the most pro-union film in the history of Hollywood," that characterization of the film emerged despite the director's original intentions.[28] According to Ritt, "we [didn't] want a union or a labor film; we wanted an entertaining, commercial one."[29] In order to meet commercial expectations in an industry that had become quite conservative, as Ritt recalled in an interview with Pat Aufderheide, the production team "came up with a notion, the relationship between the organizer and the girl, so we kept it entertaining and occasionally powerful."[30] The "artistic" choices exercised by Ritt and screenwriters Ravetch and Frank did not sit well with Jordan, however, and she eventually went public with her dissatisfaction with the end product. Jordan's primary complaint about the film was the format that the filmmakers chose to tell her story. Jordan told Eric Leif Davin, "I wanted it to be a good educational movie, not a soap opera.... If someone was going to spend that much money making a movie about me, I wanted it to be about more than two people, because it took more than two people to win a campaign involving over 3,000 workers."[31]

Although Karen Silkwood did not live to dispute the story depicted in her biographical film, her estate did contest the film's portrayal of Karen and particular aspects of her life. In an interview with *Village Voice* reporter Anna Mayo, Silkwood's father, Bill, commented that Karen was "a whole lot smarter, more intelligent than they showed her in the movie" and that she was a National Honor student who won a scholarship to Lamar College from the Business and Professional Women's Association and had plans to become a scientist.[32] Further, the film vastly oversimplifies the level of Karen's activism. According to Angela Bonavoglia, "Nowhere do we learn that she came to the plant in '72; a few months later, joined an abysmally failed strike; and was one of only twenty union members left when the strike ended."[33] Silkwood's family also resented the way the film portrayed Karen's relationship with her children. According to Mayo, in reality, Karen had taken care of her three children and drunken, adulterous, common-law husband for seven years by working several part-time jobs. When her husband decided he wanted to marry one of Karen's friends, he had his wealthy father hire lawyers to award him custody of the kids. Karen was working at Kerr-McGee so that she could eventually regain custody of her children.[34]

Both films also suffered not only from negative press, but also harsh judgment from film critics and scholars, as a result of their "loose" rendering of the facts of these real women's lives. Elizabeth Stone writes of *Norma Rae*, "At best, it's popcorn politics; at worst, it's misleading.... The problem is that Ritt and Company want to *use* Jordan's story rather than tell it." Stone also claims that "Jordan's union activities grew out of a combination of restlessness and conviction; Norma Rae's motives are trivialized, stemming only from sexual attraction that the noble Reuben resists and channels into activism."[35] *Newsweek*'s David Ansen calls *Norma Rae* "a throwback to the self-congratulatory liberal movies of the '50s sitcom agitprop which tells us that Jews are regular guys, [and] that a girl who sleeps around can have a heart of gold," and Richard Schickel of *Time* writes, "One very much wants to like *Norma Rae* better than one in good critical conscience can."[36] *Silkwood* was disparaged by, among others, critic Tom O'Brien for its "attempts to exploit the legend that has grown around [Silkwood's] name," and Suzanne Gordon for the film's failure "to give us a clear view of this woman who died defending her trade union and coworkers against a powerful employer."[37] The critical disparagement of *Norma Rae* and *Silkwood*, as well as the controversies that the films ignited, stem largely from the filmmakers' use of a politically contentious form: the Hollywood docudrama. An often contested blend of journalistic fact and narrative fiction, the docudrama "dramatizes events and historic personages from our recent memory," making its popular form and social influence a source of debate for filmmakers, film critics, and academic scholars alike.[38]

When Fact Becomes Fiction: Form and Ideology in the Docudrama

"As its name suggests, *docudrama* is a hybrid form, wedding 'documentary' material with 'drama,' particularly melodrama," according to Steve Lipkin.[39] In classical Hollywood docudramas, the melodramatic element often is emphasized because of its recognizable structure. Characterized by the heavy use of suspenseful tension, sensational episodes, and romantic sentiment, melodrama is a standard convention of the classical Hollywood style.[40] Lipkin notes that, as a major defining feature of docudrama, melodrama allows image and story to "claim a motivated, direct relationship to the events the film references."[41] Yet, the desire on the part of the docudrama's creators to maintain the tension between classical melodramatic fiction and historical fact often leads to the form's overarching failure. That is, because of the filmmakers' desire to have their film occupy a space somewhere between the historical recreation of documentary and the marketability of a dramatic narrative common to feature film, docudramas often result in neither gripping storytelling nor faithful historical record.

Norma Rae and *Silkwood* suffer equally from the limitations of such a form; in particular, the films seem to be at cross-purposes in presenting both the realism of working-class struggle and a melodramatic narrative that centers on the personal coming of age of an exceptional individual. The critical response to these docudramas often alludes to such contradictions by pointing out the inadequacies of the films' attempts to achieve a balance between a liberal sensibility and broad commercial appeal. For example, Tom Doherty calls films such as these

> issue-oriented Cinema of Quality ... films whose purported polemical intent never gets too much in the way of adventure, mystery and romance. Because such enterprises tend to lose momentum — not to mention box office — by veering from straightforward melodrama for sharp detours left of center, commercial imperatives tend to win out over political ones.[42]

Richard Blake, noting these tendencies in his review of *Norma Rae*, cautions that, "simplifying complex periods of history reduces movements to morality plays, and simplistic morality plays can be terribly hollow."[43] Terry Christensen addresses the dangers of the docudramas' emphasis on the messy and scandalous circumstances of the film subject's private life to the detriment of a more political focus on her public work and activism. Writing on *Silkwood*, he notes that, as a result, the film, "refused to make its characters easy to like or understand, and it was satisfying neither as entertainment or advocacy."[44] Further, Richard Schickel raises the issue of the "double bind" of docudrama filmmaking, arguing that these films feel "a powerful obligation to politicized mythmaking and must, in any case, try to involve the audience at a more intense and immediate, dramatic, emotional and intellectual level. The strategy, therefore, is to treat the particulars of its heroine's political activities ... almost as irrelevancies."[45]

Despite such critiques, the filmmakers stood behind their generic choices and have since attested that the docudrama form is the only way to impose a political agenda and still fulfill the obligations of Hollywood film to history. For example, in a speech delivered at The National Institute's forum "Hollywood and History: The Debate Over *JFK*," Nora Ephron recounted her experiences writing the screenplay for *Silkwood*. Ephron explained that, in doing what filmmakers do, that is, in "imposing a narrative" on a real-life event, she and Alice Arlen attempted to write, "not a movie about a heroic woman who did something heroic but rather the story of a complicated and interesting and flawed woman who quite unexpectedly did something heroic."[46] Along these same lines, Martin Ritt has defended his decision to "fictionalize" Crystal Lee Jordan's story through the character of Norma Rae by citing his recognition of "the need to idealize [the] characters in order to get the film made and to ensure that it would appeal to a national audience."[47] The end result of such a cinematic rendering of a complex life is a film that, according to Doherty, "measures the demands of entertainment against ideology, tilting the balance first one way, then the other, and finally weighs in heavier as soap opera bio-pic than soap box agit-prop."[48]

Because the docudrama acts as an interpretation of real events through the popular and persuasive media of film, the form actually functions as both entertainment *and* ideology. That is, the docudrama processes a true-life story or event into forms of cinematic fiction, such as the melodrama, while it simultaneously invites cinema audiences to believe what is being reflected back to them is "reality." What Hollywood often mirrors back to audiences, however, are visions of reality that confirm the culture's dominant ideologies. As a result, the docudramas of the late 1970s and early 1980s are representative of what Ray has termed the "New American Cinema," which, "superficially radical, internally conservative — perfectly represented its audience's ambivalent relationship to the period's developments."[49] Docudramas such as *Norma Rae* and *Silkwood* exemplify the motivations of this new cinema by providing a means for the filmmakers to approach ideologically-weighted subjects — such as feminism, liberalism, and working-class socialism — within the commercial mainstream. The primary means of achieving these ends is by combining the formal qualities of semi-documentary realism with a narrative emphasis on a strong individual whose consciousness becomes raised over the course of the film.

The films that often arise out of these motivations are part social realism, part classical Hollywood style, which accounts for the conflicting visions films such as *Norma Rae* and *Silkwood* offer. For example, both films strive in some respect to recreate the gritty realism of working-class life. In *Norma Rae*, this quality was conveyed by the work of the film's cinematographer, John Alonzo, who photographed the film in gray and brown tones to convey the depression of the southern town and the banality of the mill workers' existence. The film reveals the details of working-class culture through subtle touches, such as the people's worn-out clothing, the peeling paint on the houses, and the sweltering heat the workers face both inside and outside of the factory. Alonzo also used a hand-held camera to create a semi-documentary feel and, particularly, to capture the feelings of confinement evoked by the mill, which the opening scenes of the film also reflect.

Norma Rae's title sequence, however, oscillates between working-class realism and a sentimental classicism. The scene begins with a very stylistic, almost lyrical, montage consisting of close-ups of the various factory machines processing cotton bales into twine. The shots are accompanied by the orchestral harmonies of the original song composed for the film, "It Goes Like It Goes" performed by Jennifer Warnes. The rhythm of the edited shots quickens as the scene reveals the workers in the midst of the long lines of machines that fill the factory. The tops of the workers' heads are barely visible as they thread the machines and operate the presses. The scene emphasizes the sense of anonymous workers lost in the factory grind. A close-up, black-and-white photo of a baby appears next, followed by a shot of a page out of a scrapbook on which "Norma Rae" is handwritten. Shots of the various scrapbook photos that chart Norma Rae's childhood are then intercut with shots of the factory. This technique singles out Norma Rae as an individual apart from the others — and as the film's title character.

The final shot of the sequence imbues the factory with a dream-like quality by capturing the cotton lint that floats through the air and falls down among the fluorescent lights in images reminiscent of a snowy wonderland. The sentimentalism of the title sequence ends abruptly, however, as the deafening noise of the factory replaces the song's melodic tunes during the sudden cut to the next scene. The juxtaposition brings the viewer suddenly face to face with the harsh reality of factory life. This scene also introduces Norma Rae as a mill worker through an extreme long-shot that dwarfs her small frame among the large, thunderous machines. These establishing shots, by showing the stark realism of the factory conditions and the workers' plight, suggest that working-class oppression stems from more than just the place one occupies on the economic hierarchy — working-class culture extends into the social and environmental aspects of the workers' existence as well. These early scenes also convey the strong link between Norma Rae's personal identity — beginning with her childhood — and her economic identity as a working-class mill hand.

Silkwood also makes apparent the drudgery of factory life, where the harsh lighting and antiseptic setting of the nuclear plant stands in stark contrast to the muted, sepia-toned scenes of the Oklahoma landscape and the farmhouse Karen shares with co-workers and friends Drew and Dolly. According to *Silkwood*'s cinematographer, Miroslav Ondricek, in the film "there was to be the world of the private life of the girl, her house, her home. This was to be more romantic than the factory. I wanted this private world of Silkwood to be more melodramatic, the simple life of a girl in Oklahoma."[50] The opening scene of the film dramatically emphasizes the dichotomy between the rolling prairies, long country roads, and beautiful sunrise that characterize Silkwood's home life and the cold, gray glass and steel factory where she spends most of her days. The scene begins with a pastoral shot of a white farm house set back from the road and shaded by a grove of trees. As light banjo music starts up in the background, a small, white Honda Civic pulls away from the house and begins to travel down the dirt road. The next shot shows the car traveling on a highway, then turning into the factory. As the car approaches the security booth, the clang of the large metal gates replaces the background music. The music begins again and the pace of the film quickens as several tracking shots are edited together to show the threesome running through the factory, changing into their uniforms, and Karen taking her position on the floor. The glare of the fluorescent lighting, concrete walls, and white hazard suits worn by the employees make up the mise-en-scène. The long, uninterrupted scene that follows reveals the nuances of the interactions between the workers and the drudgery of their work day. Like those that begin *Norma Rae*, the introductory scenes of this film strike a balance between a socialist view of the realism of working-calss culture and the romantic individualism of the heroine's story.

Four. Hollywood's Working-Class Heroines

According to Peter Stead, the realist depiction of working-class living conditions evident in these films lends an appealing freshness and vitality to the stories they portray. Stead argues, however, that although "the new settings and the total command of the idiom promised a new seriousness," the films also conformed to well-established Hollywood norms by concerning themselves with "the talents, successes, and accompanying dilemmas of individual heroes and heroines."[51] Unlike most realist narratives of a socialist nature, in which the fictional subject functions as an embodiment of certain social and historical characteristics (such as a character who stands in for "the people" as a solidarity group), *Norma Rae*'s and *Silkwood*'s characterizations are marked by individualization rather than typification. Therefore, according to Annette Kuhn, the identifications posed by such mainstream working-class films "do not move readily into the terrain of either the social or the historical. [The film's] address consequently operates largely within the limits of dominant cinematic discourse."[52] That is, within these films, the social issues raised are resolved largely by shifting the emphasis from history and institutions to individual causes and effects.

Robert Ray attributes this quality of mainstream films to "Hollywood's thematic conventions [which] rested on an industry wide consensus defining commercially acceptable filmmaking. This consensus's underlying premise dictated the conversion of all political, sociological, and economic dilemmas into personal melodramas."[53] Although *Norma Rae* and *Silkwood* address issues of working-class struggle, the primary emphasis of these films remains the main protagonist's growth toward self-realization rather than any overt critique of capitalism or of the structural inequality inherent in the class system. The sentimental liberalism of these films instead offers what Michael Ryan and Douglas Kellner argue are multiple, and often contradictory, messages by suggesting a "dissatisfaction with working-class life, with the limitations capitalism imposes, and ... the need to overcome those limitations" while they also "tend to reinforce the founding values and the legitimating ideology of the class system."[54] In *Norma Rae* and *Silkwood*, the women's involvement in labor politics is taken up, for the most part, as a derivative of their personal journey toward self-actualization rather than as an explicit challenge to the structures of social and political oppression.

The initial presentation of these two film's main protagonists, Norma Rae Webster and Karen Silkwood, is particularly interesting in this regard.

Significantly, the Hollywood emphasis on humanism takes on a new twist when the paradigm of the "outlaw hero" becomes re-gendered and applied to *female* heroes. These women are portrayed as very tainted heroes, that is, they are single mothers, they drink, smoke pot, pop pills, sleep around, they are sometimes bitchy and sometimes flirty, and appear to be of questionable moral character until they begin to channel their energies into the cause of labor activism. They are both initially characterized as troublemakers and outsiders who consistently push the boundaries of convention both at work and at home. The women are shown as victims of undesirable circumstances who become incidental heroes through their desire to find an outlet for their restless energy and nontraditional impulses. These women's troubled heroism adds a new dimension to the archetype of the "outlaw hero" suggested by Ray in that these protagonist's personal difficulties are resolved through their public action; however, their activism remains overshadowed by the personal melodrama constituted by the women's sense of personal injustice that brings about her coming of age.

The first three scenes of *Norma Rae*, for example, immediately establish a view of the heroine as a feisty woman who speaks her mind, takes risks, and lives as she chooses—for better or for worse. In the very first scene, Norma shares lunch with her mother and a co-worker in the small lunch room just off of the factory floor. The din of the machines can be heard through the glass and the women have to shout in order to be heard. Norma notices her mother standing with her head in her hands and her eyes closed. Norma asks, "Momma, don't you want your lunch?" When it becomes obvious that her mother can not hear her, Norma frantically whisks her through the weaving room to the company doctor. He tells Norma Rae that this happens all the time, and that it is only temporary. Furious at the doctor's lack of concern, Norma shouts, "Well, it doesn't happen to my momma!" As Norma Rae shepherds her mother from the office, she yells, loudly enough for the doctor to hear, "Come on, Momma! They don't care about you." This very first scene demonstrates Norma's propensity toward rebellion at work, as well as the notion that her initial inclination to challenge factory management emerged out of a very personal sense of injustice. The unhealthy noise levels in the mill only became a problem for Norma Rae when it directly affected *her* momma.

The following two scenes reveal Norma Rae's personal life away from the factory and begin to show how her restlessness has led to her increasing bitterness and acts of moral indiscretion in her private affairs. After her frustrating day at the factory, Norma Rae checks on her mother (whose hearing has now been restored), soaks the pots from dinner, nags her kids about doing their homework, and, as she walks into the bedroom, sniffs her arm pit, which is soiled with sweat stains. As she removes her shirt, her father walks in and asks with suspicion, "What are you getting fixed up for?" She explains that she is going into town, and when he offers to drive her, she replies coarsely, "I'm going to J.C. Penney's to buy myself some panties and a white cotton brassiere, size 32B. You wanna come along and sit on a little stool outside the dressing room and have all the ladies look at you, then come on." "Comin' straight back?" her father asks in a defeated tone. "No. After that I'm going to the drugstore to buy myself some Kotex pads and a *Cosmopolitan* magazine," Norma Rae replies as she brushes her hair and sprays on perfume. Sitting on the bed her father asks, sadly, "Then you comin' home?" "Yeah," she replies, "after that I'll be so tired out from all the excitement, I'll be comin' home." Norma Rae's treatment of her father reveals the tension in their relationship, as well as her growing dissatisfaction with her life. It also demonstrates her father's concern, and his unspoken fear that Norma is going out to look for trouble rather than to shop for underwear.

In the next scene, Norma sits in the lobby of a motel reading a magazine, confirming her father's suspicions. An older man in a floral print shirt checks in at the desk and subtly beckons to her as he passes by. The following scene opens with Norma Rae in a motel room standing in her bra and pulling on her pants. The man from the lobby emerges from the shower and tells her he'll be back next week. As she finishes dressing she tells him, "I'm not trotting down here anymore, George," and the shaky hand-held camera shows him turn to confront her, just inches from her face. "Why, you hick," he says, "you got dirt under your finger nails, you pick your teeth with a matchbook. I see you! Shit, what the hell are you good for anyway? You come out of that factory, you wash under your armpits, you come on down here and spread your legs for a poke and you're dumping me?" George's harsh comment serves as an indictment of Norma Rae and her lifestyle, which he punctuates by hauling off and punching her in the face. Norma slams into the wall, then runs from the motel room with a bloody nose.

Back at the plant the next day, the plant supervisor, worried because he saw Norma Rae talking to the labor organizer outside of the plant, calls Norma into his office. She walks into the office and states indignantly, "Whatever it is, I didn't do it!" "Norma," he replies, "you've got the biggest mouth in this mill. 'Give us a longer break, give us more smokin' time, give us a Kotex pad machine!'" "Do it and I'll shut up," she replies. "Well, we'll do better than that. We figure the only way to close that mouth is to hand you a promotion. You're going up in the world, honey!" The promotion comes with a $1.50 an hour raise, which Norma accepts grudgingly because, even though she knows her new position as "spot checker" will not make her any friends, she needs the money. Again, this scene confirms Norma's inclination to look out for her own best interest, as well as her reputation as a woman who is not afraid to challenge authority. However, the way these early scenes develop Norma Rae's character also seems to imply that her rebelliousness also usually invites negative consequences that she must then attempt to overcome.

The early development of Karen Silkwood's character follows a very similar pattern. In the film's opening sequence, she arrives late for work at the plant and begins joking around with her co-workers. Like a naughty schoolgirl, Karen stands at her post chewing gum and blowing bubbles while sifting through plutonium and uranium oxide powder, which further accentuates her defiant and, at times, irresponsible character. As soon as the lunch bell rings, Karen runs for the door and must be reprimanded by a co-worker to "monitor" herself for contamination before she exits the room. With an over-dramatic and indignant flourish, she raises her hands in front of the monitor and dances around in a circle. The following scene shows her in the cafeteria sharing a cigarette with Drew before making what appear to be her usual rounds. With no lunch of her own, she walks from table to table taking bites of people's sandwiches or picking through their lunch containers. Some respond to her obnoxious behavior with looks of disgust, others (all men) gladly share a bite with her. The scene, however, portrays Karen as a general nuisance who willingly takes advantage of others to fulfill her own selfish needs. The next scene compounds this notion by showing Karen's attempts to guilt her co-workers into taking her weekend shift so she can visit her kids in Texas. After asking for a volunteer and receiving no response, Karen confronts each person one by one and demands an excuse for why they will not trade shifts with her. Reluctantly, one woman gives in to Karen's subtle bullying and agrees to take her shift if Karen works the following two weekends in a row.

Several scenes later, when Karen returns to work the following Monday, the film continues to cast doubt on her integrity. She finds out through the grapevine that the plant was forced to close for the weekend because of contamination in her section. Karen also becomes aware that many of the plant's employees, all of whom knew she was desperate to get the weekend off, believe she was responsible for the contamination. After her section leader asks with disdain, "Did you enjoy your weekend, Karen?" she storms out of the room and runs to the section of the plant where Drew works. On her way there a young man in the hallway whistles as she walks past and she responds with a dirty look. The next shot shows her bursting through the swinging doors yelling, "Drew! Drew! Did you hear about this thing?" "Why don't we talk about it at lunch," he responds. "I just hate people talking about me that way," she whines. After the other workers in the room air their own suspicions of Karen, Drew points to the man on his left and advises her, "Here's Quincy, here's the head of the union, talk to him. The union'll get you out of this." "Yeah, sure, O.K.," she replies, while rolling her eyes. "Karen, the company's got to blame somebody — otherwise it's their fault," Quincy explains. Blatantly ignoring Quincy's counsel, Karen turns and confronts the young man from the hallway who has now followed her into the room and continues to ogle her. "What are you lookin' at, Zachary?" she demands. Then, she rips open her jumpsuit and flashes him her bare breast while she yells at him, "Well, get lost, O.K.?" The young man runs from the room while Karen buttons back up, sticks out her tongue, and looks vaguely amused at his reaction. "Hey Karen? You ever thought of going into politics?" Quincy asks facetiously. Both Karen's behavior and Quincy's sarcastic reaction in this scene confirm the offensiveness of Karen's behavior — and suggests that she is not to be taken very seriously.

Both *Norma Rae* and *Silkwood* dramatize the circumstances of the protagonists' lives early on in ways that define them as unsympathetic characters with whom spectators may find identification difficult. The women are portrayed as not only bossy and domineering, but crude, selfish, and inconsiderate in their dealings with friends, family, and co-workers. Although they appear to be somewhat independent and free-spirited women, they also are presented as misguided in their actions and decisions.

Further, the women's overtly sexual behavior (further substantiated through allusions to their checkered sexual past) invites disapproval and disdain from the other characters in the film. From the beginning, the films appear to be building a case against the heroines through characterizations of them as selfish and unstable outsider figures, who are also naïve to the politics of the workplace. Both Norma Rae and Karen are initially presented as women whose actions in both their public and personal affairs serve no real purpose beyond their own needs for instant self-gratification. As their characters continue to develop, this early narcissism becomes the impetus for their initial entry into union politics. For both women, union activity begins as their own personal crusade, and only later do they begin to view their activism as a social and political responsibility.

In *Silkwood*, the initial spark for Karen's investigation into worker safety at the plant begins after an elderly friend, Thelma, is contaminated at work. When Dolly informs Karen that Thelma's been "cooked," Karen rushes to "decon" where the contamination victims are stripped and brutally scrubbed down in a large, tiled room lined with shower heads. Sobbing hysterically, Thelma tells Karen that now she is going to get cancer. That night, Karen becomes preoccupied with that same fear and Drew gently admonishes her on the porch, asking her, "You're just waking up to this? What do you think we're working with

Meryl Streep stars as plutonium plant worker Karen Silkwood in the Hollywood docudrama *Silkwood*. While the film attempted to craft a story of Silkwood's evolution into a corporate whistleblower and labor organizer as a testament to the courage and determination of those who fight for workers' rights, the choice of the already legendary Streep also worked to undermine the gritty realism of the working-class activist's tragic life.

over there, puffed wheat?" Several scenes later Karen herself becomes contaminated, at which point her instincts for personal survival become the initial motivation for her burgeoning activism. The next day she sits on the porch swing reading a pamphlet that had been distributed by the union, which awakens her curiosity about the health and safety conditions at the plant.

Several short scenes chronicle Karen's conversion from a blissfully ignorant plutonium worker to an impassioned and educated advocate for worker safety. Because of her contamination, the plant transfers Karen to the Metalography Division, where she assists Winston (Craig T. Nelson) in inspecting fuel rod welds. That same afternoon she witnesses him coloring in the negatives of the welds with a black magic marker and becomes even more suspicious of company practices. That night she attends a union meeting and volunteers to help organize the campaign against de-certification by serving on the union negotiating committee. When she tells Drew before bed, he chuckles and looks at her in disbelief. "Karen, let me give you a hint," he chides her, "don't flash 'em." Several short scenes later Karen is on the phone with Quincy, the union leader, giving him advice on campaign strategy. "What if we wrote the national union and told them what's going on down here, maybe they would help us," she suggests. "Well, we're not going to win the election by ourselves," she laments. "Yeah, we've got to do something, I think. You know management's puttin' up these memos now saying no union business on our breaks — that's our own time, Quincy. Yeah [pause] now, well, I think they just think they can get away with anything." These two scenes show the rapid transformation in Karen's character from an impulsive instigator to a savvy, political strategist. Her foray into activism continues to evolve, especially a few scenes later when she, Quincy, and a fellow worker fly to Washington, D. C. to meet with representatives from the national union and the Atomic Energy Commission.

The threesome appears conspicuously out of place sitting in the D.C. conference room with Paul Stone from the national office and another union representative. Karen appears nervous and intimidated in the meeting as she stammers over her words and puffs compulsively on her cigarette. After the meeting, Karen approaches the men in the hallway to inform them that the plant has been touching up negatives to cover-up faulty fuel rod welds. This scene represents a pivotal moment in the film as the men, especially Paul, validate Karen and her suspicions. "If you could get documentation, that would be very important," the union representative explains. "There's a moral imperative involved here," he informs her, "Think about it. Talk to Paul. You look like a stand-up girl." In the next scene, Drew and Karen are at Quincy's house watching slides of the trip. Several of the pictures make apparent that Karen's relationship with Paul had quickly moved beyond a professional context. In the following scene, Drew and Karen are in the car driving home when he chastises her for her involvement in the union, warning her, "People are going to lose their jobs, Karen." She parrots the union representative's words back to Drew, telling him with conviction, "There's a moral imperative here." Karen's conversion from irritating troublemaker to impassioned organizer has begun in earnest, and for the remainder of the film she becomes even more committed to exposing Kerr-McGee and initiating the fight for nuclear worker safety.

Norma Rae's coming of age follows an analogous pattern. After her promotion to spot checker, she receives the cold shoulder from many of her co-workers. Even her own father turns on her and, when she explains that she needs the raise for her kids, he yells at her, "Well, I don't need it from my kid." A few scenes later, Norma Rae realizes that no one at the plant will even speak to her anymore. She approaches an older man on his break (played by the film's director, Martin Ritt) and asks him, "What the hell is going on around here? I'm talkin' to you." He turns to her and calls her, "Fink." Norma promptly storms into the manager's office and tells him, "Nobody out there is talking to me." "Less talk, more work," the manager replies. "Yeah, well, they're my friends," she says, "and they're going to stay my friends. I'm quittin'. I'm quittin' right here and I'm quittin' right now. You're speedin' them up so you can weed them out!" "You knew all that," he reminds her. "Yeah, I was greedy and I was dumb and now I'm sorry," she concedes. Norma Rae's stand against the company begins as a remedy to her self-imposed alienation. She steps down from her management position merely to abate the ill will that has been inflicted on her by her co-workers, as well as to assuage her feelings of guilt. Two scenes later, Norma Rae decides to attend the informational meeting Reuben holds at a local church, and her transformation into an activist for the workers gradually begins.

Both *Norma Rae* and *Silkwood* focus on the women's spontaneous and unruly behavior in the first half of the films, suggesting that these protagonists' entry into activism was merely an arbitrary outlet the women chose to express their restless energy. Norma Rae's and Karen's involvement in labor politics occurs almost overnight, and without any strong sense of commitment or conviction on the part of the women. Leaving out many of the details of the larger history of how these women's involvement in the union developed over a long period of time overlooks the courage and drive, as well as the collective action, necessary for the union victories achieved by the end of the films. The films' melodramatic narratives overshadow the hard work, persistence, and commitment demanded of the female labor activist; instead, her moments of activism are reduced to just a few distinct scenes. In fact, both Norma Rae and Karen only come to view their union efforts as a worthy political cause through the unfolding of the film's second major plotline: the romantic narrative between the film's subject and the labor organizer who shows her the ropes.

In the first half of both *Silkwood* and *Norma Rae*, the heroines are portrayed as naive, immature, and in need of guidance. In both cases, they receive instructions on how to behave from the men in their lives, whether from a boyfriend, father, or boss. While the protagonist's father, boyfriend, husband, or boss may instruct her on how to act, it is not until the wiser and more principled union man enters her life that she realizes what she can become.

Although Norma Rae becomes aware of the need for factory reform through her personal experiences at the cotton mill (such as her mother's temporary deafness), it is not until she meets Reuben that she really begins to think about her own potential for activism and the social rewards of unionization. Norma first encounters Reuben when he knocks on her parents' door in one of the early scenes in the film. Reuben appears at the door and asks Norma's father, Vernon, if they might have a room he could stay in for a few weeks. When Vernon asks why, Reuben explains that he has "come to put a union in the O. P. Henley textile mill." Vernon accuses Reuben of being a Communist, agitator, and crook, and Reuben responds, "You're underpaid. You're overworked. They're shafting you right up to your tonsils. You need me." Despite Reuben's appeals, Vernon orders him off of his property. Reuben's visit arouses Norma's curiosity about him, however, and when she meets up with him again at the motel after her tousle with her illicit lover, she bombards him with questions. As Norma interrogates Reuben about his girlfriend (whose picture she notices on the bureau) and about his being Jewish, their initial attraction to each other becomes evident. While Reuben tenderly applies ice wrapped in a washcloth to Norma's bloody nose, she looks at him with a combination of curiosity and interest. The next day when Norma sees him standing outside the plant, he asks, "How's your nose?" and hands her a leaflet. "There's too many big words in here," she tells him, "If I don't understand it, they ain't going to understand it." On her way in, Norma's boss pulls her aside and asks, "That fellow a friend of yours, Norma?" "Looks like he's getting to be," she replies, and it becomes clear that Norma Rae and Reuben have already developed a bond of sorts and that, through their developing relationship, they will begin to help each other and learn from one another.

Several scenes later Norma Rae bumps into Reuben once again at the hotdog stand during a local softball game. As Norma stands talking with Reuben, a man approaches her and asks about her son. The man clearly is her son's father, Ellis Harper, and, after he leaves, she explains to Reuben the history of her relationship with Ellis. "I climbed into the backseat of his Cadillac on a rainy night six years ago, stuck my feet out the window, and got me my little Craig off that Southern gentleman," she tells Reuben. "He's never done anything worthwhile since." After they walk and talk for a bit longer, Norma turns to Reuben and asks, "What do you think of me, I wonder?" "I think you're too smart for what's happening to you," he replies. This exchange represents the beginning of Norma Rae's awakening, of which Reuben becomes the catalyst.

Later in the film, Norma Rae attends a meeting held by Reuben at a local church. Afterward, he tells her he needs her help and she responds with a pensive look. The next day Norma shows up at Reuben's motel room. "If I join up with you, will I lose my job?" she asks. "No way!" he tells her. "You can wear a union button as big as a Frisbee when you go to work," he explains, "You can talk union to any mill hand who wants to listen, as long as it's during a break. You can take union pamphlets to the mill and pass them along—and there's not a goddamn thing they can do to touch you." Norma looks at him and, with hands on her hips and wrinkled brow, she concedes, "Well, I never was a very good girl scout." "You're the fish I wanted to hook," Reuben confesses. "Well, now you got me, what're you gonna do with me?" she asks. "Make a mensch out of you," he tells her. In this scene, it becomes apparent that Norma is Galatea to Reuben's Pygmalion; all along Reuben's sights have been set on Norma and now he finally has found the opportunity to satisfy his desire and to transform her into someone he can actually respect.

The remainder of the film portrays Norma as a changed woman, more assured of herself and now focused on a cause that reaches beyond her own self-fulfillment. Norma wears a huge TWUA (Textile Workers Union of America) button to work the next day and spends her breaks convincing her co-workers to join the cause. Several scenes later, Norma approaches the reverend of her church to ask if she can borrow the church for a union meeting (with blacks and whites in attendance) the following week. She challenges him:

> Now I want to see what this church stands for. I want to see if you'll stand up in that pulpit and say there should be justice, there should be union, if you're oppressed, fight back, if you're smitten, rise up — and the Lord'll be on your side. If you don't do that, I say there's nothing in this church that's any good to me and I'll leave it flat.

The reverend responds, "We'll miss your voice in the choir, Norma." "You'll hear it raised up someplace else," she retorts, turns on her heel, and marches across the church parking lot.

Pat Aufderheide notes that, although Norma Rae "learns how to assess, value and use her strengths" and that "this focus can be exhilarating, when Sally Fields shows us a girl growing into a woman, making mistakes and learning from them, turning irritation into action," these developments in her character are merely the result of Norma's growing relationship with Reuben.[55] Norma's screen time with Reuben increases proportionately with her growing involvement in the organization of the union. For example, in a sequence about halfway through the film, Norma and Reuben are shown spending a Saturday together visiting the locals and petitioning them for their union support. Reuben and Norma are seen helping a man fix a tire, whittling wood with a group of old men in front of the country store, and talking to a farmer. At the farm, Reuben slips in a cow pasture and falls in a large pile of dung. The next scene shows Norma Rae washing out Reuben's shirt on the banks of a watering hole while Reuben swims. Norma decides to join him, and Reuben looks away while she strips down and jumps into the water next to him. The sexual tension is pronounced as Norma circles Reuben in the water, and he looks pensively over his shoulder while paddling away from her. Norma flirts with him, saying

"You've got a skinny build.... Well, you ain't got to worry 'cause you got a head on you — and you use it." The scene emphasizes Norma's fascination with Reuben, who is unlike any other man she has ever known, and demonstrates the couple's conscious effort to discipline their attraction to one another. Yet, by showing Norma's more blatant affection for Reuben, this scene also suggests that her newfound interest in labor activism may be more about the image of herself she sees reflected through her relationship with him than from a strong desire to right the wrongs of social injustice.

Similarly, in *Silkwood*, Karen's involvement with Paul Stone offers her the incentive she needed to undertake a more aggressive part in the labor activism against the plant. Paul's validation of Karen's suspicions and his belief in her abilities to expose Kerr-McGee provides her with the confidence she needs to begin the fight. When, in the very first scene after the D.C. trip, the photos in Quincy's slide show reveal Karen and Paul arm in arm, it becomes clear, especially to Drew, that Karen has begun to change. Karen returns from the meeting clearly transformed — and her association with Paul becomes part of her new identity. Several scenes later, a large meeting is held to educate the workers about plutonium poisoning and Karen and Paul sit together at a table at the front of the room along with several medical experts. After the meeting, Paul walks with his arm around Karen. When they reach her car he tells her, "I've got an early plane, Karen." "Meanin' what?" she asks. "Meaning, I don't think this is smart, us getting involved." "We already got involved," she replies matter-of-factly. "Yeah," he whispers then pauses momentarily and gets in her car, and they drive off together despite Paul's feeble protest.

The following scene shows Karen on the phone. Paul's answering machine can be heard through the phone and she leaves a message telling him that they won the union election 80–61, that she has been under a lot of pressure and, despite her success, without him there she feels very alone. This short scene illustrates Karen's dependence on Paul, and his important role in what she is doing. It also becomes clear that, without Paul, Karen is not nearly as self-assured. Also, beyond her relationship with Paul, Karen's activism is minimally represented in the film. She is shown briefly at a negotiation meeting with the company bosses and visiting her old section to ask her colleagues if she can speak to them on their break. These scenes, however, are very brief and lacking in content.

In both *Norma Rae* and *Silkwood*, the women's relationships with the labor organizer expands the women's consciousness, but the material effects are not readily apparent in the films. One consequence of the women's growing independence and political development that the films do emphasize is the impact of these changes on her personal life. Both films also include a plotline that charts the development of the women's home life and her relationship with her boyfriend or husband. Although these scenes are few once the women become involved in their activism, the content of these scenes illustrates that her political work and personal growth (as well as her attraction to her activist mentor) comes at the expense of maintaining the relationships in her private life.

In the second half of both *Norma Rae* and *Silkwood*, scenes that do not include the male labor organizer generally focus on the tension between the female heroine and her domestic partner, and thus continue to add to the melodrama. For example, Karen's relationship with Drew comprises a running plot line in the film. Before she meets Paul, Karen relies on Drew as her primary support system. He gives her advice, and comforts her after her first contamination. As soon as he learns of her affair with Paul, however, he leaves. Later in the film, after Karen's house becomes contaminated and her relationship with Paul dissolves, Drew returns and comes to Karen's rescue once again. In *Norma Rae*, the other man in Norma's life is Sonny Webster, whom she meets at the mill. Sonny becomes the most recent in a long line of men with whom Norma becomes involved, including a former husband who was killed in a bar fight. Recently divorced himself, Sonny tells Norma on their second date, "I got [my daughter] Alice and I'm alone. You got two kids and you're alone. If you could help me maybe I could help you." In the following scene Norma and Sonny are married at a small ceremony in the living room of the local Justice of the Peace. Both Drew and Sonny are represented, for the most part, as sweet, loving men who merely want to take care of the women they love. The fact that both Karen and Norma are in relationships with these ordinary, working-class men through most of the film functions to further embellish the significance of the women's attraction to the more cosmopolitan labor organizer.

Further, these domestic romantic relationships in the films explicitly dramatize the changes in the women after they become more involved in union activities. For example, in a pivotal scene in *Norma Rae*, Norma sits in the kitchen making phone calls to O. P. Henley workers late at night, urging them to get onboard with the union. Sonny, awakened by Norma's raised voice on the phone, comes into the kitchen and pulls the milk out of the refrigerator. After taking a mouthful, he spits it into the sink in a dramatic flourish, complaining, "This godam milk's sour." "I didn't have a chance to get to the market," Norma admits. With a raised voice, Sonny responds, "Well, you didn't have a chance to get to the market, did you? And you didn't get to the washing and you didn't get to the kids and you didn't get to me." "Is that right?" Norma replies with forced composure. Sonny rages on, "That's right. That's right. Damn TV dinners, the kids are going around in dirty jeans, and I'm going around without, altogether!" At this, Norma loses her temper and tears through the kitchen like a small cyclone throwing food in pots, dumping clothes in the sink and dousing them in water and soap, and yanking out the ironing board. "You want cookin'?" she yells. "You got cookin'. You want laundry? You got laundry. You want ironing? You got ironing. You want to make love, then you get behind me and lift up my nightie and we're gonna make love." Sonny gazes at her in disbelief, unable to comprehend the changes that have come over his wife.

Drew and Karen come to blows in a strikingly parallel scene in *Silkwood*. After Karen ends another phone call to Quincy regarding union matters, Drew walks in from outside and opens the refrigerator to find that there is no more beer. "You know, I don't mind somebody taking one of my beers if they replace it," he says, while grabbing a beer from Karen's hand. "Well, you're making a big deal about everything lately," she tells him. "Yup, well everything's going to hell around here!" he yells. "Meaning you're out of beer?" she retorts. "Meaning you're on the goddamn phone night and day!" Drew exclaims, revealing that his irritation stems much more from his felt neglect than lack of beer. Karen puts her head in her hands in exasperation. Both scenes suggest the women's inability to maintain both their work for the union and attention to their male companions and domestic duties. Both men's reactions also suggest that their wife's/girlfriend's work for the labor cause is tolerable, but only if it takes a back seat to her responsibilities at home. The films call attention to the issue of women's "double shift," but do not invite any particular stance on the issue. Rather, the men are stereotyped as chauvinistic jerks and the women's reactions range from ludicrous (Norma's temper tantrum) to noncommittal (Karen's silence). As a result, spectators may not find identification with either party desirable.

The dual romantic couplings found in both *Norma Rae* and *Silkwood* function in interesting ways. The women's involvement in each of their relationships (with the activists and in their home life) contribute to certain stereotypes about femininity and masculinity raised in the films. The women's relationship with her domestic partner (Norma Rae and Sonny, Karen and Drew), for example, emphasizes the traditional expectations of women's role in a male-female partnership. The women are shown, on one hand, as wanting to remain a part of such a union. Norma Rae clearly marries Sonny out of convenience, and her belief that she needs a man around, rather than for love — a conclusion hinted at by their agreement during their single-date courtship (I'll take care of you if you take care of me) and by the awkward looks they give one another after their impromptu wedding ceremony. Karen also recognizes how much she needs and relies on Drew when, after their break-up, she accidentally runs her car off the road in an effort to avoid hitting a deer. Drew picks her up and, subsequently, spends the night. Since Karen's relationship with Paul has, by that point, deteriorated, she comments to him the next morning, "If you're back, I'm really glad you're back." The couple re-unites and stays together through the remainder of the film.

Norma Rae's relationship with Reuben (although never consummated) and Karen's relationship with Paul, on the other hand, appear at the outset to be more progressive and enlightening than the women's relationship with their working-class male companions. However, the women evolve into active subjects only through their objectification by these more experienced and educated men. The union organizers mold and guide the female protagonists into the kind of women they think they should be. In making the women stronger, Reuben and Paul also achieve a more self-serving objective — they make a connection with someone on the inside who can advance the union cause for them. Both men also blatantly patronize the women on occasion. For example, Reuben constantly feels the need to correct Norma's grammar and, when the union bosses express their concern that Norma could jeopardize the campaign because of her checkered past, Reuben responds, "What do I care if she has round heels?" He also loses his temper with her when she fails to copy down a company memo for him. "Sweetheart," he yells at her, "you walk up to it, you stand there, and you copy it down word for word, line by line, you get me the date, you get me the signature, you get it all and you get it back to me." This tiff with Reuben also inspires Norma Rae to the most poignant, and most well-remembered, scene in the film. When Norma returns to the plant, she deliberately copies the memo right in front of the management, and when they call the police, she mounts a shop table, scrawls UNION on a piece of cardboard and stands defiantly for all the mill workers to see. One by one they turn off their machines in support of this bold action.

In *Silkwood*, Paul similarly belittles Karen and manipulates her into getting what he wants. For example, when she calls him from a payphone one night to relay information she has discovered about the harsh conditions the janitorial staff encounter at the plant, Paul, concerned only with the doctored X-rays, casually dismisses her by responding, "Yeah, yeah, yeah, yeah, yeah. Look, Karen it's the X-rays that are really important. Now, we're going into the contract negotiations and we want to get the guy from the *Times* down there in mid–November — that's three weeks." Interestingly, Karen's initial impulse was to do what she could to help the workers and improve conditions for them (at the initial meeting in Washington, she even brings up the poorly maintained showers in the plant). In her service to Paul, however, she risks her life to obtain information that will not directly affect worker safety, but instead cast a general suspicion regarding the dangerous production practices, and ethics, of the nuclear industry.

Through scenes such as these, the films question whether the women really can manage without the men's intrusion into their lives. More specifically, because both of these women's activism comes only through their sexual involvement with or attraction to the labor organizer, the films subtly disparage the women's eventual personal growth and liberation. These films' focus on the love interest between the working-class woman and the middle-class organizer subtly tempers the female labor activists' heroism. The path to the women's enlightenment comes as the result of these relationships. According to David Bordwell, Janet Steiger, and Kristin Thomson, narrative resolution in the Hollywood film "can work to transcend the social conflict represented in the film, often by displacing it onto the individual (the hero torn between duty and personal urges), the couple (the romance-plot taking precedence over the pretext-action), the family, or the communal good."[56] In the case of *Norma Rae* and *Silkwood*, the social conflicts (read: labor issues) of the films are, for the most part, subordinate to the two primary plot devices: the heroine's coming of age and the romantic storylines. In both films the individual hero and romantic couple plotlines unfold simultaneously through most of the narrative and, before long, the female labor activists' romantic relationships serve as the impetus for both her emerging political interests and her personal maturation. Even more problematic is that the causal effect implied by the films suggests that without Reuben, Norma Rae would not have developed the social conscience necessary to go to battle for the mill's unionization and, without Paul, Karen would have remained disorganized, unfocused, and misdirected. The logical conclusion of both films is that, had it not been for the generous guidance, and patience, proffered by the infinitely more knowledgeable and conscientious union man, the wet-behind-the-ears working-class girl likely would remain in ignorant bliss.

The women's fortitude for socially-conscious heroism is questioned further by the narrative resolution of the female characters in these films. In *Norma Rae*, the mill management responds to her defiant moment of protest by helping the sheriff escort her out of the mill and off to jail. Norma, desperate not to be sent to jail, fights with all of her might not to be put in the police car. Eventually, the two men overcome her and the next scene opens with Norma, with a despondent look on her face, being charged with disorderly conduct and led into the county jail cell. When Reuben bails her out of jail she falls apart in the car, sobbing uncontrollably into her hands. "It comes with the job," Reuben tells her, "I've seen a pregnant woman on a picket line get hit in the stomach with a club, I saw a boy of sixteen get shot in the back, I saw a guy get blown to hell and back when he tried to start up his car in the morning." While Norma continues to sob, he lectures her, "And you just got your feet wet on this one." Norma stops crying and continues to look straight ahead with a blank expression, indicating that Reuben's words have offered her little comfort. Indeed, his remarks insinuate that her act of conscience was not very significant or brave in the larger history of labor activism.

Two scenes later, Norma and Reuben stand outside of the factory as the union election takes place inside. The company supervisor announces the official count: the ballots against the union are 373, and the ballots for the union are 425. The crowd erupts into loud cheers and begins to chant, "Union, union." Hearing the celebration from outside the gates,

Norma and Reuben each take a deep breath, and begin to walk to his car. "So, what are you going to do now?" Reuben asks. "Live, what else?" Norma responds, although the vagueness of this statement sounds largely unconvincing. At the car, they politely shake hands and Reuben gets inside, ready to drive to the next factory in need of his service. Norma stands with her arms at her side, with her lips turned down as if on the verge of tears and, with no apparent plan of her own, she watches him drive away.

Karen Silkwood's story ends much more tragically. Near the end of the film, Karen arrives at work and sets off the contamination alarms on her way in. Kerr-McGee immediately dispatches a decontamination crew in white, space-like suits to her farm house. The men remove every possession in the house and begin to scrape the wallpaper off of the walls. Horrified, Karen watches as they place her children's photographs in plastic bags for proper disposal. The company boss, Mr. Hurley, asks her for a statement and she responds, her voice full of desperation, "In my own words, I'm contaminated, I'm dying." When she shows up at Drew's later that night, she compulsively pops the pills she has been shown taking more and more through the second half of the film (the epilogue reveals them to be tranquilizers). She tells Drew, hysterically, "They're killing me, they're trying to kill me. They want me to stop what I'm doing. They contaminated me, you know that? They internally contaminated me ... Drew, I'm so scared!" Clearly, Karen's resolve has been severely tested. Looking disheveled and frail in Drew's arms, Karen appears to be losing the fight against the corporate giant. After Drew and Dolly accompany her to Los Alamos to independently verify her contamination levels, Karen decides she is finally ready to meet with *The New York Times* reporter. On her way to the meeting, however, bright headlights appear in her rearview mirror and she shields her eyes from the glare. The next scene shows a tow truck pulling her demolished car down the street. Although the film's epilogue reveals that the circumstances of the accident are unknown and the police ruled her death a single-car accident, the film's inclusion of the headlights in Karen's rearview mirrors suggests that the accident was more suspicious than initially reported by the authorities who conducted the investigation. As a result, Karen's final act of protest never came to fruition and, instead, her story became the stuff of legend, making her into a martyr for the anti-nuclear power movement.

The conclusions of both films function to symbolically silence the female labor activist either through judicial incarceration — and subsequent humiliation — or through her destruction. Like the screwball comedies of the 1940s in which highly spirited and rebellious women often were silenced through physical abuse on the part of the male lead (films that Diane Carson argues wanted "to have it both ways: joyous rebellion and a status quo securely in place"), more contemporary films quell the disruptive excess of women's subversive behavior through recuperative resolution.[57] By the conclusion of *Norma Rae* and *Silkwood*, the reluctant female labor activist turns into a tragic heroine, and her ability to truly re-conceptualize social and political relations finally seems to lie just beyond her grasp or becomes remembered only as a lost promise of what could have been. While Norma stands alone after Reuben's departure, the film leaves the question of what her future might hold unanswered. Similarly, the glimpse of hope offered in the few moments of activist heroism displayed by Karen Silkwood, as well as the documents she was thought to have had in the car with her, disappear in the accident that causes her death. Each heroine's potential power, and the liberal message of the film, is diffused by the conclusion and the woman faces either an uncertain or a nonexistent future.

Norma Rae's and Karen Silkwood's tragic outcomes also may be seen as the result of the way the films re-gender the reluctant hero by characterizing the female labor activist as a tragically-flawed or tainted heroine. Significantly, *Silkwood*'s and *Norma Rae*'s depictions of their main protagonists, as problematic women who express their unpopular views willingly and flaunt their unconventional behavior for all to see, also leave their motivations for activism uncertain. *Silkwood* screenwriter Nora Ephron attributes this effect to the filmmakers' efforts to get, "closer to the truth about [Karen] than a great deal of what had been written.... A lot of which either sanctified her or attempted to blacken her entirely. Who she was was an extremely complicated, occasionally self-destructive woman who was, incidentally, a hero."[58] Yet, Karen's and Norma Rae's incidental activism may leave viewers wondering whether, as critic Doherty wonders, it has "as much to do with gut-level recalcitrance as high-flown idealism." Similarly, Christensen notes, "when she finally becomes active, we can't quite tell whether her commitment is genuine or she just likes stirring things up."[59] The focus on the unlikelihood of these women's aptness for socially-conscious heroism portrayed throughout the film creates a difficult situation for spectator identification with these women's politics and activism.

Outsider Feminism and Difficult Ideological Identifications

Norma Rae and *Silkwood* may be considered examples of popular culture's response to the feminist revolution of the early 1970s. Influenced by their leftist directors and liberal production teams, both projects were initiated with the belief that the films would "exude feminist spirit while not overtly preaching feminism."[60] Indeed, both films feature strong female characters that drive the unfolding narrative through their emerging self-actualization and enlightenment. Both Norma Rae Webster and Karen Silkwood demonstrate a defiant spirit and a proclivity toward subversive, rebellious behavior. Yet, both of these films employ a populist vision, which features an incidental heroine who learns to stand up for herself and fight the corporation by whom she feels personally betrayed, for the most part glossing over the significant issues of both capitalist oppression and feminist rebellion. Rather than explicitly detail the community effort necessary for true working-class resistance or investigate the larger causes of patriarchal domination and women's oppression, *Norma Rae* and *Silkwood* construct a melodramatic rendering of the outlaw hero (in this case heroine): a radical individualist who initiates a showdown on behalf of a demoralized community and, in the end, is punished. According to Ray, a film like *Norma Rae* only "*seems* different because it employs the standard Hollywood strategy of assimilating (and co-opting) a fashionably dissident *topos* potentially threatening to the prevailing ideology — in this case, feminism, defused by having Norma Rae appear dependent on the male labor organizer."[61] The overarching messages of these subtly feminist-focused films, then, are not so different from that of the more conservative films of the mainstream cinema. Through the myth invoked by the classical Hollywood narrative, the films' attempts at social criticism are reconciled through their resolutions, in which the status quo is restored.

Philip Green views such conflicting visions as the result of Hollywood's confrontation with feminism. He argues that, because contemporary mainstream films have been produced under the rubric of the gender-conscious conditions prominently structured by the feminist cultural revolution of the 1970s, many films contain slippages and evasions in their reproduction of dominant ideology.[62] In *Norma Rae* and *Silkwood*, however, I would argue that an opposite strategy operates: because they are docudramas about women, the films appear to be feminist ruminations on a woman's struggle against oppressive forces, yet they actually use the feminist movement's founding issues to disempower the female protagonist. Most conspicuous in this regard are the conflicting images the films produce of the "liberated" woman and the way the films address issues of the public and the private.

Both Norma Rae and Karen Silkwood are represented, particularly in the first half of the films, as outsiders. The women are antagonists, not only because of their role as labor agitators, but in all aspects of their lives. From the beginning, both films paint a portrait of the female protagonist as a woman who is outside of the mainstream, whose lifestyle flies in the face of convention, and whose personality most people find somewhat abrasive and difficult to take. For example, Norma Rae initially is presented as a combatant in all of her relationships — she fights with her father, her lover, her kids, and her boss. At one point in the film, she even begins to battle the other volunteers during the union campaign. After Norma reprimands a male worker for showing up late to a union meeting, Reuben rebukes her bluntly, "Mouth, you're too muscular. You can't come down that hard on a man and leave him his balls. Easy — Jesus, if you were in the state department we'd be at war." Norma responds by saying, "You're right, I've got a big mouth. You know cotton mill workers are known as trash to some. I know the union's the only way we're going to get our own voice — make ourselves any better. I guess that's why I push." Norma Rae's big mouth has finally found a respectable outlet in the film; however, Reuben's indictment of Norma's growing public power also confirms that the activist woman will always remain an outsider, even within the union campaign she helped to organize.

Karen evokes a similar reaction as she becomes more vocal about Kerr-McGee's negligence. In one scene late in the film, Karen sits in the lunchroom with her co-workers and, when she overhears someone talking about a missing kilo of plutonium, she writes it down in a small notebook she carries with her. "Why are you writing it down? ... You won your election!" one of her colleagues asks. "We are still negotiating a contract, here,"

Karen informs her. "Well, uh, why don't you just concentrate on uppin' our wages and skip over what is none of our business," the woman answers in exasperation while some of the other workers look at Karen in disgust as they file out of the room. "This is our business, honey," Karen corrects her. At that, the woman gustily throws her lunch in the trash and, as she runs from the room, turns and yells, "Karen, I like my job!" Karen is left sitting at the table completely alone, alienated from the people she believes she is trying to help.

According to Doherty, "Karen's problem is that she can't keep her categories straight: she takes work personally. Even before her anti-nuke consciousness gets raised, she's a subversive element in the workforce because she won't leave her humor, tears, or sexuality at home."[63] In fact, both Norma Rae and Karen share the same problem and their personal faults, conflicts, and inadequacies often overwhelm their public efforts at activism and social change. In this way, the films make little distinction between the women's active involvement in labor issues and the struggles that complicate her personal life. The woman's "problem" in these films becomes her inability to find her true identity somewhere between the heroism of her public work and the challenges of her private life, an ongoing struggle to which she often falls victim.

Parallel scenes in both *Norma Rae* and *Silkwood* address the conflict generated as the result of the women's dual roles. In the next to last scene in *Norma Rae*, for example, Sonny confronts Reuben after he has returned Norma from jail, telling him, "She had one call and she called you.... You come in here, you mix her up, you turn her head all around. She's all changed. I didn't want that, I didn't want her to be a forerunner. What's going to happen to us now?" Similarly, when Drew decides to leave Karen, she follows him out to the car and he tells her, "Sweetheart, it's like you're two people — and I'm in love with one of them. The other one's — " "Just a real pain-in-the-ass," Karen finishes his thought for him. Both Sonny and Drew are disgruntled because their wife/girlfriend has found something beyond the home to fulfill her needs, and left him behind like a neglected housewife.

These moments in the films, as well as Sonny's and Drew's earlier tantrums over the women's inability to manage her responsibilities at home with her commitment to the union, could be explained as the films' response to the "personal is political" slogan assimilated into cultural discourse as a result of the second-wave feminist movement. *Norma Rae* and *Silkwood* do not incorporate such discourses into the narrative, however, or question the societal conventions that work against Norma's and Karen's adoption of such a philosophy. Instead, the films appear to validate Sonny's and Drew's complaints by shifting spectator identification to the men during these moments in the film. The men are both redeemed in the films when their complaints about their "changed" women are immediately followed by touching, sentimental confessions. After Sonny expresses his dissatisfaction with the "new" Norma to Reuben, he walks into the bedroom and asks Norma Rae if she ever slept with Reuben. "No, but he's in my head," she responds sadly. "I'm going to see you through getting tired, getting old, I'm going to see you through anything that comes up," Sonny assures her, "And there's nobody else in my head, just you." Likewise, before Drew drives off, and as the violin music surges in the background, he runs back to Karen, embraces her one last time and reassures her, "I really loved it, baby." In this way, the men appear caring and rational and the women seem inconsiderate and ungrateful because of the way they have treated these stand-up guys.

On the whole, the female labor heroines are represented in these films in a manner that may make spectators' identification with the women difficult. These female protagonists are, for the most part, portrayed as atypical women who have messy lives and a bad attitude. Their overt sexuality, such as the cleavage and nipples that show through Norma's tight, V-neck T-shirts and the mini-skirts and cowboy boots worn by Karen, makes them appear trashy rather than feminine. Further, because the women are portrayed by the well-known stars Sally Field and Meryl Streep, even the women's working-class mannerisms seem faintly contrived. Because these "ordinary" individuals are embodied by these "extraordinary" actresses, the notion of the difficulty of these women's working-class struggle becomes more difficult for spectators to accept.

A further consequence of a strong focus on the individual women, who are played by prominent stars, is these films' blatant omission of the notion of collective struggle. According to Aufderheide, because *Norma Rae* (and I would argue *Silkwood* as well) uses the female protagonists' personal growth as the thread of the story, "the conflicts the movie focuses on limits [viewers'] understanding of her development and its social import."[64] The films are not only bereft of any notion of solidarity, but are, in Green's words, "*hommages* to individual heroism."[65] The films' lack of comprehension of the collectivity involved in union victories also functions to idealize the personal growth of the female protagonist and attribute the positive outcomes to her individual transformation (as prompted by the outside union organizer). Consequently, the films do little to explicitly critique the socio-economic contexts that constrain the working-class culture to which the female protagonist belongs. According to Jasmine Paul and Bette J. Kauffman: "Glorification of The Individual has consequences, particularly for groups engaged in struggle for social change.... The 'exceptional' woman and working-class person so incorporated satisfies popular demand for representation without invoking class and gender struggles that might seriously undermine the veneer of male-female and management-labor relationships."[66] Similarly, *Norma Rae* and *Silkwood*'s emphasis on the individual struggle of the female heroine limits the films' potential for the expression of a progressive political message. Despite their faults, however, *Norma Rae* and *Silkwood* should be recognized as Hollywood's best attempt to address the feminist consciousness and movement toward social progressivism prevalent during the late 1970s and early 1980s. In light of where the film industry would take women in the even more conservative climate of the 1980s and 1990s, *Norma Rae* and *Silkwood* represent daring Hollywood portrayals of archetypal politicized women — a phenomenon that did not emerge again in either the mainstream or independent cinema for nearly two decades.

CHAPTER FIVE

Negotiating Feminist Politics in the Third Wave
Labor Struggle and Solidarity *in* Live Nude Girls Unite!

> "It didn't matter how aggressive, or Jewish, or smart, or witty, or, you know, strong I was, personality didn't provide me with good working conditions, being part of a group — organizing a successful union effort did."
> — Julia Query, *Live Nude Girls Unite!*

Sometime during the summer of 1996, among the burlesques, strip bars, and peep shows in San Francisco's club district, a strange thing happened. A group of women marched with large picket signs while chanting, "2-4-6-8, don't go in to masturbate." Although one may assume these were conservative women on the frontlines of the culture wars protesting the smut and corruption of the porn industry, on closer inspection several of the women could be seen wearing pink tee-shirts that read "Bad Girls Like Good Contracts." The picketers were, in fact, the exotic dancers themselves protesting their employer, a popular peep show. This scene is one of many in an intriguing feminist labor documentary that brings the experience of sex workers to a mainstream audience. In 1996, a group of women in San Francisco decided to fight back against what they deemed were unfair, and ultimately sexist, labor practices and organized a unionization campaign against their employer, The Lusty Lady exotic dance club. *Live Nude Girls Unite!* is a low-budget production that chronicles the dancers' efforts to unionize in order to improve their working conditions. The project was the brainchild of producer and co-director, Julia

Query, who decided that she and her fellow workers' efforts to unionize exotic dancers should be documented for posterity.

The film serves as a record of these sex workers' struggle to improve their working conditions and overturn unfair employment practices. The strippers' primary complaint was that they were being illegally photographed through the peepshow's one-way windows, and their performances were showing up without their consent or compensation on the Internet and in amateur porn videos. After the management refused to remove the one-way glass, informing the women that amateur porn stardom was an occupational hazard they had to accept, the women turned to the Exotic Dancers Alliance, a San Francisco sex worker advocacy group, for advice. The EDA put them in touch with local 790 of the Service Employees International Union (SEIU) and the strippers' unionization campaign began in 1995.

Over a year later, in 1996, the women went through with a National Labor Relations Board union election and won 57–15. They named their SEIU chapter the Exotic Dancers Union and entered the contract negotiation phase.[1] *Live Nude Girls Unite!* documents the collective struggle of the strippers versus the Lusty Lady's management (and their team of anti-union lawyers) over the following year. After the labor negotiations had come to a close, Query realized that the hundreds of hours of video she had accumulated were too unwieldy for her to manage on her own, so she recruited Vicki Funari, a documentary filmmaker and former stripper, to serve as editor and co-director. The resulting film functions as part autobiographical account of Query's life as a stripper turned union activist, part educational labor video, and part forum for feminist debate over the status of the third wave and the need for a revision of the second-wave's "the personal is political" slogan, particularly with regard to female sex workers in America.

In this chapter, I demonstrate how this unique film expands our knowledge of contemporary women's cultural status by portraying an aspect of some American women's experiences not often depicted in the mainstream mass media: namely, the ongoing economic and gender oppression that women continue to face in their daily lives, even at the beginning of the twenty-first century. I argue that *Live Nude Girls Unite!* provides an alternative glimpse of feminism's current ideological status through its blend of social commentary, feminist politics, and personal melodrama, which exposes the political evolution, as well as the contradictions, that embody the shift to third-wave feminist activism. More importantly, given ongoing debates about the merits of the third wave, this film invites spectators to reconsider their ideas about what constitutes gender oppression and offers a productive perspective on the responsibilities of coalition politics. Through these women's analysis of their political situation, the film rhetorically addresses complex issues such as the complicated distinctions between victimizer and victim in contemporary gender politics, women's appropriation of sex work as a form of empowerment, and the dominant culture's insistent attempts to regulate working women's private and public lives. The women's collective bargaining in the end stands in for a larger scheme representing women's bargaining power within the patriarchal institutions that continue to exist, and often remain unexamined, in our twenty-first-century culture.

Documenting the New Feminist Revolution

Beginning sometime in the late 1990s, the mainstream media predicted the timely death of second-wave feminism, one of many *fin de siècle* reflections on the status of twentieth-century American social experiments. Feminism's unfortunate collision with the cult of celebrity and an era of heightened individualism (bordering on neurotic self-obsession) was quickly interpreted by the media as a harbinger of the movement's demise.[2] While popular culture offered up Ally McBeal and Bridget Jones as single women grappling with the legacy of the feminist revolution, a group of young, attractive, and outspoken female critics hit the media circuit to critique previously established feminist ideologies about gender politics. These "popular press feminists," such as Katie Roiphe, Naomi Wolf, and Christina Hoff-Sommers, peddled their best-selling books over the airwaves by convincing talk show hosts that feminism was no longer necessary or relevant to contemporary women.[3] The media's coverage of both the incarnation of "postfeminism," exemplified by popular representations of thirty-something women conflicted between their professional and personal identities, and these new critics' attempts to dismantle liberal feminism, particularly as it is theorized and practiced by academic feminists, soon took on the nomenclature of the "third wave." Third-wave feminists, as interpreted by the mainstream media, represented an opposition to feminism's second wave. As a means of distancing themselves from earlier feminists, this group of women emphasizes individualism, personal rather than political empowerment, and power feminism, which wields women's feminine sexuality as a tool for economic and social gain.[4]

While the media may conflate the notion of postfeminism and the ideologies of the third wave, academic theorists have offered clear distinctions between the two in terms of their characteristics and objectives. Karrin Vasby Anderson and Jessie Stewart delineate two conceptions of third-wave feminism: that of the popular media and culture from the 1990s forward and that of the scholarly community of the 1980s and 1990s.[5] In the media, third-wave feminism is indistinguishable from postfeminism, in which women, whether they claimed the "feminist" label or not, "positioned themselves in opposition to feminists of earlier generations, repudiating the supposed racism of their foremothers, focusing on self-transformation rather than on collective political action, and reveling in the endless contradictions that characterize their identities."[6] Third-wave feminism in the academy, however, was initiated by younger scholars concerned with the second wave's failure to contemplate issues of racial and sexual differences, as well as this new generation of scholars' incorporation of poststructuralism, postmodernism, and postcolonialism into contemporary feminist theorizing.[7] Yet, another vein of third-wave feminism represents a combination of the oppositional feminism promoted by the popular media and the new academic feminism culled from late twentieth-century theoretical perspectives: the rise of the "new movement" feminist manifestos.

In 1995, two anthologies self-proclaimed as speaking the "voice" of the "next feminist generation" and "telling the truth and changing the face of feminism" were published by representatives of the third wave.[8] Rebecca Walker, daughter of second-wave feminist writer Alice Walker, edited the anthology *To Be Real*, while Barbara Findlen, former editor of *Ms.* magazine, edited the collection *Listen Up*. Both volumes reflected the thoughts, feelings, and expressions of a diverse group of women who had grown up with second-wave feminism, but could not claim to embrace all of that movement's ideals or find its resonance within their own lived existence. The reality of these women's experiences also was shaped by the Reagan/Bush era. Lisa Marie Hogeland notes, "The increased tendency to pathologize any kind of oppositional politics" that resulted in "a climate in which passionate political commitments seem crazy" left special interests, such as feminism, demonized in the larger political culture.[9]

The published collections by those proclaiming to represent the third wave consist primarily of autobiographical, anecdotal, or personal reflections on topics such as the multiplicity of cultural identities, reproductive rights, sexual harassment and abuse, eating disorders and definitions of femininity. These works have been critiqued by second-wave feminists for failing to recognize the connections of these issues to those already addressed in the second wave. For example, Natalie Fixmer and Julia T. Wood argue that the contributions of the third wave thus far have been historically uniformed and politically ineffectual. They conclude that "third wave feminists' efforts to understand their own movement and to develop and deploy effective political strategies would be enriched by a fuller understanding of the second wave, particularly the radical feminists who developed insights and strategies that seem remarkably similar to [third-wave] politics."[10] Third-wave academic feminists have continued the critique by characterizing much third-wave discourse as overly individualistic, theoretically abstract reflections that fail to inform or inspire the coalition politics necessary to further develop the movement. Academic third wavers Leslie Heywood and Jennifer Drake note in *Third Wave Agenda: Being Feminist, Doing Feminism* that previous third-wave anthologies have presented a version of feminism "that relies, for the most part, on personal anecdote for their definitional and argumentative strategies" and that "the writing rarely provides consistent analysis of the larger culture that has helped shape and produce those experiences."[11] Similarly, third-wave writers Rory Dicker and Alison Peipmeier contend in their collection of academic essays, *Catching the Wave: Reclaiming Feminism for the 21st Century*, "that this generation needs a politicized, activist feminism that is grounded in material realities and the cultural productions of life in the twenty-first century."[12]

In response to these critiques, Amber E. Kinser recommends ways that third-wave feminism can "position feminists in rhetorically and politically advantageous space," namely by being able to "confront the relationships between feminism, *struggle*, and social change, and ... what it means to live in the margins."[13] There are, however, some women of the next generation who are already meeting the challenge called forth by

Kinser and feminist critics of the third wave. The film *Live Nude Girls Unite!* depicts the year-long saga of such young, working-class women. In this low-budget independent documentary, a group of exotic dancers struggle to find ways to negotiate their own agency within the constraints of ingrained systems of patriarchy, and in a service industry that had been largely condemned by their feminist foremothers. This feminist-produced film and its focus on working women functions rhetorically to broaden our understanding of American women's experience beyond the often monolithic view of third-wave feminism usually offered in the American media, while it also reveals young women's capacity for radical activism and organized opposition to challenge gender oppression on multiple levels.

Live Nude Girls Unite! is a rare example of a product, even within the contemporary independent film industry, through which we can explore the politics and debates that have characterized third-wave feminism and its critique. In this film, cultural discourses and political visions are produced by the women workers that move beyond the individualism and vague, "theory-free" generalities common to much of the third-wave generation's reflections on feminism's contemporary status. In addition, through this film, the complexities of women's capacity for coalition politics are examined, which include not only women's gendered identifications, but also those affiliated with various ethnic and social classes, such as working-class culture. In response to this challenge, the film advocates a solution through the cooperative enterprise of labor organizing, which represents the socialist hope and political possibilities that feminist solidarity can effect. More importantly, this film informs spectators that the potential for feminist praxis and collective action still exists, even among the members of the "third wave."

According to Query, once the dancers had gained national attention and "made it onto the national joke monitor with Jay Leno, we all starting feeling very protective of our story. So I started videotaping."[14] The film cost 120,000 dollars and grossed just under 150,000 dollars in art house showings, finding its most public outlet through early-morning airings amongst the various skin-flicks on the Cinemax cable network in 2001. Shot on a High 8 Handycam video camera and 16 mm film, *Live Nude Girls Unite!* has the look of a home video and the subversive appeal of the documentaries produced in the 1970s by the second-wave feminist movement.[15]

Live Nude Girls Unite! was praised by reviewers for its innovation, wit, and activist focus. A. O. Scott of *The New York Times* notes that the film "displays its share of exposed flesh, but at heart it's a movie about work, part of the rich tradition of labor documentaries that includes Barbara Kopple's *Harlan County, U.S.A.* and *American Dream*."[16] Amy Taubin of *The Village Voice*, however, recognizes the film as a standout in that tradition, writing that the film is "wickedly funny. Its subversive comic style is an antidote to the absence of humor in ... Barbara Kopple's classic labor doc, *Harlan County, U.S.A.*"[17] Other reviewers commended the film for its deft handling of complex political and feminist issues. Loren King of *The Boston Globe* writes, "The film, and its participants, take the issues that are raised seriously, but temper what could be a strident political diatribe with humor and insight" and Saul Austerlitz of *Cineaste* notes, "The film astutely recognizes sex work as a fault line in contemporary feminism and considers the strippers' battles for respect the equivalent of 1960s activism."[18]

As an independently produced, written, directed, and edited documentary, *Live Nude Girls Unite!* takes the figure of the female labor activist further into the margins than any other film of the twentieth century. The film's appeal may stem from its combination of a social realism blended with a secondary plot device that adds a melodramatic flare; this style allows the film to balance its progressive messages and innovative aesthetics with a classical convention that remains accessible to spectators looking for a good story. One of the film's strengths as a representation of contemporary feminism is the way it contemplates numerous cultural contradictions. For example, the film invites debate regarding whether the sex industry is exploitation or empowerment and the legitimacy of women's right to view sex work as a legitimate labor practice, while simultaneously exposing the challenges of one young woman's third wave struggle over how to justify her chosen professional identity in light of her own enlightened politics and progressive feminist principles.

Turning Contradiction into Coalition

The contradictions inherent in women's roles has riddled the feminist movement since its conception, beginning with first-wave feminists' disagreements over whether to utilize or challenge norms of traditional femininity in the name of women's rights, and continuing with second-wave feminists' attempts at making the personal political, a paradox unique to the rhetorical campaign for women's liberation.[19] The third-wave movement reflected in *Live Nude Girls Unite!* exemplifies a continuity with this feminist foundation built on attempts to rectify the inherent contradictions of female identity politics. However, the move toward forming a collective identity *by embracing* such contradictions and plurality is a new development in the feminist movement. Helene Shugart has noted that "third wavers' predilection for contradiction may well be reflective of a more sophisticated understanding of, tolerance for, and acceptance of difference, thus enacting the pluralism that even most second-wavers acknowledge is not characteristic of second-wave feminism."[20] In fact, third wavers tend to embrace such pluralism in an effort to resolve complex tensions they recognize as having gone unaddressed in the second-wave movement, such as emboldening women *both* personally and politically.[21]

According to Heywood and Drake, the "lived messiness" of the third wave is what defines it:

> People who *are* white *and* black, gay *and* straight, masculine *and* feminine, or who are finding ways to be and name none of the above; successful individuals longing for community and coalition, communities and coalition longing for success; tensions between striving for individual success and subordinating the individual to the cause; identities formed within a relentlessly consumer-oriented culture but informed by a politics that has problems with consumption.[22]

Indeed, at the very heart of *Live Nude Girls Unite!* lies the contradictions that also characterize third-wave feminist politics: to find opportunities and strategies that allow women individually to negotiate contradiction in affirmative ways while they also give voice to a politics of coalition, and acknowledgement of cultural production and sexual politics as key sites of struggle that allow feminists to both use and resist power structures to fuel their struggles for justice.[23] While the primary plot of the film charts the working women's collective odyssey of union activism, a secondary plot line chronicles Julia's individual dilemma of "coming out" to her mother as a stripper (she had already come out as a lesbian). Through the device of this double plot, the film blends the overarching socialist theme of women workers joining together for a united cause with a compelling,

Five. Negotiating Feminist Politics

personal story about one female labor activist's individual evolution and the challenge of negotiating her own public and private identities.

The film begins with what appears to be home video of a small child (only her hand is shown) holding a bunch of multi-colored crayons and filling in the outlined image of Martin Luther King Jr. in a coloring book. Folksy guitar chords play in the background and, in voice-over, a woman states, "I was born in 1968, the day before Martin Luther King Jr. was assassinated." The next shot cuts to an adult hand opening a photo album and a close-up on the first page, which features a picture of a woman with a young girl sitting on her lap. The voice-over continues, "My mom raised me to believe in freedom, justice, and equality for all." The device of having one of the primary labor activists in the film narrate the story from her own unique, personal perspective, imbues the film with melodramatic interest and invites spectators to personally connect with this young woman and her plight. This opening scene of the film, which functions as a prologue of sorts, also reveals the cultural context in which many of the third wave's ideas of plurality were formed. Being raised by a politically liberal, second-wave feminist mother is what allowed this third waver to recognize diversity and difference as something to celebrate, respect, and protect. Perhaps because of this influence, many third wavers "recognize the complexity of injustice and the intersection of multiple injustices, and respond with similarly complex formations for activism."[24]

The woman in voice-over continues, "I dreamed of fighting the good fight," while the picture of the woman and child dissolves into a standard school portrait of a girl around age eight. The music abruptly changes to a bluesy, horn-heavy burlesque tune, while the camera focuses in on a woman's feet in a pair of silver, platform shoes. As the camera pans up her body, a woman in a blonde wig wearing a sheer pink dress and matching headband is seen lounging on a red velvet drape. Her one hand is placed over her breast as she looks demurely away from the camera. The woman in voice-over confesses, "But, I never dreamed that my first attempt at labor activism would be as a stripper," while the woman on screen turns to face the camera and breaks into laughter. This moment stands in stark contrast to the folksy and sentimental opening scene of the film; the laughing woman appears to be poking fun at both the seriousness of the previous scene and at the narrator's confession. The subject's simultaneous direct address to the camera and blatant laughter also rupture the veneer of the camera's seductive gaze, which provides the film with a satirical edge while it also suggests the impulse toward transgression that characterizes the remainder of the film. This tone continues in the next shot, which features a sign that, partially in neon, partially in animation, provides the film's title: the sign reads "Live Nude Girls" until a woman's hand opens a tube of lipstick and scrawls "Unite!" underneath.

The opening of the film presents Julia, the film's narrator, as a woman in her late-twenties who appears to have experienced a fairly common upbringing by a politically progressive mother, which later led to her socially-conscious views. Also, since the film never formally introduces her to the audience (we only figure out her name from others' references to her), she also maintains an anonymous quality that allows for greater identification from the audience. Her current career path, as a stripper, is explained as a choice made in an effort to fulfill both her desire to pursue her less-well-paying creative goals of becoming a writer and comic and her need to bring home enough money to pay the rent. Julia explains that a friend suggested that she take a job at the Lusty Lady, "because it had a reputation as the hip, feminist peep show with good working conditions. I was comfortable showing my body, especially since there was no cigar-chomping boss — most of the managers were women."

The film compiles a number of various films styles, including newspaper clips and news footage, talking-head interviews, home video, and animation. This combination of styles adds a texture to the film that provides a female perspective on work and labor politics, a humorous quality that makes its political messages more palatable, and a strong view of the women who participate as active subjects in the film's narrative. Much of the film's narrative consists of a mix of behind-the-scenes footage of the peep show (Julia explains how the quarter-operated boxes work, for example) and the dancers' dressing room, as well as interviews with the strippers and footage of them participating in the union campaign. The interviews serve to build an argument for women's rights through documentation of the female workers' grievances, their early organization efforts, and a month-by-month chronicle of their collective bargaining struggle. The film also employs a cinema verité style, which captures the offstage politics that unfold inside the peepshow.

In one of the early scenes in the film, the women are shown in a dressing room preparing for their performance. While a very thin blonde woman with short, spiky hair undresses, Julia asks two women sitting in front of the mirror, "So, what's the object of putting on make-up?" "It's like a mask," one woman responds, "It's like getting ready for the circus." As one woman puts on eye shadow, the blonde, who is now naked, begins brushing out a long blonde wig, and a petite Asian woman, who is also naked, walks past and scratches her rear end. Another woman identified as "Jane" explains, "It's kind of fun to be in a little disguise." The blonde woman walks over to the camera and puts on her wig, while Julia comments, "Suddenly she's heterosexual! Wink, wink!" The women depicted in this brief scene immediately challenge stereotypical representations of exotic dancers. The women shown in the film are of various ethnicities and body types, some have tattoos, others have body piercings, and one has prominent and unflattering tan lines, none of which reflect the airbrushed, glossy images of women seen in pornographic media. The scene is shot with a minimalist style that portrays these ordinary women workers in their daily routine preparing before a shift, presenting them as acting subjects with a voice, rather than merely objectifying their bodies on film. The women's comments also reveal them as willing participants in the construction of themselves as a product for their customers, a perspective that reflects third-wave women's "emphasis on paradox, conflict, multiplicity, and messiness ... as a result, we are able to see the constructed nature of identity as well as the ways in which gender may be a performance that can be manipulated and politically altered as it is performed."[25]

In scenes such as this, the film addresses the complex issue of female agency, particularly when agency is constrained by both ingrained patriarchy and capitalism. Perhaps the most provocative aspect of *Live Nude Girls Unite!* is this exploration of the paradox of a woman's maintenance of her subjectivity through her own, conscious, objectification. According to one of the dancers interviewed, Decadence/Kristina, who reveals being a social worker by profession and dancing on her "off days": "I loved it, actually. I felt that it was a very strong thing to use my sexuality, my feminine power in a way that made me feel good and in a way that profited me — that I was finally being paid what I was worth, which I was not in my job before." By exposing the inside cultural politics of the sex industry from the perspective of those who make up its workforce, the film invites spectators to question some of the myths surrounding views of strippers and other sex workers as objectified and exploited victims. Such a politics is, according to Shugart, Waggoner, and Hallstein, characteristic of the third wave's "embracing of contradiction so that apparently inconsistent political viewpoints coexist in the name of third-wave feminism.... Third-wavers seek to embrace sexual desire and expression, freeing it from the limits of patriarchy and heterosexuality as well as from what they perceive to be the anti-sex sensibilities of second-wave feminism."[26]

By featuring the strippers in interviews talking about their feelings and experiences, the film presents its women subjects as thoughtful, articulate, and savvy. Although a few of the women in the group are single, working mothers trying to stay off of welfare, the majority of the 70 dancers at the Lusty Lady had entered the sex industry by choice. Commenting on her own decision to become an exotic dancer in an article about the film in *SF Weekly*, Query argues:

> When you're a young woman out in the world, you're sexually harassed and are often asked to do things that are sex work-oriented — to be emotionally available to men, to provide attention, to wear make-up, and look good. If you have an awareness of this, the obvious leap is to go ahead and get paid for it.[27]

A similar attitude is repeated a number of times throughout the film by different women with their own unique insights into the sex industry. A dancer referred to as "Tara" explains that "sex work is a form of work. The sex industry is an industry that pays people's bills, pays people through school, raises children, helps people start small businesses." At this point, the film cuts to a shot of "Tara" in a tattoo parlor creating a piece of body art for a customer. She goes on to explain that for her, sex work goes beyond the material. She views her profession as "a sacred act," adding, "there's a life force in it, and it's healthy, and I consider myself to be providing a spiritual service — a sexual, spiritual service." "Naomi," a fellow dancer, reflects on the connection she felt with other women in the club, "I loved dancing in a little room with other women, it was like a weird pajama party. I liked the music, the lights, and I liked the fact that the customers looked like these little things in boxes.... What we all have in common is that we're all in it for the money."

Julia's own perspectives on stripping are revealed through a running commentary intercut throughout the film that consists of soundbites from her stand-up routine. In one of these interludes, she informs her comedy club audience, "But I love working at a peep show because I've never worked with so many women who have college degrees — mostly women's studies and philosophy. It's like they figured out what to do about patriarchy — take their money!" By showing the various ways that these diverse women came to sex work as a profession, the film begins to express a feminist politics that deconstructs the stereotypical notion of "stripper." The self-reflective observations that these women offer through their interviews reveal that many of these workers view their career choice as an act of negotiation or performed compliance, a pragmatic strategy for exploiting the patriarchal power hierarchy.

The film's celebration of a diversity of women's different perspectives also exposes varied responses to the contradictions and social obstacles of women's exploitation, and demonstrates women's ability to adapt individual female experience and use it in transformative ways. Fixmer and Wood have identified this as a founding gesture of the third wave, a feminism that

> engages differences and multiplicities within and between women that were ignored by predecessor feminist movements; works to build a new kind of solidarity that recognizes and brings together blurred, overlapping, and sometimes contradictory facets of women's identities that were often compartmentalized by feminists in other eras, and incorporates feminism into everyday life more than previous feminist movements.

However, it is these women's shared sense of injustice at the hands of capitalist power that eventually forces them to recognize the benefits of female solidarity and collective confrontation for creating spaces to resist social and political domination. Through these women's transformation from workers to activists, the film challenges cultural beliefs about modern feminists by re-defining young women's ability to maintain their personal empowerment while also forging a united feminist politics as we move through the twenty-first century.

Mapping New Boundaries for Feminism: From Personal Empowerment to Political Action

For second-generation feminists, the slogan "the personal is political" in many ways highlighted women's recognition that they needed to revision their personal identity and relationships before they could achieve the systemic political changes for which the movement was fighting. One of the most prominent critiques of third wavers, according to Catherine Orr, is that their "'feminist' practices become matters of personal style or individual choice and any emphasis on organized intervention is regarded as naïve and even oppressive to women," which she believes demonstrates a "lack of theoretical, historical, or organizational resources under which third wave feminists seem to be laboring."[28] Part of this conception also has been informed by the media's portrayal of the third wave as "a revision of feminism that encourages women's private, consumer lifestyles rather than cultivating a desire for public life and political activism."[29]

For Julia, however, the "personal" was not merely about how feminism has changed her lifestyle, but also how her third-generation feminist politics would affect her complex relationship with her second-generation feminist mother. The focus on this mother-daughter drama adds a very female-centered perspective and an intriguing private dynamic to the film. About a third of the way through the film, the scene opens with another shot of the photo album (and the accompanying guitar music) from the introduction, lingering over a number of Polaroid snapshots while Julia explains, "My mom had taught me that I could be anything. My mom was a nice Jewish girl and her parents expected her to marry a doctor. She rebelled. She became a doctor." The shot then cuts from the photographs to a home video of a little girl on her mother's lap reading *Free to Be ... You and Me*. Query continues, "She was a divorced mother in the 1970s who told me not to be ashamed of my body, to feel entitled to pleasure, to be independent and strong." The shot cuts to an overhead close-up of a copy of *Our Bodies, Ourselves* lying on a table. As the film speeds up, feminist academic books are piled on top of the first book, and include titles such as Michel Foucault's *The History of Sexuality*, *Sex, Power and Pleasure* by Mariana Valverde, *Sex Work: Writings By Women in the Sex Industry* edited by Frederique Delacoste and Priscilla Alexander, and Simone de Beauvoir's *The Second Sex*. Julia explains her own feminist development: "In graduate school I wrote a paper analyzing the feminist debates about the sex industry. Even though I argued that sex work should be understood as just that — work — I didn't tell my classmates or my mother about my job in the industry." Julia's comments draw attention to a major theme of the film: the stigma that she felt for making the economic decision to enter the sex industry, despite her enlightened and political views on the feminist interpretations of sex work.

About a quarter of the way through the film, the "problem" is introduced into the plotline. A clip from ABC's prime-time news show *20/20* reveals the identity of Julia's liberal feminist mom — Dr. Joyce Wallace, a New York internist who also moonlights as an advocate for the safety of female prostitutes. The narrative periodically returns to the mother-daughter conflict and, at one point, Julia recalls that she first realized that "all sex workers are scorned" as a child when her mother was the frequent recipient of protests and even bomb threats for providing health services to women in the sex industry. An element of suspenseful tension is provided for the spectator when Julia and her mother are both invited to the First International Conference on the Legalization of Prostitution in Van Nuys, California, as guest speakers, and the film builds anticipation for the impending confrontation. Julia explains her reason for keeping her profession a secret:

> My mom and I were both fighting for sex workers. I wanted her to see us as allies, as on the same side. We were both feminists, but feminists have disagreed about the sex industry for years. Some people say the sex industry is oppressive to all women, and some people say that working in the sex industry can be empowering. But, after hours of dancing and watching hundreds of men "come" and go, I just found it boring.

Julia decides that she must confess the nature of her professional career to her mother and arranges a meeting with her before the conference. With cameras rolling, she tells her mother that she is not only at the conference in support of the strippers' unionization efforts, but that she also works in the industry. Her mother, clearly disappointed and hurt, lashes out: "I came to this conference as somebody who was going to present and I don't want to have attention on anything else other than my work." After Query comforts her by rationalizing that, because they have different last names, no one would connect them, her mother laments: "You put me in an awkward position because I don't want to tell people that you're not my daughter, you are my daughter!" Yet, as tears begin streaming down her face, Julia's mother admits, "And I don't want it known that Dr. Wallace from New York, who is an expert, has a daughter who's in the smut business. You know, I think it takes away from *my* professional message." She concludes, "We have to swallow pride in almost any kind of work, but it's better to work with your mind than to work with your body." This heart-wrenching moment, between a mother and daughter each struggling to maintain both of their linked identities through their sacred bond, as well as their separate identities as individuals, may resonate with female viewers in particular. At the end of the scene, Julia describes the universal nature of such mother-daughter tensions when she states in voice-over: "We weren't talking just about sex work anymore. It was *the* fight — the same old fight, the same old dance. Each of us wondering: 'Am I a good mother?' 'Am I a good daughter?'"

The dramatic tension between mother and daughter also provides an outlet for the film to explore the debate among feminists over whether sex work exploits or empowers women. King notes that "this ultra-modern mother/daughter moment is one of the most uncomfortable and revealing aspects of the film."[30] The confrontation between Julia and her mother symbolizes the differences between the two feminist generations. Julia's mother symbolizes the idealistic and theoretical feminist tenets about women's subjugation that had formed the basis of the second-wave movement's activism twenty-five years earlier. As the film unapologetically shows, however, women like Julia and her fellow co-workers are demonstrating what the philosophies preached by their mothers may become when put into practice. At one of the contract negotiation meetings, the union negotiator explains her own position as a second-wave feminist activist trying to really understand women who do this kind of work. Summer, one of the dancers, responds, "It seems like a very simple issue to me. This is my body and these are my reproductive organs and I'm going to do with them as I please — and it seems strange to me that another woman would say, 'Well, yeah, actually you know, someone can tell me what I can do with my body and what I can't do.'" Another dancer adds, "It was always my understanding that the feminist perspective was about enabling women to have a choice." The film then cuts to an animation that visually illustrates this evolution by showing a 1970s feminist activist in bell bottoms and a T-shirt holding her bra over a fire in one hand and a picket sign in the other juxtaposed with a stripper, topless in a red g-string and heels, dangling her bra in front of a man with one hand while holding a fist full of money in the other. The liberation and equality of the second wave has entitled the next generation to exploit their femininity *and* independence as they see fit.

More than two decades after the height of the second-wave movement, *Live Nude Girls Unite!* demonstrates that women are still fighting the same battles; however, what has been won for them by second-wave feminism is a greater freedom of choice over how they want to conduct their lives — even if that often involves choosing what kinds of battles they would like to fight. According to Orr, the third wave "assumes that the women's movement took care of oppressive institutions, and that now it is up to the individual women to make personal choices that simply reinforce those fundamental societal changes."[31] Julia and the other women of the third wave demonstrate through the film (and particularly through her commentary in her stand-up routines) that they feel that their work liberates them by providing control over their female subjectivity — including use of their bodies and the manner in which they are perceived by men.

The film astutely illuminates the hypocrisy of a cultural politics that divides women's roles and identities into categories such as private versus public, and personal versus political. The film suggests that, because of the very nature of the sex industry, the strippers' daily existence instead blurs these divisions — the women are paid to publicly perform very private acts. Further, the film's documentation of their political efforts as part of the unionization campaign exposes the boundaries between the public and the private even further. The explicit gender politics raised by the film become most poignant when, during the hostile negotiations between the management, the anti-union law firm, and the strippers, the depth of societal beliefs about women's roles becomes painfully clear.

After negotiations had dragged on for three months, management attempted to formally declare the strippers' job "fun," which the film includes as a commentary to expose the problematic assumption that the women are not engaged in public "work" and they must experience personal enjoyment from their "dancing." As a result, the strippers decide to initiate a work slowdown. The women designate one day "No pink day," a day when they will dance with their legs closed. While Julia explains this bargaining tactic in voice-over, a shot of the outside of the peep show reveals a "No Contract — No Pussy" sign placed on the crotch of the female figure (outlined in pink neon) that advertises the Lusty Lady's exotic dance club/peep show. Oddly, the corporate lawyers representing the management were not nearly as concerned about the work slowdown as they were with the women's use of the word "pussy." When the workers also included the term in their proposed contract, the lawyers accused the women of "sexually harassing themselves." One lawyer explained his ire over this term to the union shop steward at a meeting, which she recalls in the film: "We asked him to defend why he thought that the company had the right to put those kinds of limits on our free speech and he said, 'Well, I don't let my kids talk that way, why should I let you?'" Throughout the film, the management and their lawyers consistently regarded the women with this patronizing attitude, and seemed skeptical of the women's tenacity and political proficiency. The women prove them wrong, however, by conducting a civil, organized, and patient campaign. In the end, the dancers' demands were met and a contract was ratified in 1997, making the Lusty Lady the only unionized strip club in the United States. The film's documentation of the women's unity throughout the long battle toward securing a contract that protected them as workers rhetorically demonstrates how the women's solidarity was activated as a means of political change.

Embracing the Collective: From Bargaining to Activism

The majority of the second half of the film documents the women in the corporate boardroom where the contract negotiations take place. These scenes add a stark realism to the film that invites spectators to consider the extent to which the strippers' daily routines are a form of manual labor (despite the lawyers' contention otherwise), and to identify with the women's political savvy and determined commitment with regard to their work for the union campaign. Further, by documenting the women's efforts to overcome such domination, the film also challenges stereotypical depictions regarding third-wave feminists' capacity for political organization and public activism. Another frequent critique of third-wave feminists has been that they eschew collective politics and public activism. Shugart

Opposite page: Writer, director, and producer Julia Query reveals the inner workings of a San Francisco peep show in the labor documentary *Live Nude Girls Unite!* The film presents a complex view of third-wave feminism as the women in the film contemplate the relationship between sex, work, and contemporary women's rights.

Five. Negotiating Feminist Politics

explains that the third-wave philosophy has been defined as "individually liberating in that it absolves women of responsibility to the collective. Rather than shouldering the burden of all women, third wavers are responsible to and for themselves."[32] Others have argued that "empowerment takes on a different meaning in this new feminism ... not in collective terms, as with the second wave, but in very individualistic terms. Being empowered in the third wave sense is about feeling good about oneself and having the power to make choices, regardless of what those choices are."[33] According to Heywood and Drake, however, the collective impulse is not absent in the third wave, but rather they envision "a coalition-politics activism that defines itself, and its politics, through the multiple subject positions and diverse community affiliations of its members."[34]

A primary impetus for the women's decision to collectively organize in the film was unequal representation among the dancers and the way that the club's management exploited the women's differences. The club did not allow the dancers to call in sick, if you could not find someone to replace your shift, you risked losing your job. This was not an easy task, however, since club policy indicated that your replacement "had to have skin and hair as light as yours or lighter, her breasts had to be as big as yours or bigger." Julia laments, "We were all classified by race, hair color, and breast size." In addition, workers of color were given far less shifts in the schedule (since management scheduled only one minority woman per shift) and, as Julia explains, "in the higher paid, one-on-one fantasy talk booth, called Private Pleasures, management wouldn't schedule black dancers at all." "Naomi," an African American dancer, recalls, "At first I felt it was me, then I started to look at the schedule and I noticed that it was not just me, I noticed that the other three black girls were never in booth." The management claimed that black dancers were not as marketable as white dancers, therefore it would not be as profitable to schedule them. This was one of the first workers' rights issue that the women organized around, as "Jane" explains in the film: "It doesn't matter if a specific race is more or less marketable than another race because it's illegal. You can't classify workers on the basis of race."

Other issues that fueled the workers' sense of injustice included a vague disciplinary policy that led to frequent firings and the lax enforcement of the no camera policy in the booths. The management also had enacted policies that prohibited any worker from reaching the top wage position. "Naomi" explains the situation, "When you get to like $18 an hour, you suddenly looked different. You were told that you were unattractive, overweight, suddenly cut down in shifts or written off the schedule altogether. So, basically, everyone operated up under this fear." A missed meeting or showing up for a shift a few minutes late could result in not receiving a scheduled raise or, worse, being knocked back down to starting wage. After the women began comparing their stories and experiences, similar to the consciousness-raising activities of the second wave, they decided that "enough was enough" and agreed to unionize. Julia reflects on this moment: "Here amid the neon lights, the fake hair, and the high heels was the good fight I dreamed of fighting."

As the women initiate their unionization campaign at the Lusty Lady, they also begin to reach out to other strippers throughout the San Francisco industry to chart the capitalist exploitation that had become increasingly oppressive to sex workers over the past decade. The film includes a segment in which workers interviewed from throughout the industry, including those working in strip clubs, peep shows, lap dancing and other one-on-one "pleasure" venues, speak from their particular experiences as devalued women workers in a patriarchal industry. The film provides a kind of Marxist socialist analysis of the evolution of the sex industry, and the resulting de-evolution of the sex worker (which is depicted through a cartoon showing reverse Darwinism, in which a stripper evolves into an ape wearing a pink bikini.) As one of the dancers astutely (albeit crudely) comments,

> People assume, "Oh, well, see, you guys are being exploited, you deserve it." Almost, like, don't you know exotic dancers are exploited whether or not you want to believe it or not? It's, like, yeah, but they're not exploited just because they are exotic dancers, it has to do with the fact that the club's fucked up, the management's fucked up, they're not getting their tips. If all of that was in place, then, no, I don't think they would be exploited just because they're job is selling pussy.

Throughout the months of negotiation, the film also highlights a few of the experiences that exemplified the women's growing solidarity, such as their first picket (on behalf of a fellow dancer, Summer, who was fired for union activity), and the camaraderie built through endless meetings in which the women represented themselves at the bargaining table (since the exotic dancing industry did not yet have a union representative). At one point, "Jane," a member of the bargaining committee, describes the industry's response to the women's collective action as a kind of "reverse therapy," as the women were forced several times each month to spend 12 hours in a horrible, beige room, "just getting hammered on that you're not going to get this thing that you thought was so important to you, and that all of these people are counting on you to get for them." The women on the bargaining committee devoted almost two years of their lives to make the industry a better place for all women workers, those who had come before them, their colleagues, and those who would come after.

Through this documentary's chronicle of these workers' year-long battle with management and union-busting lawyers, which ultimately earned them a contract that guaranteed them sick pay, health insurance, and better conditions for workers of color, spectators are shown that the tenets of the American labor movement are still alive, although the movement may have been declared dead by the dominant culture. *Live Nude Girls Unite!* demonstrates that upholding the values of community over individualism and equality over exploitation and domination can make a difference. For example, in the last scene Julia explains why she feels joining the union was important for her, stating: "It didn't matter how aggressive, or Jewish, or smart, or witty, or, you know, strong I was, personality didn't provide me with good working conditions, being part of a group — organizing a successful union effort did."

Conclusion

In considering the significance of image-based politics and its connection to U.S. political culture, and feminism in particular, Shawn Parry-Giles has noted that "we live in a time where politics is all about images and where images are all political," and she urges rhetorical critics to "recognize the salience of such images, continue to critique these images ... and produce images of feminism that help achieve the political ends of the movement."[35] Along similar lines, Bonnie Dow has asserted, "I find it imperative that feminist criticism address the strategies through which the mass media tend to offer consumers interpretations of the 'reality' of an issue that differ in important ways from the 'reality' that many women experience."[36] This essay makes some inroads into this call for greater critiques of political images of feminism, in this case, the feminism of the twenty-first century. By providing a representation of third-wave feminism in terms of both its ideological discourses and its materialist practices, I argue that *Live Nude Girls Unite!* functions as a provocative rhetorical artifact that provides strategic images through which the dynamics of contemporary feminist politics and debate may be better understood. Further, as a documentary produced by third-wave feminists to depict their own politics and perspectives, the film also may be seen as an example of genuine social change, as well as an intervention against what passes for feminism today both in the mass media and in the real world.

Live Nude Girls Unite!, in the vein of the documentary tradition, conveys a sense of legitimate realism by employing the authenticity of this cinematic form to address various social themes, such as gender oppression and collective action, more profoundly than those constructed by the largely conservative portrayals of third-wave feminism in the mainstream media. Julia, the film's producer and protagonist, demonstrates the ways in which she and the other strippers must constantly negotiate the challenges and contradictions of their chosen profession with their public role as political activists, and how that negotiation impacts their personal lives as women, daughters, and mothers. For these women workers, often the complex and ambiguous lines between the public and private, personal and political, are blurred because the very nature of the sex industry disrupts the boundaries between them.

In this independent film's revolutionary effort to navigate contradiction, re-imagine the boundaries between the public and the private, and overturn the power hierarchies related to class and gender oppression, it also advocates a resistive, third-wave feminist subculture through the demonstration of the effectiveness of collective action for social and political change. In Hollywood, however, the female labor activist of the twenty-first century would struggle with similar issues, while recognizing both the benefits and costs of feminism and collective action in an era of individualism and lifestyle politics.

CHAPTER SIX

Hollywood's Feminist Labor Heroines Moving Into the Twenty-first Century
Have We Really Come a Long Way?

"Not personal? That's my work in there — my sweat, my time away from my kids. If that's not personal, I don't know what is."
— Erin Brockovich, *Erin Brockovich*

"Yeah, I'm a beautiful girl ... I could find a guy to take care of me. I'm done lookin' to be taken care of. I want to take care of myself, take care of my kids."
— Josie Aimes, *North Country*

After declaring the second-wave feminism of the 1970s and 1980s dead, in the 1990s the mainstream media, and particularly Hollywood, began to co-opt a "brand new feminism" culled from its interpretation of third-wave goals and ambitions being marketed by popular press feminists, such as Roiphe, Hoff-Sommers, and Wolf. According to Dow, the media cast the revelations of these authors as a call for "feminists to abandon the structural analysis of patriarchal power, to embrace individualism, and to reach out to the millions of women (all feminists in their hearts, they imply) who have been turned off or disempowered by the emphasis on victimage."[1] The motivations of such "power feminism," rather than the "victim feminism" of the earlier generation, also resonated seamlessly with a classical Hollywood character arc: the exceptional individual who overcomes great odds to secure the American Dream, sweeping others like them up in a final communal strategy, despite the resistance of both friends and enemies. Hollywood's new post-feminist character-type generally consists of a central female protagonist on a "narrative quest," in which the independent woman (without a man) searches for self, combining realpolitik feminism with a sense of personal fulfillment.[2]

Such post-feminist media portrayals, according to Dow, while enhancing "awareness and acceptance of the range of choices women can make about how to lead their lives," also has reinterpreted, and consequently reversed, the "personal is political" slogan that defined much second-wave feminist ideology. Dow notes, "The political is personal, it tells us, as a set of political ideas and practices is transformed into a set of attitudes and personal lifestyle choices. Feminist politics become feminist identity. Feminist identity, in turn, is defined by appearance, by job, by marital status, and by personality, not by political belief or political practice."[3] The consequence of an emphasis on feminist lifestyle rather than politics has manifested itself in mainstream Hollywood films through a thematic emphasis on the American cult of individualism. While this focus may urge women to make something of themselves, it also, according to Susan Douglas, emphasizes "our isolation from and competition with other women. The political has been collapsed into the personal so that you, the lone individual, are all that matters."[4] As Jennifer Drake similarly notes, such mass media portrayals also emphasize "competitive individualism, the American work ethic, consumerism, and catfighting, all in feminism's name."[5]

This chapter maps the evolution of the female labor heroine in Hollywood at the transition between the twentieth and twenty-first centuries through an examination of two mainstream films: *Erin Brockovich* (2000) and *North Country* (2005). Although produced two decades later, these films are remarkably similar to *Norma Rae* and *Silkwood* in their overarching narrative and character developments. While *Norma Rae* and *Silkwood* emphasized the limitations of victim feminism, and presented women's liberation as a problem with no clear solution, *Erin Brockovich* and *North Country* portray their working-class heroines as women in a post-feminist era utilizing the entitlements gained from the second wave in an effort to make improvements in their individual lives. Both films feature down-and-out women who elbow their way into traditionally male-dominated professions in order to make a better life for themselves and their kids. The women become dismayed by what they find there (exploitation of a working-class community by big business in *Erin Brockovich* and corporate-wide sexual harassment in *North Country*), and become unwitting crusaders in a fight to make things right. The films' narratives focus on the women's' individual journeys of self-revelation and adoption of feminist sensibilities, which also represent the embodiment of the lifestyle feminism that has become the hallmark of Hollywood's representation of women's issues in the post-feminist media era. The heroines of these films accept the current patriarchal and capitalist system, but focus on their own opportunities for equality within that system, won for them by the legal precedents set by second-wave feminism. These women, I argue, merely "try on" a feminist identity for their own personal advantage, however, the lack of commitment to any explicit feminist politics results in these Hollywood films' failure to productively challenge the exploitative nature of a gendered and classed patriarchal capitalist society. Finally, the women's work on behalf of the collective is presented as a means to an end, rather than a conscious act of altruism on the part of these working-class women activists.

An analysis of these two films in the context of their cinematic predecessors also makes clear their similarities to the previous establishment and independent films considered in this book so far, and how the distinctions between those modes of construction influence the film industry's depth of engagement with socio-political issues. Considering these various representations of the female labor heroine over a period of fifty years and through three feminist eras (pre-second-wave, second-wave, and post-feminism), as well as during a decades-long decline of the American labor movement, the conservatism of Hollywood's portrayal of feminist and socialist ideas stands in marked contrast to the independent film industry's efforts to demonstrate the continued existence — and strength — of these ideologies. I conclude this chapter by examining the rhetorical implications of these tensions between representations of the female labor heroine in the mainstream and on the margins through comparative analyses of *Erin Brockovich* and *North Country* with the other films previously discussed.

Hollywood Conservatism in The Age of Reagan

Hollywood's consistently conservative portrayal of female labor activism in the last decades of the twentieth century and entering into the twenty-first century is partly due to changes in the film industry, and partly the result of the steady decline of the labor movement in the United States over the previous few decades. Both shifts may be regarded as symptomatic of the Reagan years in United States history — a period when the impact of a political and economic policy overhaul penetrated every aspect of American social and cultural life, and had its greatest effects on the working class. According to Jasmine Paul and Bette Kauffman, "Depictions of working-class life fell by the wayside as economic and political climates hardened toward the working class in the 1980s and 1990s.... In these decades, people worked harder, employers made greater demands, and media validated materialism more than before."[6] The effects of Reaganomics and the adverse fiscal conditions that followed (including high unemployment and a nationwide recession) greatly influenced the decline of the American labor movement, which already had been losing ground since the end of World War II. Union membership had grown quickly in the 1930s, from 3.4 million members in 1930 to more than 10 million in 1941. "Union density" peaked from 1945 to 1946 and again in 1954, when 35 percent of workers were union members. The number of union members continued to grow over the next two decades, from 17 million in 1954 to 20.2 million in 1978. By 1983, however, membership had dipped to 17.7 million (20.1 percent of workers) and, by that decade's end, unionization efforts were virtually nonexistent and the progress that had been made in the previous half century had been largely eroded. By 2001, the percentage of workers belonging to unions had reached a 60-year low of just 13.5 percent.[7]

Hollywood also fell under the influence of the Reagan administration during this time. The first White House occupied by a former actor cultivated an enthusiastic relationship with the film industry forged through a mutual commitment to both technology (from the military weaponry of the "Star Wars" Defense Initiative to the technical innovations glamorized in the *Star Wars* film series) and conservative ideology (republican ideals shaped in response to the Cold War against the Soviet "evil empire").[8] In the years following the release of *Norma Rae* and *Silkwood*, Hollywood entered a phase that some have characterized as "the Age of Reagan." According to Robert Sklar, the majority of films produced during the Reagan administration in the 1980s revived and reshaped the World War II adventure tale and, in the process, paired values such as unity and heroic self-sacrifice with more demeaning messages of imperialism, racism, and sexism.[9] Similarly, Michael Ryan and Douglas Kellner note that, under Reagan's leadership, "the revived conservative social movements managed to turn back many of the liberal and social gains of the preceding fifty years."[10]

A by-product of these cinematic tendencies, and of the general cultural ideals predominant during the Reagan years, was an emphasis on an exaggerated masculinity in films. Susan Jeffords notes that in film representations from *Rambo* to *Terminator*, "the depiction of the indefatigable, muscular, and invincible masculine body became the linchpin of the Reagan imaginary. These hard bodies came to stand not only for a type of national character — heroic, aggressive, determined — but for the nation itself."[11] The cultural and ideological landscape of this period, then, left little room for strong, independent women — especially in Hollywood feature films. Rather, according to Susan Faludi, the lesson proffered by films featuring working women during the 1980s, including such films as *Fatal Attraction* (1987), *Baby Boom* (1987), *Broadcast News* (1987), and *Working Girl* (1988), among others, was that "American women were unhappy because they were too free; their liberation had denied them marriage and motherhood."[12]

Yet, while the spectacle of cyborgs, action heroes, and extraterrestrials dominated the film industry in the 1980s, an underground film movement was building that would eventually pose a challenge — albeit a subtle one — to the mainstream excesses of the Hollywood cinema. Although the blockbuster mentality of the Hollywood marketplace appeared to have overwhelmed the industry, the remnants of an "identity cinema" established by committed filmmakers in the 1960s lurked just beneath the surface. In the mid–1980s, various enterprises were established (such as Robert Redford's Sundance Institute) in an effort to aid up-and-coming filmmakers in developing independent projects and screening the completed works for critics and distributors.[13] In addition, the new commercial outlets that had emerged during the decade, such as home video rentals and cable TV, created a niche market for this revival of the independent film movement. Such independent productions usually were based on scripts written by the filmmakers themselves, featured no-name actors, were shot on 16 mm film, and cost well under one million dollars. Yet, the occasional independent film enjoyed overwhelming financial success, such as director

Steven Soderbergh's breakthrough indie *sex, lies and videotape* (1989), which earned over 25 million dollars, including nearly 10 million dollars in rental sales for Miramax, the film's distributor.

The success of Soderbergh's low-budget, high-grossing film quickly attracted industry attention. By the mid–1990s, films such as *Clerks* (1994) and *The Brothers McMullen* (1995), each of which were produced for under 250,000 dollars and grossed 3 million dollars and 10 million dollars respectively, confirmed the ability of independent films to garner both critical praise and box-office revenue. Subsequently, 1996 was dubbed the "Year of the Independent" when four out of the five films nominated for the Best Picture Academy Award (including *The English Patient, Fargo, Shine,* and *Secrets & Lies*) were independently-produced films. The undiluted — and unprecedented — profit potential of these films became impossible for Hollywood studios to ignore, and before long the major conglomerates began to form their own "independent" divisions or simply purchased already-established independent distributors (such as the Walt Disney Corporation's purchase of Miramax). The result of this industry change, according to Claudia Puig, is that the indies, which once provided an alternative to the commercialism of studio movies, "instead have become Hollywood's darling. In the process, some of Hollywood's crassness has worn off on them.... Consequently, the line between independent films and more mainstream studio pictures has grown increasingly blurred."[14] In addition, a number of films released by the major studios in recent years, such as *L.A. Confidential* (Warner Bros., 1997), *A Simple Plan* (Paramount, 1998), and *Rushmore* (Disney, 1998) have taken on the look and feel of independents by featuring an explicitly artistic and innovative style, as well as more probing themes and subject matter.[15] Given these changes in what had come to define Hollywood films at the close of the twentieth century, *Erin Brockovich* and *North Country* are both typical of independent-style films within the mainstream media industry, reflecting the movement in turn-of-the-century Hollywood filmmaking to color issue-oriented cinema with commercial appeal.

Directed by the famous progenitor of the indie revival, Steven Soderbergh, *Erin Brockovich* reflects the director's inclination for loosely-conveyed realism accomplished through hand-held camera work and a dressed-down plot. Yet, the advertising for the film subtly belied the restraint and low-gloss spontaneity usually associated with Soderbergh productions by announcing, "Julia Roberts is Erin Brockovich." The tagline suggested that, despite the look of the film, it was a product of the industry — for only a Hollywood production budget could accommodate the 20 million dollar salary Julia Roberts now regularly demands. A David-and-Goliath story about a working-class girl versus a ruthless corporate giant, *Erin Brockovich* was written by Susannah Grant and became an instant box-office success, as well as an award-show gem. The film grossed more than 250 million dollars (28 million of which was earned during opening weekend) and continues to earn profits in both video and DVD sales, as well as through cable television revenues. The popular film also won seventeen awards in 2001, many of which went to Julia Roberts for her featured performance, including an Academy Award for Best Actress.

The plotline for *Erin Brockovich* originated with Brockovich's L.A. chiropractor, who found the environmental crusader's story so intriguing she passed it along to another client, Carla Santos Shamberg, a film producer. Shamberg then pitched the idea to her husband, Michael Shamberg, a partner with Danny De Vito and Stacey Sher in the production company Jersey Films. Believing that Brockovich's tale was ideal subject matter for a film, Carla Santos Shamberg decided to become the executive producer on the project and Jersey Films bought the options to Brockovich's story. The team then asked screenwriter Susannah Grant to meet with Brockovich and to begin assembling the screenplay. Grant, the acclaimed writer behind a number of female-centered films, including *Pocohantas*, the 1995 Disney feature; *Ever After* (1998) featuring Drew Barrymore; and *28 Days* (2000) with Sandra Bullock, took on the task of compressing a five-year period in Brockovich's life into a two-hour movie. The next step for the film team from Jersey Films was to sign a major-name actress to the title role, and they chose Julia Roberts. According to the published shooting script for the film, Roberts "was thrilled to play the title character."[16] The production team then approached Soderbergh, who they had previously worked with on the film *Out of Sight* (1998). According to co-producer Michael Shamberg, Soderbergh was the logical choice since "[Erin's] story is so dramatic and funny and big on its own, that we wanted someone who would keep it grounded and real. There is never anything sentimental or overblown and glossy about Steven's work. We knew he would take this classic story and keep it classic."[17] Soderbergh signed on to the project because he found the strong, linear screenplay that "was performance-driven and had a female protagonist who was in every scene of the film" an appealing challenge.[18]

Erin Brockovich was generally well-received by critics, many of whom compared the film to *Norma Rae* and *Silkwood*, or the more recent *A Civil Action* (1999), an environmental legal drama starring John Travolta. Kenneth Turan of *The Los Angeles Times*, for example, describes the film as an "irresistible, hugely satisfying feminist fairy tale that turns 'Norma Rae' into the protagonist of 'A Civil Action' and makes us believe it."[19] David Ansen, in his review for *Newsweek*, notes, "Like 'Norma Rae,' this is a story of an unlikely and uneducated heroine who spearheads the fight for justice," and Robert Ebert describes the film as: "'Silkwood' (Meryl Streep fighting nuclear wastes) crossed with 'A Civil Action' (John Travolta against pollution) plus Julia Roberts in a plunging neckline."[20] Peter Travers of *Rolling Stone* writes, "For a true story about water pollution, cancer and mountains of legal briefs, 'Erin Brockovich' is outrageously, even shamelessly, entertaining. Unlike 'A Civil Action,' which took a muted approach to a similar topic, Erin is as loud as its heroine."[21] Joe Morgenstern offers great praise for the film as well, writing in his review for the *The Wall Street Journal*: "This is a terrific movie ... that's as funny, romantic and justifiably self-confident as any seen on the screen since Hollywood's golden age. I thought I'd had enough of truish-life stories about working women taking on corporate adversaries, as in 'Silkwood' or 'Norma Rae,' but 'Erin Brockovich' ... caught me up and turned me around."[22]

Like *Erin Brockovich*, *North Country* features one of Hollywood's most celebrated actresses, Oscar winner Charlize Theron, who won Hollywood's most coveted award for another biographical turn as serial killer Aileen Wuornos in *Monster* (2003). *North Country* was the work of Participant Productions, a new film company dedicated to "changing the world one film at a time." Directed by Nikki Caro, the critically-acclaimed director of the art-house film *Whale Rider* (which won an Independent Spirit Award in 2004 for best foreign film) and a native New Zealander, the film has the perspective of a Hollywood "outsider" working within the constraints of the Hollywood style. The screenplay, written by another Hollywood newcomer, Michael Seitzman, was adapted from the 2005 book *Class Action: The Story of Lois Jensen and the Landmark Case That Changed Sexual Harassment Law* by Clara Bingham, and so features a distinctly female perspective. The film also featured Woody Harrelson, Sissy Spacek, and

Julia Roberts as Erin Brockovich displaying her "assets" as a receptionist/burgeoning legal aid and primary investigator into the contamination of the water supply in the working-class community of Hinkley, California. Brockovich's character is an ambivalent heroine in the film as she struggles between the dictates and rewards of a patriarchal and capitalistic culture for women of the working-class and a rebellious resistance of those conventions.

Frances McDormand. Although the film was generally well received by critics, and garnered Academy Award nominations for Best Actress and Best Supporting Actress, it was a colossal failure by Hollywood standards, grossing only $18 million dollars, little more than half of its $35 million dollar budget.[23]

While reviews of *Erin Brockovich* focused on the film's feminist heroine, various critics of *North Country* lauded the film for its emphasis on both working-class issues and sexual harassment in the workplace. David Edelstein, in his review of the film for *Slate* online, for example, observes, "The theme isn't just sexism, but the changing American economy — the blue-collar towns slowly dying, their hangers-on living a dog-eat-dog life, with the bitches the first to go."[24] Roger Ebert's review for the *Chicago Sun Times*, notes that "'North Country' is one of those movies that stir you up and make you mad, because it dramatizes practices you've heard about but never really visualized."[25] Others commended the film for its overarching moral perspective. According to Steve Persall of the *St. Petersburg Times*, "*North Country* is a working-class feminist morality tale eclipsing Norma Rae and Erin Brockovich in that narrow category of filmmaking," and Manohla Dargis of *The New York Times* characterizes the film a "a star vehicle with heart — an old-fashioned liberal weepie about truth and justice."[26] David Rooney, writing for *Variety*, notes, "it remains an emotionally potent story told with great dignity, to which women especially will respond."[27]

Both *North Country* and *Erin Brockovich* employ a melodramatic style to tell their morality tales, similar to that found in earlier films about female labor activists, an aesthetic choice that compresses the history of a real-life event into the formula of a Hollywood docudrama. According to Grant, as the film's screenwriter this was her greatest challenge, since "any life is complex, and Erin's, especially in the years of the PG&E trial, was labrynthine. Writing the script was a matter of figuring out which parts of the labyrinth were essential to the story I was telling; which were germane; which were expendable; and which were inessential."[28] Turan notes that what is most exciting about *Erin Brockovich* is "how old-fashioned it is at its core. It uses standard Hollywood building blocks like big stars and a Cinderella story line laced with laughter and tears and reminds us why they became standard in the first place."[29] Indeed, both films resonate with the social-consciousness and populist sentiment inherent in the Hollywood idealism of a bygone era. Like *The Pajama Game*, *Norma Rae*, and *Silkwood* before them, *Erin Brockovich* and *North Country* follow the classical Hollywood tradition by focusing on two major plotlines: the female heroine's personal growth through her public activism, as well as her personal struggles with family, romantic relationships, and members of the community. However, such a formula has its limits in a film portraying social protest and collective action. In *North Country*, for example, the story of a group of real women's experience in the mining industry is collapsed into a Horatio Algers tale of one woman's efforts to achieve stability, financial security, and independence amidst the colossal odds stacked against her. The tagline for the film reveals this theme: "All she wanted was to make a living. Instead she made history." This choice on the part of the filmmakers also was the focus of much of the criticism about the film from reviewers. Ruthe Stein of *The San Francisco Chronicle* comments, "Oddly in a movie about women's rights, the other actresses aren't given much to do," and Kenneth Turan observes in his review for the *Los Angeles Times*, "While it's a truism that movies have to take dramatic license to make complex stories fit into finite time frames, it is depressing to come across a movie whose over-eagerness to convince us makes us reject it rather than embrace it."[30]

Both films also temper the classical Hollywood melodramatic story arcs by also incorporating shades of the non-obtrusive style and manufactured realism usually found in independent cinema. The great majority of the scenes in *Erin Brockovich*, for example, are shot with a hand-held camera, which creates a voyeuristic feel throughout the film, as if the spectator actually is privy to an unfolding reality. Adding to the realist technique is the film's use of mise en scene: Erin's house is run down and bug-infested, the scenes in Hinkley were shot on location in the actual town just across from the PG&E plant, and the shots inside Ed's law office evoke the disheveled, fluorescent-lit, claustrophobic existence of an overburdened lawyer on the verge of retirement. Similarly, *North Country* uses a realist style to convey the vast, emptiness of the Minnesota mining town and the lonely existence of single mom, Josie Aimes. As Rooney notes,

> Aided immeasurably by the gritty, unvarnished textures of Chris Menges' widescreen camera work, which gives the film both physical and emotional majesty, Caro creates a vivid sense of the women's isolation and powerlessness. This climate of fear and wariness is achieved not only through scenes depicting the indignities they suffer, but also in the sheer brute presence of the mine itself: a big, clanking industrial monster squatting in the middle of a vast landscape blanketed in snow.

For all of their attempts to capture the realism of working-class existence, however, these films also remain true to the tenets of the classical Hollywood style prevalent in mainstream films. The films focus almost entirely on the main protagonist, the outlaw heroine, charting her episodic growth and personal transformation into a full-fledged crusader for those who have been disempowered and exploited.

Erin Brockovich's fiery protagonist and her path to redemption, and *North Country*'s barrier-breaking activist driven by righteousness and courage, also share many similarities with the Hollywood female labor heroines that graced the silver screen in earlier decades. These twenty-first-century protagonists combine the independence and intelligence of Babe Williams of *The Pajama Game*, the fierce determination and restless energy of Norma Rae Webster in *Norma Rae*, and the brass and fearlessness of Karen Silkwood in *Silkwood*. All five of these women also are portrayed in the films as women on the margins of the workplace: Babe, whose position as head of the union grievance committee distinguishes her from her co-workers; Norma Rae, whose promotion to spot-checker alienates her colleagues; Karen, who becomes shunned by workers fearful of losing their jobs; Erin, who represents a threat to her colleagues (both sexually and professionally), and Josie, who has infiltrated an all-male industry under the protection of sexual equality in the workplace rulings. Although Erin's legal fight for financial reparations on behalf of the working-class citizens of Hinkley differs somewhat from the union-focused struggles of the other heroines, Erin's narrative development is strikingly similar to that of the other female protagonists, especially Norma Rae and Karen. *Erin Brockovich* begins by characterizing its female protagonist as an unlikely, and clearly tainted, heroine. Initially presented as spirited but misguided, the female heroines of *Norma Rae*, *Silkwood*, and *Erin Brockovich* grow and transform in such ways that, by the films' conclusions, their conversion appears miraculous and somewhat inauthentic. Similarly, in *North Country*, much of the plot hinges on a scandalous incident in Josie's past, which has led to her being characterized as "nothing but trouble," and a "cheap whore," her whole life. It is not until the end of the film that the truth about the misconceived situation in Josie's history is revealed.

Here We Go Again: Individual Heroism and Personal Redemption For Women of The Working-Class

Erin Brockovich opens with a shot of the female protagonist answering questions during a job interview. The interviewer is off-screen and the camera focuses in on Erin. Her appearance is somewhat unconventional: her eyes are made-up with light blue eye shadow that extends far beyond her eyelids, fading out slightly above her high eyebrows. Her hair is arranged in a large, beauty-pageant style bouffant and she is wearing a low-cut, flowered dress with thin straps. The next scene cuts to a shot of Erin standing against a wall outside of the building where the interview took place smoking a cigarette (a familiar shot that evokes past screen images of street-walking prostitutes). As the credits begin, she grounds her half-smoked cigarette into the sidewalk with her high-heeled sandal and walks to her car. When she approaches, she notices a ticket under the windshield wiper and mumbles, "Oh, fuck!" As she opens the door, she yells, "God damn it!" and inspects her now damaged fingernail. The scene ends with Erin pulling out of the parking spot and, as she crosses the intersection, being hit by a driver who runs a red light.

Two scenes later Erin sits on the witness stand testifying against the man who hit her. After a brief montage that shows Erin, in a neck brace and a very low-cut dress, describing her situation of trying to raise three kids with no husband and a large debt, the defense lawyer asks her, "Is your ex-husband helping you out?" "Which one?" she asks. "There's more than one?" he responds with surprise. "Yeah, there's two," she retorts, the irritation evident in her voice. "Broke, three kids, no job? A doctor in a Jaguar must have looked like a pretty good meal ticket," the lawyer insinuates. "That asshole smashed in my fucking neck!" Erin yells, enraged by his attempt to incriminate her.

The next scene shows Erin arriving home after her day in court to three hungry kids and a ramshackle house crawling with water bugs and bereft of food. A brief montage follows that summarizes several days in which Erin places a number of unsuccessful job calls found through the classifieds, which propels her to return to Ed Masry's law office and sternly inform him: "There's two things that aggravate me, Mr. Masry: being ignored and being lied to." While Ed stammers an apology, she tells him with her voice raised, "I don't need pity, I need a paycheck. And I've looked, but when you've spent the last six years raising babies, it's real hard to convince someone to give you a job that pays worth a damn," then, after flashing a look toward the secretary staring at her in disbelief, she snaps, "You getting every word of this down honey, or am I talking too fast for you?" From the start, the film portrays Erin as gruff, foul-mouthed, bitter, and barely able to keep control over her life. Not afraid to speak the truth, Erin frequently crosses the line of conventionality and, as a result, quickly offends or alienates nearly everyone who comes in contact with her.

North Country's introduction of its female protagonist echoes that of *Erin Brockovich*, in which the main character is initially demoralized and her character and personal choices are called into question. The film opens with an idyllic scene of a little, blonde girl in pajamas admiring the ornaments on a Christmas tree then sitting with a half-dressed Barbie doll and brushing her hair with a comb. The tone quickly turns as an old Chevy comes skidding through the snow-packed driveway, and the girl's mother looks out the window and then ushers her daughter upstairs. In a voice-over narration you hear the same woman say in a distinctive Minnesota accent, "Lady, you sit in your nice house, your clean floors, your bottled water, your flowers on Valentine's Day," as the scene switches to a courtroom with the woman on the witness stand. She continues, "and you think you're tough? Wear my shoes — tell me tough. A day in the pit, tell me tough." The shot cuts to a female lawyer, who condescendingly remarks, "I'm sure we're all sufficiently impressed, Mrs. Aimes." "There's no Mrs. here," the woman on the stand states as the scene abruptly shifts to a shot of her now lying on the kitchen floor and coming to consciousness. She struggles to pull herself to her feet, then rinses the blood from her mouth and face in the kitchen sink. The scene cuts back to the courtroom with the woman stating, "No, I didn't go to the police." "What did you do?" the lawyer asks. "What I had to," the woman states and she is shown leaving the house with the little girl, who is now sobbing, and gently easing her daughter into a pick-up truck. Her teenage son stands in the doorway, asking accusingly, "We're not coming back, are we?"

The cross-cutting continues as the woman drives to her parents' home, and the lawyer continues to question the woman we now learn is Josie Aimes. She receives a warm and concerned welcome from her mother (Sissy Spacek), and a cool reception from her father (Richard Jenkins), just back from a night-shift at the mine, who asks, "Did he catch you in bed with another man, is that why he laid hand on ya?" Immediately, Josie is established as a single, working-class mother and domestic abuse victim struggling to do what is best for her children. She is also cast as a potentially loose woman with a checkered past (through the courtroom interrogation that establishes the fact that she is un-married, her two children are from different men, and she has never revealed the father of her first child that she had at age 17).

In a manner very much like Norma Rae and Karen Silkwood, both Erin and Josie find an outlet for their rebelliousness and a means of providing for their families through unusual avenues that they believe will bring them closer to "the American dream." The prime outlet for Erin is through her job processing files, when she discovers an energy comapany's (PG&E) attempts to exploit the working-class community of Hinkley, California. Having been down on her own luck for so long, Erin transforms overnight from a victim to a crusader in classic Hollywood form, and turns her own tenacity and personal resentment into an activist energy in order to fight for others who share her same working-class plight. Of course, she does not accomplish this redemptive turnaround alone; she is helped by two men in her life. Her relationship with Ed provides the impetus for her activism when he gives her "permission" to further investigate the Hinkley case. Erin's journey to enlightenment and heroism would have been impossible without Ed's legal expertise and, more importantly, his financial backing. Ansen notes that "Finney, with his boiled-potato face and alarmed eyebrows, is a masterful comic foil for Robert's needling, lower-class rage. They're a great beauty-and-beast team."[31] Although they never become romantically involved, Ed and Erin spat like a husband and wife and she spends considerably more screen time with him than her actual romantic partner, next-door neighbor, George.

George comes to Erin's rescue early in the film by volunteering to take care of her kids during the day while she begins collecting the evidence she needs to incriminate PG&E. Reminiscent of Norma Rae's husband Sonny and Karen's live-in boyfriend Drew, George is kind, compassionate, and easy-going. George and Erin quickly begin a romance, but he just as quickly tires of Erin's inattention and preoccupation with the Hinkley case. In one scene, when Erin has arrived home late from work yet again, and is cranky as usual, he informs her, "what I'm thinking is, you oughta either find a different job or a different guy. 'Cause there may be men who don't mind being the maid and getting nothing in return, but I sure as shit ain't one of them." As in *Norma Rae* and *Silkwood*, the female protagonist's male companion provides the voice of conscience that challenges the woman's attempts to transcend her traditional role as a domestic wife and mother. *Erin Brockovich* also invites sympathy for George, rather than Erin, when he tells Erin that he had bought her a pair of earrings at the mall one day and decided the next time she said or did something nice he would surprise her. "Know how long ago that was?" he asks her, "Six months." By inviting spectators' identification with the thoughtful and loving George, this scene works to subtly disparage Erin for her selfishness in making her work a priority over her personal relationships.

Similarly, in *North Country*, Josie's life quickly turns around when she runs into an old friend who convinces her to apply for a job at the mine. From a mining family herself, Josie is skeptical, since the mines "are no place for women," a sentiment reinforced by her father's response to Josie's decision to seek work at the mine, "So, you want to be a lesbian now?" He adds, "Do you have any idea how many accidents there have been since this whole thing started. Somebody's going to get killed cause of them women." Josie joins a small group of women who broke through the gender barrier in the iron mines of northern Minnesota by taking advantage of the Equal Opportunity Act during the 1970s and 1980s. One there, however, she becomes quickly dismayed by the sexism present at the mines, both institutionally and through the appalling behavior of the men working there who resent the women's presence. The harassment begins with the corporate-mandated gynecological exam to rule out pregnancy before the women are hired, then continues on the women's orientation, in which the mine manager states, "The doc says you look darn good under those clothes. Sense of humor, ladies, rulo numero uno." While showing the women around the mine, a fellow worker walks by and whispers, "Cunts," and the intimidation only increases over the coming weeks with the women tormented through degrading graffiti on the mine walls, sex toys and semen in their lockers, and verbal and physical abuse.

After suffering through a few months of this appalling treatment, Josie tries to speak to her father about the working conditions at the mine (he ignores her), then she approaches Gloria, the friend who got her the job. As a union representative, Gloria had initiated a number of reforms in order to improve working conditions for the women, such as port-o-potties in the pits, however, she feels that the "mining mentality" is just something she and the other women must accept. Coincidentally, Gloria is diagnosed with ALS early in the narrative, which also conveniently takes her out of the fight, as she is the most likely character to initiate a protest on behalf of the women. Instead, Josie, inspired by the Anita Hill hearings she sees on television, tries to rally her female co-workers to lodge a group complaint, but they refuse and begin to turn against her in fear that if she "stirs up trouble" they may lose the well paying jobs they have come to depend on. Alone and alienated, like each of the Hollywood female labor heroines before her, Josie lodges an individual complaint and attends a meeting with Mr. Pearson, the mine owner. Pearson states that he is willing to help her out, by allowing her to tenure her resignation immediately, rather than require a two-week notice. When Josie says she's not interested in resigning, he advises, "I suggest you spend less time stirring up your female co-workers and less time in bed with your male co-workers and more time working on your job performance."

Josie returns to work and the harassment escalates: the women discover vulgar threats written in feces on their locker room walls, one woman is held inside a port-o-potty while the men tip it over, and Josie is nearly raped in an abandoned mine shaft. Josie confronts her tormentor, a guy she's known since high school named Billy Sharp, in the cafeteria in front of everyone. The women distance themselves from her and the men, and even those who had previously chosen to stay above the fray now step forward in Billy's defense. Josie leaves in tears and decides to quit, then goes

In *North Country*, Josie Aimes (played by Charlize Theron) confronts a group of male co-workers that have been harassing her and other females at a Minnesota mine and later becomes the successful plaintiff in the nation's first sexual harassment lawsuit, which changed sex discrimination policies in the workplace. In the film version of Aimes's story, however, her personal character is constantly being called into question by members of the community and, consequently, her efforts on behalf of the other women at the mine are initially met with hostility and suspicion, which taints the power of her labor activism over the course of the film.

to see Gloria's friend Bill, a lawyer, for advice. "I want to sue the mine, the company, all of them," she tells him. He initially tries to dissuade her by reasoning that even when you win, you don't win because in corporate lawsuits right has nothing to do with the real world. He explains that "you're like Anita Hill," and they call it the "nuts and sluts defense," the corporation makes the case that either the woman filing the suit is nuts and imagined the harassment, or she's a slut and asked for it.

Bill initially advises Josie to find another job, but when she persists he agrees to take on the case if she can find other women to participate in a class action suit, the only way around the nuts and sluts defense. Like Erin, Josie depends on the help of a man to carry out her mission. However, unlike in the other films, *North Country* does not integrate a romantic plot into the film, rather the relationship between Josie and Bill stays at the level of mutual respect and innocent flirtation.

Hollywood Heroines and Feminist Contradictions

One of the most interesting aspects of both *Erin Brockovich* and *North Country* is the means through which the films address the contradictions of modern feminism, in contrast to most mainstream films and their cinematic predecessors. For example, one of the most talked about aspects of *Erin Brockovich* was the title character's wardrobe, which consistently displayed what has come to be Brockovich's most identifiable feature in real life and on film, her well-endowed chest. In fact, almost every film review made tribute to this part of the film heroine's anatomy. For example, Thomas Doherty describes the film as "a buoyant tribute to American mammary-centricity stuffed into a legal payback melodrama."[32] Ansen suggests that "Jeffrey Kurkland's wittily tacky costumes could have been nominated for best supporting actress by themselves."[33] Travers notes that Erin "jiggles like a babe from *Baywatch*."[34] Turan accuses her of "an encyclopedic knowledge of the uses of cleavage."[35] This aspect of Erin's character adds an interesting dimension to the film that in some ways illustrates what Yvonne Tasker describes as Hollywood's "insistent equation between working women, women's work and some form of sexual(ised) performance." [36] The camera's (and male characters') gaze often lingers on Erin's breasts or pans down her body (often clad in tight-fitting and revealing outfits), which may be interpreted as a form of objectification of the female protagonist commonly found in Hollywood representations of working women. Erin's displays of female sexuality, however, also are advanced as a means of feminist empowerment in the vein of third-wave feminism and similar to the strippers in *Live Nude Girls Unite!*. In these instances, Erin's self-confessed use of her anatomy as a political weapon presents her sexuality as a powerful tool of her subjectivity. For example, when Ed asks Erin, "What makes you think you can just walk in [to the Water Board] and find what we need?" without missing a beat, Erin replies, "They're called boobs, Ed."

In *North Country*, the contradictions of feminism reflect more the backlash found so often in popular culture that advises women to be wary of the gains achieved through the second-wave feminist movement because they always come with a price. For Josie, her job at the mine allows her to support her kids and live on her own for the first time without having to depend on a man or her parents (a few weeks after she starts her job, she also buys a dilapidated house close to the mines). However, the achievement of the American dream for Josie is fraught with danger, isolation, and in the end, regret due to the sexist environment in which she is forced to toil in order to make a decent living. Although the sexual harassment testimony that Josie offers during the lawsuit brings the feminist critique of patriarchal institutions into bold relief in the film, in the end the film privileges Josie's long and difficult individual struggle over her and the other women's collective feminist victory.

In the post-feminist style, both films also similarly offer a strong sense of the women's often uncomfortable negotiation of their public careers with their private lives. One of the secondary plot lines of *North Country* is Josie's strained relationship with her adolescent son, which is made even more difficult by the strain of the lawsuit. As members of the community refer to Josie as a rabble-rouser and "mining whore," her son starts to pull further away from her and begins to echo the labels and slurs he has heard used to describe his mother. Josie also loses the support of her family for a time, until her mother makes her own feeble attempt at launching a feminist critique of her own situation by leaving her husband a sandwich and a note before moving out of the house and into a motel. Although early on in *Erin Brockovich* the film invites the spectator to view Erin's resistance to her domestic role from George's hurt and angry perspective, in other scenes the film also invites consideration of this issue from Erin's view. In one scene, while driving through the desert on her way back from Hinkley, Erin learns that her youngest daughter spoke her first word that afternoon. Then, as George describes in detail how it happened, Erin presses her lips together and blinks away her tears until she can no longer hold them back and begins to sob. Later, near the end of the film, Ed accuses her of getting too emotional and of making the case against PG&E personal when it should remain professional. "Not personal?" she yells. "That's my work in there — my sweat, my time away from my kids. If that's not personal, I don't know what is."

Erin proves how personal the case has become in the next to last scene of the film when she asks George to accompany her to Hinkley so he could see what he had helped to do. Once there, she "personally" informs one of the plaintiffs, Donna Jensen (Marg Helgenberger), that she has been awarded five million dollars in the settlement, and as Donna cries tears of relief and gratefully embraces Erin, the triumphant activist heroine looks over Donna's shoulder at George and smiles through her own tears. While *The Pajama Game* suggests that the heroine must choose between public activism and personal happiness (and she eventually embraces the latter) and *Norma Rae* and *Silkwood* disparage their heroines for personalizing their work and neglecting their personal lives, *Erin Brockovich* and *North Country* both attempt to show the female labor heroine's sense of personal (and in Josie's case, professional) sacrifice and the arduous consequences of making such a choice to work toward the greater public good.

Unlike the female activists in *Norma Rae* and *Silkwood* who are, in the end, punished for their newfound liberation, Erin Brockovich and Josie Aimes both experience the happy ending also enjoyed by Babe in *The Pajama Game*. Rather than celebrate at a company pajama party, however, Erin is rewarded with a spacious, corporate office with floor-to-ceiling windows and a two million dollar bonus. Josie is finally redeemed during the trial when, after 12 years, it is finally revealed that she was raped by a teacher in her high school, which is how she became pregnant with her son. Once her moral character is restored, everything else falls into place. Her son comes around and recognizes his mother's love and devotion, and the other female miners finally stand behind Josie and provide the needed ballast for the class action suit. In many ways, *Erin Brockovich* and *North Country* represent the logical conclusion to the trajectory of Hollywood's depictions of the female activist over the previous five decades: in a post-feminist world, a woman has the right to "choose" her feminist fight, but she will never find the "balance" between her personal life and her public work. As long as she embraces the ways of capitalism, however, in the end everything is tidily resolved.

Finally, while the fairy-tale happy ending of *Erin Brockovich* may have somewhat tempered the film's political ambitions, Julia Robert's star turn as the strident and sexually provocative Brockovich served to further dilute its transformative power. As a mega box-office star, Julia Roberts dominates any film in which she is featured. Noting the strength of her screen persona, many reviewers discussed Robert's propensity for overshadowing the character she portrays. For example, Ebert notes that, "in every single scene, she upstages the material," and Ansen asserts, "You never forget you're watching Julia Roberts, possessor of the most incandescent smile in Hollywood."[37] Similarly, Charlize Theron, even covered in mine soot and dressed in a yellow work jumpsuit, is radiant and picturesque. Stein notes, "Charlize Theron's beauty initially makes her not terribly believable as a woman forced to blast ore and haul rocks for a living."[38] Like that of Doris Day, Sally Field, and Meryl Streep, Julia Roberts' and Charlize Theron's glamorous star personas inhibit a realistic portrayal of the female heroine and function to distract spectators from the "ordinary" struggles of the working-class.

Possibilities and Limitations for the Female Labor Heroine in Film: A Comparative Analysis

Over time, various cinematic incarnations of the female labor activist have emerged as a response to the changing historical and cultural contexts of three distinct periods in American social history: the 1950s, the 1970s, and the year 2000. The earliest of these representations include *Salt of the Earth*'s Esperanza Quintero, a Mexican American working-class mother transformed through her militant participation in a mining strike and *The Pajama Game*'s Babe Williams, a no-nonsense union representative torn between love (with the company supervisor) and duty (to her striking co-workers). Like the "transitional women" included in Brandon French's study of women in American films of the fifties, Esperanza and Babe "are often torn between [their] desire for a conventional, secure lifestyle and [their] longing for an unconventional, adventurous, largely uncharted course of action."[39] In the end, Esperanza experiences a transformative emergence by taking on a new, if temporary, public identity, while Babe chooses to abandon her independence as a worker and activist for a more traditional role as the dutiful wife of the company boss.

The documentaries *Union Maids* and *With Babies and Banners* recover the experiences of female union activists who had made the transition from women's more traditional roles to active participants in the American labor movement during an even earlier period, the 1930s. The women's stories are told within the rhetorical milieu of the second-wave feminist movement of the 1970s, and reveal that these women's capacity for political activism, and the obstacles they faced as a result of their forays into the public sphere, remained forty years later. Two mainstream films of the same era also captured women's efforts to achieve equality and liberation through their attempts to challenge working-class and gender oppression. *Norma Rae* portrays a worker who takes a stand for labor reform in a southern cotton mill and *Silkwood* features a martyred activist who broke the bonds of convention and exposed the faults in the nuclear power industry's safety regulations for its workers. Responding to women's expanding roles as a result of the feminist movement, the films portray these women as they face the dual struggle of balancing their private lives with their public activism. By the films' conclusions, however, both women are shamed and punished for their attempts to reconcile such a double existence.

The transition from the twentieth to the twenty-first century brought three productions that carried on this tradition of reality-based films featuring enterprising women of courage and determination: *Erin Brockovich*, *North Country*, and *Live Nude Girls Unite!*[40] All three films re-imagined the figure of the labor heroine featured in the films of years past, offering an updated spin on the cinematic representation of the female activist.[41] Like the other films included in this study, the differences between these two films — both thematically and ideologically — reveal the profound gap between the independent cinema's representations of the female labor heroine and those produced within the Hollywood establishment. Released at the turn of the twenty-first century, *Erin Brockovich*, *North Country* and *Live Nude Girls Unite!* reveal how cinematic representations of the woman labor activist have been updated and transformed from the previous films produced in the 1950s and 1970s. An examination of these late twentieth-century and early twenty-first-century heroines provides significant findings regarding the evolution of cinematic constructions of female activism, while also further exposing the conservatism of Hollywood's treatment of gender and social issues and the progressive challenges to those dominant views found in the independent cinema.

Despite the focus of *Erin Brockovich*, *North Country*, and *Live Nude Girls Unite!* on strong female protagonists and their proclivity for mixing sex (or, at the very least, sex appeal) and politics, the three productions are really quite different. An examination of these representations of female labor activists within the context of their cinematic predecessors also reveals how the evolution of the Hollywood heroine has remained fairly static, while the labor heroine of the independent films has gone further into the margins and become increasingly progressive. *Erin Brockovich* and *North Country*, for example, released in the post–Reagan era and the aftermath of the dissolution of labor unions in the mainstream culture, represents the nearest example to the union women of the past. Although still an activist of sorts, Erin Brockovich is cast alone in her fight for the working class and, in the end, winds up saving herself through the same capitalist mechanisms that she was initially working against. Josie Aimes is perhaps the most progressive of all of the Hollywood heroines in her feminist fight against sexism in the workplace, however, the choice to engage in this feminist protest was made only in an effort to maintain her high-paying job in a male-dominated industry. Both Erin's and Josie's actions, then, represent the post-feminist media's depiction of feminism as a lifestyle choice rather than a political identity.

A comparative analysis of these films illuminates the rhetorical tensions that emerge among Hollywood and independent films and their various forms, and explores how they express their social and political themes and invite certain ideological identifications. These tensions arise largely because of the distinct modes of production for these two films. *Erin Brockovich* and *North Country* are fairly large-budget, Hollywood-produced films based on the real-life stories of two ordinary women who, in an effort to improve their own lives, decided to fight back against the exploitation of women and the working-class and also improved the lives of others along the way. *Live Nude Girls Unite!* is an extremely low-budget documentary that chronicles exotic dancers' (from San Francisco's Lusty Lady) efforts to collectively unionize in order to improve their working conditions. The film was produced and directed by fellow Lusty Lady dancer, Julia Query, and the story is told through the perspective of the group and addresses the benefits of a coalition feminist and socialist politics. The rhetorical tensions made apparent through an investigation of these three films reveals how they follow the ideological trajectory established by their cinematic predecessors both within and independent of the Hollywood establishment.

While all three films employ a combination of the realist style and elements of melodrama in an effort to portray the lives and activism of their female heroines, *Erin Brockovich* and *North Country*, following the path of the Hollywood films that came before, tend to privilege classical Hollywood melodrama over realism in an effort to provide narrative coherence to the heroine's story. *Live Nude Girls Unite!*, in the vein of the independent films that preceded it, employs a sense of realism through the social authenticity of the documentary form that allows the film to address social themes, such as gender oppression and collective action, more profoundly. As in the previous Hollywood films, these choices produce in *Erin Brockovich* and *North Country* a focus on the heroine's individualistic, and sometimes unsuccessful, struggle against a prescribed feminine destiny. In contrast, *Live Nude Girls Unite!* repeats the format of the previous independent films by focusing on the struggles of working-class women within a larger social/historical situation. These tensions create stereotypical representations of working-class women in the Hollywood films, while the independent films present a more individual subjectivity for their female protagonists.

Erin Brockovich, *North Country*, and *Live Nude Girls Unite!* also differ with regard to their treatment of ideological issues raised by the films' themes and the manner in which they portray the female labor heroine — distinctions that also exist among the previous Hollywood products and their independent counterparts. The earlier Hollywood films, for example, implicitly address socio-political issues, such as women's onerous occupation of both the public and the private spheres. While *The Pajama Game*, *Norma Rae*, *Silkwood*, *Erin Brockovich*, and *North Country* raise the issue of this difficulty for women, they portray the public and private spheres as inherently incompatible for women, and as an inevitable and impossible choice the women are forced to make. As a result, when the women represented in these films try to occupy both the public and private realm, they fail and are subsequently disparaged, shamed, or punished so that the status quo remains in tact. In the independent films, on the other hand, explicit challenges to the status quo are raised and the female heroines question the very limiting and gendered structures of the public and the private, as well as the consequences they must face as they consistently try to blur those boundaries. *Salt of the Earth*, *Union Maids*, *With Babies and Banners*, and *Live Nude Girls Unite!* present women's attempts to find ways to inhabit both the public and private spheres, which also allows them to challenge the domination of society's gendered hierarchy.

The view of the status quo offered by these films is further influenced by the differing ways establishment films and independent films present the female labor heroines as models for female subject identification. Following the pattern established by the Hollywood films, which offer the well-known actresses Doris Day, Sally Field, and Meryl Streep, *Erin Brockovich* and *North Country* feature mega-box-office stars Julia Roberts and Charlize Theron. The labor heroines portrayed by these women invite responses from spectators that are hampered by the undeniable presence of the women's star persona, thus creating an interpretive distance between the glamorous movie star and the ordinary working-class women they portray. On the other hand, the independent films' presentation of real women rather than actresses (such as Julia Query who wrote, produced, directed, and stars in *Live Nude Girls Unite!*) lends a personal authenticity to the films with which female spectators may relate and identify.

The comparison of these three films reveals the disparate paths that Hollywood and the independent film industry have taken over the past few decades. While the figure of the female labor heroine may represent a progressive alternative to most incarnations of women on the big screen, the differences in the political and ideological impact of independent versus Hollywood films is significant. The concluding chapter of this book will map such tensions and reveal the complex history of female labor films over five decades.

CHAPTER SEVEN

Fifty Years of Female Labor Activism in Film
Mapping the Rhetorical Tensions

In a 2001 essay for *Entertainment Weekly*, Ty Burr argues that the female labor heroine is one of the Hollywood archetypes that almost always insures an actress an Academy Award nomination and he describes this coveted role as consisting of "leading ladies who defy tradition, refuse to play it safe—and end up finding themselves."[1] According to Burr, the ingredients for the transformative roles featured in films such as *Norma Rae*, *Silkwood*, and *Erin Brockovich* (and I would add *The Pajama Game* and *North Country*) are straightforward: "Take a pre-feminist naïf—it helps if she's way down the economic ladder—then have her slowly wise up to political/corporate corruption as well as her own power to change things for the better."[2] These women are best summarized by the label Burr provides: "Women on the verge."[3] Women such as Babe Williams, Norma Rae Webster, Karen Silkwood, and Erin Brockovich stand on the precipice of liberation, political action, and feminist resistance, but in the end their transformation remains unfulfilled, unconvincing, or seemingly inauthentic. Their momentary acts of rebellion quickly lead to their recuperation back into the safety of domesticity, the utopian lure of the capitalist way, or the ultimate silence of death. In contrast, the women featured in independent films, such as *Salt of the Earth*, *Union Maids*, *With Babies and Banners*, and *Live Nude Girls Unite!*, represent women who are not merely on the verge, but have defiantly crossed a line and welcome the consequences. These independent films offer examples of the long, difficult, and collective struggles for progressive change enacted by radical activist women who blatantly transgress the social order. In part, these distinctions are a result of the political-economic factors involved in the production of these films, which have greatly influenced the forms these films have taken, as well as the ideological stance they invite from spectators.

When cinematic representations of the female labor activist are analyzed consecutively over a fifty year span, the compelling differences that arise are most clearly attributable to the distinctions between mainstream Hollywood products and those projects produced by independent filmmakers. That is, with regard to the nine films included in this study, the means through which these films were produced clearly affect the content that spectators receive in important ways. Although half of the films examined in this study were produced by the Hollywood industry with various degrees of independence on the part of the films' creators (ranging from the strict industry standards for the Warner Bros.–produced *The Pajama Game* to *Erin Brockovich*, a mainstream film directed by a former independent artist), they remain fairly similar in their more conservative portrayals of the female labor heroine — which eventually reify dominant ideologies about women's place in society. The remaining films, which were created independently of the Hollywood industry, on the other hand, offer formal aesthetics and ideological discourses that challenge the status quo, most often owing to the lack of constraint on the producers' progressive motivations. As a result, the independent films are frequently very personal, artistic creations on the part of their creators designed to challenge spectators' ways of thinking, and possibly provoke them into social action. In contrast, the films coming out of Hollywood often fall prey to formulaic patterns that in many ways undermine the female heroine's power, thereby satisfying the need to reach a broad spectrum of the filmgoing public in order to insure commercial success.

The reason for this diversity in the representations of the female labor activist may begin with the origin of these films' productions (inside or outside of the Hollywood industry); however, these disparities may be better understood as arising from an array of factors constitutive of certain tensions that emerge out of the differences in the films' formal attributes, both aesthetic and thematic, as well as the way the films construct or position spectators. The rhetorical function of these tensions determines the depth of feminist and socialist expression the films achieve and the degree to which they maintain or challenge dominant ideologies. The spectrum

Seven. Fifty Years of Female Labor Activism in Film   191

of meanings offered by these films is the result of four rhetorical tensions identified through a comparative analysis of five Hollywood films featuring female labor heroines and their four independent counter-parts released during three distinct historical periods. Through an investigation of the way these nine films privilege either a realist or classical formal style; the manner in which they present their female protagonist's subjectivity; the degree to which they challenge the political status quo; and their differing portrayals of working-class heroines, ranging from real-life women to Hollywood stars, I demonstrate both their rhetorical limitations and the rhetorical possibilities for cinematic engagement with gender and class politics.

Through an analysis of these nine films, I explored how the aesthetic form and thematic content of the films contributes significantly to their potential for social and feminist empowerment. All but one film — *The Pajama Game* — is based on or documents a real-life event and, as a result, almost all of the films use some combination of cinematic realism and the more dramatic form of the classical Hollywood style. Realism, which is typically defined as an objective rendering of the world through film, functions to create the cinematic effect of an undistorted reflection of authentic truths and the genuine struggles of everyday life. Filmmakers often attempt to "capture" such realism on film by using natural lighting, location shooting, long shots that include views of the surrounding environment rather than close-ups or point-of-view shots, editing for continuity rather than aesthetics, and untrained or little-known actors. Such a style functions rhetorically in a number of the films featured in this book because these creative choices construct the appearance of an uncompromising view of the social and environmental conditions that oppress members of the working class.

Of all of the films discussed in this project, *Salt of the Earth* applies the realist technique most persuasively by re-creating the unrelenting and harsh conditions of the Mexican Americans' struggle for survival in the desert mining village in which the subjects of the film live and work. *Norma Rae, Silkwood, Erin Brockovich,* and *North Country* also incorporate certain aspects of realism through the manner in which they construct the sparse and dilapidated conditions of the heroines' home life and the unhealthy and dangerous conditions in which they work. In *Live Nude Girls Unite!, Union Maids,* and *With Babies and Banners,* the realist style is used as a political tool to demonstrate the genuine experiences of women as workers through old news footage and the women's recollections in interviews in the earlier films, and through the behind-the-scenes videos of the women's sex work and labor negotiations included in the later film.

Most of the films also blend these realist elements with a dramatic form or overarching narrative in an effort to impose the rhetorical coherence of a story onto the film, while still displaying the stark social realism of working-class people living in America as an interesting backdrop. In an effort to do this, films such as *The Pajama Game, Norma Rae, Silkwood, Erin Brockovich,* and *North Country* employ the paradigm of the classical Hollywood tradition. This mode of filmmaking has been defined by David Bordwell, Janet Staiger, and Kristin Thompson. According to these authors, the Hollywood tradition remains the dominant model of feature filmmaking, which includes "a distinct mode of film practice with its own cinematic style and industrial conditions of existence."[4] The style is made up of two main characteristics: the package-unit system, which includes the collaboration of scriptwriter, producer, and star usually through the matchmaking of the studio, and the formal operations of the paradigm, such as the use of big stars in type roles, reluctant heroes and clear-cut villains, generic conventions, and a double plot line (generally public/private or work/romance). Adherence to such a paradigm allows mainstream films, in particular, to render even a somewhat progressive subject through traditional means. These standard devices make invisible the processes of filmmaking, thus disguising any pervasive ideologies and taming the central political issues of the film. The most distinctive characteristic of this style, which is demonstrated through the analysis of the Hollywood films included in this study, is how these films allow the personal goals of the characters to take precedence over the social issue. In this way, the films' protagonists are situated in a largely ambivalent position with respect to the social problem — in this case with regard to the women's involvement in social activism.

The Hollywood films are not the only films to utilize aspects of this formal style, however. *Salt of the Earth*, for example, incorporates a traditional plot that features standard elements of melodrama, as well as the dual storylines of the individual heroine's transformative emergence into a public actor and the romantic plotline charting the husband and wife's relationship. The film also employs the resources of classical filmmaking, such as framing, camera angles, editing, and sound track to underline its themes. *Salt of the Earth*, however, utilizes these elements to highlight the overarching social themes of the film, while *The Pajama Game* uses Hollywood sound stages, Technicolor, and editing for dramatic effect to distract attention from the film's social issues. Further, the Hollywood films also combine the elements of the classical style into a melodramatic rendering of the female labor activists as "outlaw heroines"—outsider figures who disrupt the order only to be recuperated back into the status quo (Babe's acceptance of domesticity in *The Pajama Game*, for example) or destroyed (such as Karen Silkwood). The independent films, on the other hand, employ such stylistic features of the classical style as a device to address certain social issues, such as the focus on gender roles through the romantic plotline in *Salt of the Earth* or the aspects of the feminist debate over sex work that are illuminated through the feminist mother-daughter relationship in *Live Nude Girls Unite!*

The manner in which these films construct the female labor heroine constitutes another significant rhetorical tension that emerges from a comparative analysis of these films. This tension determines the extent to which representations of the female labor activist in these films conform to or challenge traditional views of women as expressed through patriarchal culture. The independent films attempt to present the women to spectators as active and independent subjects by using the films to document the lived experiences of these women in society, and by appropriating images and ideals circulating within feminist discourses. These films often attempt to call into question or reject stereotypical images of women and offer an alternative to the more conventional and conservative representations offered through classical Hollywood cinema. For example, *Salt of the Earth* shows women breaking with tradition and entering the public sphere, *Union Maids* and *With Babies and Banners* reveal women's capacity for collective organization and militancy, and *Live Nude Girls Unite!* demonstrates the political resourcefulness of a group of smart, articulate, and intellectual women fighting for a cause they believe in. The mainstream films, in contrast, construct representations of women that often fall short of these goals and, for the most part, construct characters that are overly sexualized, objectified through the spectators' gaze, and subordinated to men, as demonstrated in the films *Norma Rae*, *Silkwood*, *Erin Brockovich*, and *North Country* specifically, and more generally in *The Pajama Game*. As a result, the heroines of these films appear one-dimensional, their authority and control is limited, and they are ultimately vilified, domesticated, or destroyed, whereas the independent films present images of women that are complex, strong, intelligent, and independent.

The cumulative examination of these nine films also reveals how they construct meanings differently depending on the degree to which the films contribute to feminist and socialist discourses. That is, the exploration of how these films related their socio-political messages to the larger culture within the context of a given historical period reveals the various films' potential to explicitly critique the status quo and the hierarchy of power relations related to gender and class. Each of these films invite spectators to think about issues of diversity through both the representation of disenfranchised voices and their efforts to challenge or overturn stereotypical constructions of femininity or misinformed assumptions regarding class and ethnicity. For example, the independent films explicitly address issues such as the division of the public and private as they work to expose those oppositions and the consequences for marginalized groups. The more mainstream films, on the other hand, invoke similar issues but do not explicitly problematize the division and its effects. For example, by the last scenes of *Salt of the Earth*, the film emphasizes woman's role as problem-solver and activist and challenges the division between the public and the private by subverting the men's and women's roles in the community. The film also demonstrates the working-class community's achievement through their transcendence of these divisions. *The Pajama Game*, on the other hand, provides a glimpse of women's growing independence, but this liberation is quelled by the end as the film reconciles the public with the private at the pajama party. In this fairy-tale marital union, both capitalism and patriarchy emerge triumphant — the factory workers make up with management and Babe merges into a domestic union with the factory supervisor.

The films' various means of portraying the female labor heroine also constitute a rhetorical tension identified through an analysis of these nine films. By focusing on the spectator positions offered through these films, this aspect of the analysis explores how the films present the struggle of working-class women and uphold them to female spectators as role models to be emulated. The independent films, through their employment of real-life women, feature activists with whom the audience can easily identify. Women such as Julia Query, or the ladies sitting around the kitchen table in *Union Maids* and *With Babies and Banners*, are presented as unexceptional women who took on exceptional feats. Such representations may serve as productive models for spectators to emulate. The Hollywood films, on the other hand, use well-known stars such as Doris Day, Sally Field, Meryl Streep, Julia Roberts, and Charlize Theron — a choice that often serves to distract spectators from the real-life characters these films are intended to portray. Often, when spectators watch characters played by established stars, they bring to the film a kind of layered relationship with the character established through knowledge of the star's persona, personal life, and former roles, as well as the role of the character currently being executed. In *The Pajama Game* or *Erin Brockovich*, for example, Doris Day's and Julia Robert's charisma and fame in many ways overshadows their characters, making them difficult figures with whom ordinary women could identify.

The feminist and class conflicts in the nine films examined in this project function with various degrees of conservatism and radicalism and each represent both the challenges facing women and members of the working class while also demonstrating their political power. All nine films, I believe, contain the potential to produce both conventional representations of working-class women in patriarchal culture and progressive discourses that create opportunities for social change and a movement toward greater equality and justice. However, some films do a better job than others and the distinctions can largely be seen in the differences between the independent films and those produced by the Hollywood establishment.

Viewing the trajectory of independent films dealing with labor and feminism, it is clear that there has been a definite forward progression with regard to the gains made through the feminist movement. For example, in *Salt of the Earth*, we see women who work to gain better conditions for their roles in the private sphere, and so they must enter the public sphere momentarily to do so. In the feminist documentaries *Union Maids* and *With Babies and Banners*, groups of real women explicitly convey their frustrated and sometimes successful attempts to deal with the public world of work and power, but continue to struggle with the conflicting identities that emerge from their attempts to manage their responsibilities in both the public and the private spheres. Finally, in *Live Nude Girls Unite!*, the lines between the public and private are blurred because the very nature of the sex industry disrupts the boundaries between them. Also, Julia, the film's protagonist, demonstrates the ways in which she and the other strippers must constantly negotiate the stigma attached to their chosen profession with their public role as political activists, and how that negotiation impacts their personal lives as women, daughters, and mothers.

Additionally, through these independent films, spectators are shown that the tenets of the American labor movement are still alive, although the movement may have been declared dead by the dominant culture. These films show that upholding the values of community over individualism and equality over domination can make a difference. For example, in the last scene of *Live Nude Girls Unite!*, Julia explains why she feels joining the union was important for her, stating: "It didn't matter how aggressive, or Jewish, or smart, or witty, or, you know, strong I was, personality didn't provide me with good working conditions, being part of a group — organizing a successful union effort did."

The Hollywood films show the demise of the union mentality and by the twenty-first century mainstream union films are almost non-existent. The reason for this becomes clear when one notes that the protagonists in these films are primarily individualists who are ambivalent to the ways of capitalism, but merely enter the world of labor activism as a diversion from their self-destructive and unsatisfying personal lives. These films feature a kind of reluctant labor heroine who, although she finds her voice and initiates some progress in the world of work and labor, ultimately is relegated back to the domestic sphere (Babe), jailed (Norma Rae), ostracized by family and community (Josie), or destroyed (Karen Silkwood). Only Erin Brockovich appears to have changed for the better; however, she never attempts to engage in union activity, only to right the wrongs of a corporation that has exploited and endangered the unwitting members of a working-class community. Significantly, when Erin eventually wins the case against PG&E and become a success, she quickly joins the lifestyle of the corporate lawyers she earlier presumed to hate, and embraces the principles of capitalism.

The findings from the analysis of these nine films featuring labor heroines and their cumulative effect encourage a cross-cultural awareness of film's participation in processes of cultural and social change. Considering these films together shows how both Hollywood and independent films have responded to cultural discourses circulating around gender and class issues over three historical periods. Through this analysis, it becomes evident that the rhetoric of Hollywood films more often functions to reign in or question the gains made by the feminist and labor movements through the films' resolutions, thereby reconfirming dominant ideology and the political status quo. The films *The Pajama Game*, *Norma Rae*, *Silkwood*, *Erin Brockovich*, and *North Country* are characterized by an ambivalence that simultaneously confirms and transgresses the contradictions of modern feminism in their portrayals of the female labor heroine as both independent and vulnerable to the conventions of patriarchal culture. In contrast, the independent films *Salt of the Earth*, *Union Maids*, *With Babies and Banners*, and *Live Nude Girls Unite!* provide spectators with a perspective on the world that subverts the structures of the dominant culture and, particularly, of patriarchal ideology. In their efforts to reimagine the boundaries between the public and the private and overturn the power hierarchies related to class and gender oppression, these independent films establish a resistive subculture through their demonstration of the effectiveness of collective action for social and political change. Despite their differences, each of these films is significant to our understanding of resistance and domination, and heroism and oppression, in that they all, in various ways, draw attention to the cultural and political situations and capacity for activism of those on society's margins.

Chapter Notes

Introduction

1. Bonnie Dow, *Prime-Time Feminism: Television, Media Culture, and the Women's Movement Since 1970* (Philadelphia: University of Pennsylvania Press, 1996), xv.

2. See, for example, Sloan, *The Loud Silents*; Kevin Bronlow, *Behind the Mask of Innocence* (Berkeley: University of California Press, 1992); and Garth Jowett, *Film: The Democratic Art* (Boston: Little, Brown and Company, 1976).

3. Sloan, *The Loud Silents*, 3.

4. Peter Roffman and Jim Purdy, *The Hollywood Social Problem Film: Madness, Despair, and Politics from the Depression to the Fifties* (Bloomington: Indiana University Press, 1981), x, 7.

5. See Steven J. Ross, *Working-Class Hollywood: Silent Film and the Shaping of Class in America* (Princeton: Princeton University Press, 1998); John Bodnar, *Blue-Collar Hollywood: Liberalism, Democracy, and Working People in American Film* (Baltimore: The Johns Hopkins University Press, 2003); Peter Stead, *Film and the Working Class: The Feature Film in British and American Society* (New York: Routledge, 1989); David James and Rick Berg, eds., *The Hidden Foundation: Cinema and the Question of Class* (Minneapolis: University of Minnesota Press, 1996); Paul Thomas, "'I Could Have Been A Contender': Hollywood Discovers the Working Class?" *Film Library Quarterly* 12 (1979): 58–63; Lynn Garafola, "Hollywood and the Myth of the Working Class," *Radical America* 14 (1980): 7–15; and Al Auster, et al., "Hollywood and the Working Class: A Discussion," *Socialist Review* 9 (1979): 109–121.

6. Ross, *Working-Class Hollywood*, 241.

7. Bodnar, *Blue-Collar Hollywood*, 227.

8. Frank R. Walsh, "The Films We Never Saw: American Movies View Organized Labor, 1934–1954," *Labor History*, 27 (1986): 564–580. See also Ken Margolies, "Silver Screen Tarnishes Unions," *Screen Actor*, 23 (1981): 43–52; William J. Puette, *Through Jaundiced Eyes: How the Media View Organized Labor* (Ithaca: Cornell University Press, 1992); Tom Zaniello, *Working Stiffs, Union Maids, Reds, and Riffraff: An Organized Guide to Films About Labor* (Ithaca: Cornell University Press, 1993); Gay P. Zieger and Robert H. Zieger, "Unions on the Silver Screen: A Review Essay on *F.I.S.T.*, *Blue Collar*, and *Norma Rae*," *Labor History*, 23 (Winter 1982): 67–78; and Frank Stricker, "Hollywood Meets the Unions," *New Labor Review* 2 (Fall 1978): 111–118.

9. Margolies, "Silver Screen," 43.

10. Stricker, "Hollywood Meets the Unions," 118.

11. A number of scholars who have lamented the absence of films that take seriously labor and working-class issues will mention the exception of *Norma Rae* or *Salt of the Earth*. Yet, none of these scholars have adequately examined the reason for the difference between these and other labor films — namely the nontraditional images they present of women. See for example, Garafola, "Hollywood and the Myth," and Walsh, "The Films We Never Saw." An exception is Edward Benson and Sharon Hartman Strom, "Crystal Lee, Norma Rae, and All Their Sisters," *Film Library Quarterly*, 12 (1979): 18–23, which examines a number of films that "have tried to escape Hollywood conventions about class and sex roles and have worked to confront the issues of women's liberation." Another is Enid M. I. Sefcovic, "Cultural Memory and the Cultural Legacy of Individualism and Community in Two Classic Films about Labor Unions," *Critical Studies in Media Communi-*

cation 19 (September 2002): 329–351, which acknowledges but does not fully explore the feminist agenda in *Salt of the Earth*.

12. Sonya Michel, "Feminism, Film, and Public History," in *Issues in Feminist Film Criticism*, ed. Patricia Erens (Bloomington: Indiana University Press, 1990); 238–249.

13. Anne Mattina, "'Rights as Well as Duties': The Rhetoric of Leonora O'Reilly," *Communication Quarterly* 42 (1994): 204–205. See also, Mary E. Triece, *Protest & Popular Culture: Women in the U.S. Labor Movement, 1894–1917* (Boulder: Westview Press, 2001).

14. Mari Boor Tonn, "Militant Motherhood: Labor's Mary Harris 'Mother' Jones," *The Quarterly Journal of Speech* 82 (1996): 16.

15. Tonn, "Militant Motherhood," 16–17.

16. Linda Dittmar, Janice R. Welsch, and Diane Carson, "Introduction," *Multiple Voices in Feminist Film Criticism*, eds. Diane Carson, Linda Dittmar, and Janice R. Welsch (Minneapolis: University of Minnesota Press, 1994), 3.

17. Judith Mayne, "Review Essay: Feminist Film Theory and Criticism," *Signs* 11 (1985): 81–100.

18. Mayne, "Review Essay," 83. See also Judith Mayne, *The Woman at the Keyhole: Feminism and Women's Cinema* (Bloomington: Indiana University Press, 1990).

19. Douglas Kellner, *Media Culture: Cultural Studies, Identity and Politics Between the Modern and the Postmodern* (New York: Routledge, 1995), 2. See also Michael Ryan and Douglas Kellner, *Camera Politica: The Politics and Ideology of Contemporary Hollywood Film* (Bloomington: Indiana University Press, 1988).

20. Christine Gledhill, "Image and Voice: Approaches to Marxist-Feminist Film Criticism," in *Multiple Voices in Feminist Film Criticism*, eds. Diane Carson, Linda Dittmar, and Janice R. Welsch (Minneapolis: University of Minnesota Press, 1994), 109–123. See also Christine Gledhill, "Pleasurable Negotiations," *Female Spectators*, ed. Deidre Pribram (New York: Verso, 1988), 64–89; and Judith Mayne, *Cinema and Spectatorship* (New York: Routledge, 1993), 93. For a related argument, see Celeste Condit, "The Rhetorical Limits of Polysemy," *Critical Studies in Mass Communication* 6 (1989): 103–122.

21. Elayne Rapping, *The Movie of the Week: Private Stories Public Events* (Minneapolis: University of Minnesota Press, 1992), xii.

22. Martin J. Medhurst and Thomas W. Benson, eds., *Rhetorical Dimensions In Media: A Critical Casebook*, 2nd ed. (Dubuque: Kendall/Hunt, 1991), 444.

23. For a similar approach to a rhetorical analysis of films, see Susan Mackey-Kallis, *Oliver Stone's America: "Dreaming the Myth Outward"* (Boulder, CO: Westview Press, 1996).

24. According to Thomas Benson, "For modern rhetorical criticism, a meaning-centered approach brings to the text a curiosity not simply about the structure of the texts, nor about the clues to the author revealed by the text, nor about the extent to which the text mirrors 'reality,' but also about the ways in which the text invites an audience to make meanings." See Thomas W. Benson, "The Rhetorical Structure of Frederick Wiseman's *Primate*," *Quarterly Journal of Speech*, 71 (1985): 204.

25. Gledhill, "Image and Voice," 14.

26. Gledhill, "Pleasurable Negotiations," 74.

27. Mayne, *Cinema and Spectatorship*, 3.

Chapter 1

1. *Return of the Secaucus, 7*, dir. John Sayles, 1981; *Salt of the Earth*, dir. Herbert Biberman, perf. Rosaura Revueltas and Juan Chacón, Independent Production Company, 1954; for a discussion of *Salt of the Earth*'s recurrences, see James J. Lorence, *The Suppression of Salt of the Earth: How Hollywood, Big Labor, and Politicians Blacklisted a Movie in Cold War America* (Albuquerque: The University of New Mexico Press, 1999) 194; Tom Miller, "Class Reunion: *Salt of the Earth* Revisited," *Cineaste* 13.3 (1984): 31; Tom Miller, rev. of "The Suppression of *Salt of the Earth*: How Hollywood, Big Labor, and Politicians Blacklisted a Movie in Cold War America," by James J. Lorence, *Cineaste* 25.3 (2000): 60; *A Crime to Fit the Punishment*, dir. Stephen Mack and Barbara Moss, narrator Lee Grant, Mack and Moss, 1982. *Salt of the Earth* also was recently the focal point of a made-for-cable movie based on the life of Herbert Biberman, the film's director. See *One of the Hollywood Ten*, dir. Karl Francis, perf. Jeff Goldblum and Greta Scacchi, Alibi Films International, 2000.

2. Brandon French, *On the Verge of Revolt: Women in American Films of the Fifties* (New York: Frederick Ungar Publishing, 1978), xv. See Daniel J. Leab, "How Red Was My Valley: Hollywood, the Cold War Film, and *I Married a Communist*," *Journal of Contemporary History* 19 (1984): 61. For a greater discussion of the controversy surrounding historiography of the Cold War, see Charles Maier, "Marking

Time: The Historiography of International Relations," *The Past Before Us: Contemporary Historical Writing in the United States*, ed. Michael Kamman (Ithaca: Cornell University Press, 1980).

3. Dan Georgakas, "Union-Sponsored Radical Films," *Encyclopedia of the American Left*, ed. Mari Jo Buhle, Paul Buhle, and Dan Georgakas, 2nd ed. (New York: Oxford University Press, 1998), 846.

4. Miller, "Review," 59.

5. Lorence, *The Suppression*, 7.

6. See Douglas Gomery, *The Hollywood Studio System* (New York: St. Martin's, 1986).

7. The notion of an independent film during this period had a much different significance than independent films today. During the time of *Salt of the Earth*'s production, John Howard Lawson defined independent productions in this way: "Production which is independent in a creative sense must be free from monopoly control, free from the class domination of the bourgeoisie, and — this is a condition which is in some respects most difficult to guarantee — free from the ideology of the dominant class." John Howard Lawson, *Film in the Battle of Ideas* (New York: Masses and Mainstream, 1953), 117.

8. Lisa Kernan, "'Keep Marching, Sisters': The Second Generation Looks at *Salt of the Earth*," *Nuestro* 9 (May 1985): 24.

9. William Lafferty describes the semi-documentary as a feature film that originated in the U.S. after World War II and involves a topical subject filmed in a "documentary" or "realist" manner. Also, film historian Jack Ellis defines the semi-documentary as a kind of "fiction filmmaking that stayed close to actuality" and that "fits into one ... more or less distinct sub-species of the fictional film with documentary tendencies — films based on fact, on real persons, or incidents." See William Lafferty, "A Reappraisal of the Semi-Documentary in Hollywood, 1945–1948," *The Velvet Light Trap* 20, (1983): 23; and Jack C. Ellis, *A History of Film* (Englewood Cliffs, NJ: Prentice-Hall, 1979), 239.

10. Dorothy B. Jones, "Communism in the Movies: A Study of Film Content," *Report on Blacklisting: Vol. I — the Movies*, ed. John Cogley (New York: Fund for the Republic, 1956), 219.

11. See Jones, "Communism" 218–221 for a more detailed discussion of the changes that the motion picture industry underwent between 1947 and 1954. Jones also notes that in 1954 the tradition of "social realism" seemed to be restored through the popular film *On the Waterfront* (Columbia), which won Academy Awards for best picture, writer, director, and producer. What Jones fails to note is that *On the Waterfront* may be seen as an anti–Communist picture that symbolically sanctioned cooperation with the HUAC investigations of 1947.

12. Larry May, "Movie Star Politics: The Screen Actors' Guild, Cultural Conversion, and the Hollywood Red Scare," *Recasting America: Culture and Politics in the Age of the Cold War*, ed. Larry May (Chicago: University of Chicago Press, 1989), 143.

13. May, "Movie Star," 128.

14. Ceplair and Englund, *The Inquisition*, 16.

15. For a more detailed account of the CSU labor strikes and the conflict between CSU and IATSE, see Mike Nielsen and Gene Mailes, *Hollywood's Other Blacklist: Union Struggles in the Hollywood System* (London: British Film Institute, 1995), especially chapter, 5.

16. Ceplair and Englund, *The Inquisition*, 212.

17. Quote by Alliance member John Lee Mahin reported in *Variety*, 7 February 1944: 5.

18. Ceplair and Englund, *The Inquisition*, xiv.

19. Although historians disagree as to what constituted the beginning of the Cold War in America, some note the now famous speech, officially titled "Sinews of Peace," delivered by Winston Churchill on March 5, 1946 as a hallmark event that hastened Americans' adoption of a Cold War ideology. In this speech, Churchill also blamed the Soviet Union for the "iron curtain that [had] descended across the Continent." Winston Churchill, "Sinews of Peace," Westminster College, Fulton, Missouri, 5 Mar. 1946, online, Speech and Transcript Center at George Washington University, Internet, 16 July 2001.

20. Eric Johnston, "Utopia is Production," *Screen Actor* 14 (April 1946): 7. For a discussion of Johnston and the culture of anti–Communism in Hollywood, see May, "Movie Star," 125–153.

21. The HUAC investigations of 1947 were not, in fact, the government's first attack on the Hollywood industry, but may be the most famous given their association with the legend of the "Hollywood Ten." The U.S. government began sending probes into the movie industry in the summer of 1938 when Martin Dies, the present chairman of HUAC, released a report charging that Communism was "rampant" in Hollywood. Dies would continue

investigations in 1940, fact-finding missions would be held in California by Senator Jack Tenney, and in 1945 the U.S. Chamber of Commerce issued a report on *Communist Infiltration in the United States*, which warned that Communists were seeking to gain control of the entertainment and information media. For more on these early investigations, see Howard Suber, "Politics and Popular Culture: Hollywood at Bay, 1933-1953," *American Jewish History* 68 (1979): 523-528.

22. May, "Movie Star," 143.

23. See Suber, "Politics" 530. The members of the "Hollywood Ten" included: producer Adrian Scott, directors Herbert Biberman, Lester Cole, and Edward Dmytryk, and scriptwriters Dalton Trumbo, Alvah Bessie, John Howard Lawson, Albert Maltz, Samuel Ornitz, and Ring Lardner, Jr.

24. Nora Sayre, *Running Time: Films of the Cold War* (New York: The Dial Press, 1978), 19. Sayre notes the difficult choice between pleading the First Amendment versus the Fifth: those pleading the First were sent to prison for contempt, those pleading the Fifth, declining to be called as witnesses against themselves, dodged a jail sentence but were tainted as Communists and often lost their jobs as a result. See also Richard M. Fried, *Nightmare in Red: The McCarthy Era in Perspective* (New York: Oxford University Press, 1990), 77.

25. Richard Maltby, "Made for Each Other: The Melodrama of Hollywood and the House Committees on Un-American Activities, 1947," *Cinema, Politics, and Society in America*, eds. Philip Davies and Brian Neve (Manchester: Manchester University, 1981), 147.

26. Robert Sklar, *Movie-Made America: A Cultural History of American Movies*, rev. ed. (New York: Vintage Books, 1994), 265.

27. Ayn Rand's directives are quoted in John Cogley, ed. *Report on Blacklisting: Volume 1—The Movies* (The Fund for the Republic, 1956), 11.

28. Quoted in Ceplair and Englund, *The Inquisition*, 416-417.

29. George Lipsitz, "Herbert Biberman and the Art of Subjectivity," *Telos* 32 (1977): 180; Herbert Biberman, *Salt of the Earth: The Story of a Film* (Boston: Beacon Press, 1965), 32.

30. Lorence, *The Suppression*, 47-48.

31. As stated by Paul Jarrico to Stephen Mack and Barbara Moss during an interview included in the documentary film *A Crime to Fit the Punishment*.

32. See Miller, "Class Reunion." For a more in-depth discussion of the difficult circumstances faced in the making of *Salt*, see also Lorence, *The Suppression* 65-90 and Deborah Silverton Rosenfelt, *Salt of the Earth* (Old Westbury, NY: The Feminist Press, 1978), 126-135.

33. Paul Jarrico and Herbert Biberman, "Breaking Ground: The Making of *Salt of the Earth*," *Celluloid Power: Social Film Criticism from The Birth of a Nation to Judgment at Nuremberg*, ed. David Platt (Metuchen, NJ: The Scarecrow Press, 1992), 480. This article originally appeared in *California Quarterly* 3 (1953).

34. Originally reported, along with quotes from other press accounts, in Paul Jarrico's chronology of production, which is reprinted in part in Rosenfelt, *Salt*, 131.

35. Jarrico and Biberman, "Breaking Ground," 480.

36. "Reds in the Desert," *Newsweek* 2 Mar. 1953: 27.

37. Rosenfelt, *Salt*, 131.

38. "Silver City Troubles," *Newsweek* 16 Mar. 1953: 43.

39. For a more detailed history of the obstacles against distribution of the film, see Lorence, *The Suppression*, especially chapters 5 and 6, and Biberman, *Salt*.

40. Pauline Kael, *I Lost It At the Movies* (Boston: Little, Brown and Company, 1965) 331, 342.

41. "'Salt'—One Brand," rev. of *Salt of the Earth*, dir. Herbert Biberman, *Newsweek* 29 Mar. 1954: 87.

42. "Salt & Pepper," rev. of *Salt of the Earth*, dir. Herbert Biberman, *Time* 29 Mar. 1954: 92; Rev. of *Salt of the Earth*, dir. Herbert Biberman, *Variety* 17 Mar. 1954: 1.

43. Rev. of *Salt of the Earth*, *Variety*, 1.

44. Bosley Crowther, "'Salt of the Earth' Opens at the Grande—Filming Marked by Violence," rev. of *Salt of the Earth*, dir. Herbert Biberman, *The New York Times* 15 Mar. 1954: 20.

45. Quoted in Murray Schumach, *The Face on the Cutting Room Floor: The Story of Movie and Television Censorship* (New York: Harper and Row, 1964), 129.

46. Brian Neve, *Film and Politics in America: A Social Tradition* (New York: Routledge, 1992), 201.

47. Linda Dittmar, "The Articulating Self: Difference as Resistance in *Black Girl*, *Ramparts of Clay*, and *Salt of the Earth*," *Multiple Voices in Feminist Film Criticism*, eds. Diane Carson, Linda Dittmar, and Janice R. Welsch (Minneapolis: University of Minnesota, 1994), 400.

48. Various scholars have noted the difficulties of such filmmaking practices, primarily because these productions are often accessible only to an educated minority. See Christine Gledhill, "Image and Voice: Approaches to Marxist-Feminist Film Criticism," *Multiple Voices in Feminist Film Criticism*, eds. Diane Carson, Linda Dittmar, and Janice R. Welsch (Minneapolis: University of Minnesota, 1994), 117.

49. Rosenfelt makes similar claims in her critique of *Salt of the Earth*, see Rosenfelt, *Salt* 147. For more on *Salt*'s adherence to Hollywood convention see, Patrick McCarthy, "*Salt of the Earth*: Convention and Invention of the Domestic Melodrama," *Rendezvous: Journal of Arts and Letters*, 19 (1983): 22–32.

50. Jarrico and Biberman, "Breaking Ground," 479.

51. For a discussion of this use of such characterizations in socialist realism, see Annette Kuhn, *Women's Pictures: Feminism and Cinema*, 2nd ed. (New York: Verso, 1994), 137.

52. Although often mistakenly conflated, Marxism, socialism, and Communism are three independent but related philosophical tenets. It is important to note with regard to the analytical interpretation of *Salt of the Earth* that the Marxist critique offered through the film is not to be misaligned with the hyperbole of Communist doctrine that has become so vilified in late twentieth-century public memory.

53. Arnaldo Bocelli, quoted in Millicent Marcus, *Italian Film and the Light of Neorealism* (Princeton: Princeton University Press, 1986), 18.

54. Gerald Mast and Bruce F. Kawin, *A Short History of the Movies*, 6th ed. (Boston: Allyn and Bacon, 1996), 342.

55. Marcus, *Italian Film*, xiii–xiv.

56. According to Marcus, Neorealism lasted only seven years, generated a little over twenty films, failed at the box office, and fell short of its didactic and aesthetic aspirations, including the goal of both educating and elevating the tastes of Italian moviegoers. See Marcus, *Italian Film*, xvi.

57. Peter Morris, "Salt of the Earth," *Celluloid Power: Social Film Criticism from The Birth of a Nation to Judgment at Nuremburg*, ed. David Platt (Metuchen, NJ: The Scarecrow Press, 1992), 489.

58. Lipsitz, "Herbert Biberman," 178–179.

59. Mast and Kawin, *A Short*, 342.

60. The casual insertion of Spanish dialogue in certain scenes of the film provides another interesting example of how the filmmakers attempted to capture the reality of the Mexican Americans' lives. As Ella Shochat and Robert Stam note, most American films of the time presumed "to speak for the other in *its* native idiom ... Hollywood proposed to tell the story of other nations not only to Americans, but also for the other nations themselves, and always in English." Thus, the inclusion of some native dialogue within the film represents another way that *Salt of the Earth* resisted the conventions of mainstream Hollywood filmmaking. See Ella Shochat and Robert Stam, "The Cinema After Babel: Language, Difference, Power," *Screen* 26.3 (1985): 36.

61. Rosenfelt, *Salt*, 149.

62. Margo Kasdan, "'Why are you afraid to have me at your side?': From Passivity to Power in *Salt of the Earth*," *The Voyage In: Fictions of Female Development*, eds. Elizabeth Abel, Marianne Hirsch, and Elizabeth Langland (Hanover, NH: University Press of New England, 1983), 260.

63. Lillian S. Robinson, "Out of the Mine and into the Canyon: Working-Class Feminism, Yesterday and Today," *The Hidden Foundation: Cinema and the Question of Class*, eds. David E. James and Rick Berg (Minneapolis: University of Minnesota Press, 1996), 174.

64. Jarrico and Biberman, "Breaking Ground," 478.

65. This function of voice-over is described in Sarah Kozloff, *Invisible Storytellers: Voice-Over Narration in American Fiction Film* (Berkeley: University of California Press, 1988), 63, 129.

66. Robinson, "Out of the Mine," 182.

67. Robinson, "Out of the Mine," 182.

68. Kuhn, *Women's Pictures*, 141.

69. See Robinson, "Out of the Mine" 174. Also, this argument is similar to the one Linda Dittmar makes about the use of "the articulating self" in three films about marginalized women and their eventual emergence. See Dittmar, "The Articulating Self," 398.

70. Gledhill, "Image and Voice," 118.

71. Jack Cargill, "Empire and Opposition: The 'Salt of the Earth' Strike," *Labor in New Mexico: Unions, Strikes, and Social History Since 1881*, ed. Robert Kern (Albuquerque: University of New Mexico Press, 1983) 185.

72. Rosenfelt, *Salt*, 94.

73. Stephen Powers, David J. Rothman, and Stanley Rothman, *Hollywood's America: Social and Political Themes in Motion Pictures* (Boulder, CO: Westview Press, 1996), 155.

74. Marjorie Rosen, *Popcorn Venus: Women, Movies and the American Dream* (New

York: Coward, McCann & Geoghegan, 1973), 245.

75. See Jackie Byars, *All That Hollywood Allows: Re-reading Gender in 1950s Melodrama* (Chapel Hill: University of North Carolina Press, 1991), 115–116 for a discussion of women's roles in the social problem melodramas of the fifties.

76. Kasdan, "Why Are You Afraid," 269.

77. Gary D. Keller, "The Image of the Chicano in Mexican, United States, and Chicano Cinema: An Overview," *Chicano Cinema: Research, Reviews, and Resources*, ed. Gary D. Keller (Binghamton, NY: Bilingual Review/Press, 1985), 35.

Chapter 2

1. Brandon French, *On the Verge of Revolt: Women in American Films of the Fifties* (New York: Frederick Ungar Publishing, 1978), xxii.

2. Jackie Byars, *All That Hollywood Allows: Re-reading Gender in 1950s Melodrama* (Chapel Hill: University of North Carolina Press, 1991), 8.

3. Marjorie Rosen, *Popcorn Venus: Women, Movies and the American Dream* (New York: Coward, McCann & Geoghegan, 1973), 209–210.

4. Rosen, *Popcorn Venus,* 214.

5. Molly Haskell, *From Reverence to Rape: The Treatment of Women in the Movies,* 2nd ed. (Chicago: The University of Chicago Press, 1987), 230.

6. Byars, *All That Hollywood,* 85.

7. French, *On the Verge,* xxi.

8. Molly Haskell, *Holding My Own in No Man's Land: Women and Men and Film and Feminists* (New York: Oxford University Press, 1997), 5.

9. French, *On the Verge,* xxi.

10. Richard Bissell, *7½ Cents* (Boston: Little, Brown, 1953); *The Pajama Game,* dir. George Abbott and Stanley Donen, perf. Doris Day, John Raitt, Eddie Foy Jr., Carol Haney, Warner Bros., 1957.

11. Christine Gledhill, "Introduction," *Stardom: Industry of Desire,* ed. Christine Gledhill (New York: Routledge, 1991), xiv.

12. Richard Dyer, *Stars.* New ed. (London: British Film Institute, 1999), 31.

13. Richard de Cordova, *Picture Personalities: The Emergence of the Star System in America* (Urbana: University of Illinois Press, 1990), 13.

14. Pam Cook, *Screening the Past: Memory and Nostalgia in Cinema* (New York: Routledge, 2005), 128.

15. Adrienne L. McLean, *Being Rita Hayworth: Labor, Identity and Hollywood Stardom* (New Brunswick: Rutgers University Press, 2004), 6.

16. Andrew Klevan, *Film Performance: From Achievement to Appreciation* (New York: Wallflower Press, 2005), 103.

17. Alan Gelb, *The Doris Day Scrapbook* (New York: Grosset & Dunlap, 1977), 13, 10.

18. Haskell, *Holding My Own,* 26.

19. Hollis Alpert, "Enough! Enough!," *Saturday Review* 17 Nov. 1956: 29.

20. Cameron Shipp, "Hollywood's Girl-Next-Door," *Cosmopolitan* Apr. 1956: 63.

21. Rosen, *Popcorn Venus,* 302.

22. Ethan Mordden, *Movie Star: A Look at the Women Who Made Hollywood* (New York: St. Martin's Press, 1983), 247

23. Kenneth Turan, "Doris Finally Gets Her Day," *The Los Angeles Times* 18 Jan. 2001: 6.

24. Dyer, *Stars,* 30–32.

25. Dwight Macdonald, *On Movies* (New York: Berkeley-Medallion Edition, 1971), 137.

26. Haskell, *Holding My Own,* 22.

27. Haskell, *From Reverence,* 4.

28. For example, Garth Jowett writes that musicals "emerged into their second 'golden age' in the late 1940s and 1950s;" Robert Matthew-Walker notes that Hollywood musicals reached the height of their early success by 1940, but it was not until after World War II that the golden age of the musical began; and Richard Fehr and Frederick Vogel note that "the period from 1950 to 1958 merits the title of the Golden Age of Film Musicals." See Robert Matthew-Walker, *From Broadway to Hollywood: The Musical and the Cinema* (London: Sanctuary Publishing, 1996), 48; and Richard Fehr and Frederick G. Vogel, *Lullabies of Hollywood: The Movie Music and the Movie Musical, 1915–1992* (Jefferson, NC: McFarland & Co., 1993), 223.

29. Gerald Mast, *Can't Help Singin': The American Musical on Stage and Screen* (Woodstock, NY: The Overlook Press, 1987), 290.

30. Andrew Dowdy, *The Films of the Fifties: The American State of Mind* (New York: William Morrow, 1973), 123.

31. Fehr and Vogel, *Lullabies* 2–3.

32. In early 1953, Bissell and musical producer Abbott approached composing team Richard Adler and Jerry Ross (who would go on to score the now-legendary *Damn Yankees* two years later) to see if they would be interested in writing a musical treatment for Bissell's book *7½ Cents.* Adler and Ross agreed and the foursome began assembling a creative team of artists new to the musical theater,

Notes — Chapter 2

most of whom would later become Broadway legends. Bob Fosse was hired as the show's choreographer, and the roles of the main characters were staffed by John Raitt, Janis Paige, Eddie Foy Jr., and Carol Haney.

33. Rev. of *The Pajama Game*, dir. George Abbott and Stanley Donen, *Time* 9 Sept. 1957: 110; Gelb, *The Doris Day*, 93.

34. Rick Altman, "Introduction," *Genre: The Musical*, ed. Rick Altman (Boston: Routledge & Kegan Paul, 1981), 5.

35. Fehr and Vogel, *Lullabies*, 3.

36. Dowdy, *The Films of the Fifties*, 123.

37. Fehr and Vogel, *Lullabies*, 222–223.

38. Matthew-Walker, *From Broadway*, 190.

39. Philip K. Scheuer, "Fast, Furious Musical Film Made of Stage Hit," rev. of *The Pajama Game*, dir. George Abbott and Stanley Donen, *Los Angeles Times* 30 Aug. 1957: 6.

40. Rick Altman, *The American Film Musical* (Bloomington: Indiana University Press, 1987), 360.

41. Jane Feuer, *The Hollywood Musical*, 2nd ed. (London: The Macmillan Press, 1993), ix.

42. David Bordwell, *Narration in the Fiction Film* (Madison: University of Wisconsin Press, 1985), 157.

43. Feuer, *The Hollywood Musical*, 7.

44. Feuer argues that, within its texts, "the musical makes use of a repertory of techniques usually associated with modernist art." These techniques include fragmentation of space; multiplying and dividing the human figure into splits, doubles, or alter egos; placing a premium on expressions of spontaneity, group choreography, and a naturalization of technique; the employment of direct address, as well as multiple and divided characters; and the insistence on multiple levels of reality, such as the continuity between dream images and waking life. Feuer, *The Hollywood Musical* x.

45. Stacy Wolf, *A Problem Like Maria: Gender and Sexuality in the American Musical* (Ann Arbor: The University of Michigan Press, 2002), 10.

46. Haskell, *Holding My Own*, 4.

47. Patricia Mellencamp, "Spectacle and Spectator: Looking through the Musical Comedy," *Ciné-tracts* 1 (1977): 29.

48. Wolf, *A Problem Like Maria*, 31.

49. Feuer, *The Hollywood Musical*, 29.

50. Jim Collins, "Toward Defining a Matrix of the Musical Comedy: The Place of the Spectator Within the Textual Mechanisms," *Genre: The Musical*, ed. Rick Altman (Boston: Routledge & Kegan Paul, 1981), 138.

51. Wolf, *A Problem Like Maria*, 4–23.

52. Lea Jacobs and Richard de Cordova, "Spectacle and Narrative Theory," *Quarterly Review of Film Studies* 7 (1982): 302.

53. Mellencamp, "Spectacle," 32.

54. The notion of "to-be-looked-at-ness" refers to Laura Mulvey's influential essay "Visual Pleasure and Narrative Cinema" in which she argued that "It is the place of the look that defines cinema, the possibility of varying it and exposing it.... Going far beyond highlighting a woman's to-be-looked-at-ness, cinema builds the way she is to be looked at into the spectacle itself." See Laura Mulvey, "Visual Pleasure and Narrative Cinema," *Issues in Feminist Film Criticism*, ed. Patricia Erens (Bloomington: Indiana University Press, 1990), 38.

55. Mellencamp, "Spectacle," 28.

56. Altman, *The American*, 164.

57. Simone de Beauvoir described the woman in love in her groundbreaking feminist doctrine *The Second Sex* in 1952. Beauvoir outlines the way women are "taught" to behave in certain ways within romantic relationships and stresses that these actions have nothing to do with the laws of nature, or the nature of a woman, but that they are a reflection of the difference in men's and women's situations in society. Beauvoir states: "For woman ... to love is to relinquish everything for the benefit of a master. As Cécile Sauvage puts it: 'Woman must forget her own personality when she is in love.... A woman is nonexistent without a master. Without a master, she is a scattered bouquet.'" See Simone de Beauvoir, *The Second Sex*, trans. and ed. H.M. Parshley (New York: Vintage Books/Random House, 1952), 713.

58. Ken Margolies, "Silver Screen Tarnishes Unions: Hollywood Movies Have Given Workers a Black Eye," *Screen Actor*, 23 (1981): 48.

59. Martin Sutton, "Patterns of Meaning in the Musical," *Genre: The Musical*, ed. Rick Altman (Boston: Routledge & Kegan Paul, 1981), 195.

60. Martin Sutton makes a similar conclusion about the representation of Babe in *The Pajama Game*. See Sutton, "Patterns," 195.

61. Wolf, *A Problem Like Maria*, 31.

62. McLean, *Being Rita Hayworth*, 26.

63. Altman, *The American*, 27.

64. Shari Roberts, "'The Lady in the Tutti-Frutti Hat': Carmen Miranda, A Spectacle of Ethnicity," *Cinema Journal* 32.3 (1993): 3–4.

65. Molly Haskell recounts the near-tirade of women at a feminist luncheon in New York who blamed their blighted existence on "'those films of the fifties in which Doris Day ended up in the kitchen, glued to her frying pan and

apron." See, Haskell, *Holding My Own,* 23. Also, in *The Pajama Game,* this occupation of the domestic situation may also be seen as a role Babe had already taken on in the absence of her mother, as her father's caretaker.

66. Gelb, *The Doris Day,* 150.
67. Pam Cook, "Star Signs," *Screen* 20.3/4 (1980): 83.
68. Gelb, *The Doris Day,* 150.
69. Pam Cook, "Border Crossings: Women and Film in Context," *Women and Film: A Sight and Sound Reader,* eds. Pam Cook and Philip Dodd (Philadelphia: Temple University Press, 1993), xv.
70. Phillip Auslander, *Performing Glam Rock: Gender & Theatricality in Popular Music* (Ann Arbor: The University of Michigan Press, 2006), 233.

Chapter 3

1. Patricia Erens, "Women's Documentary Filmmaking: The Personal Is Political," *New Challenges for Documentary,* ed. Alan Rosenthal (Berkeley: University of California Press, 1988), 555.
2. Eileen Ogintz, "The Strike That Made Labor History," *Chicago Tribune* 19 Oct. 1978: 5.
3. Sonya Michel, "Feminism, Film, and Public History," *Issues in Feminist Film Criticism,* ed. Patricia Erens (Bloomington: Indiana University Press, 1990), 238.
4. Julia Lesage, "The Political Aesthetics of the Feminist Documentary Film," *Issues in Feminist Film Criticism,* ed. Patricia Erens (Bloomington: Indiana University Press, 1990), 222.
5. *Union Maids,* dir. Julia Reichert, James Klein, and Miles Mogulescu, perf. Stella Nowicki, Sylvia Woods, and Christine (Kate) Ellis, New Day Films, 1976.
6. *With Babies and Banners,* dir. Lorraine Gray, perf. Genora Johnson and members of the Women's Emergency Brigade, New Day Films, 1978.
7. For an excellent essay on the stylistic and substantive features of consciousness-raising as a rhetorical strategy within the women's liberation movement, see Karlyn Kohrs Campbell, "The Rhetoric of Women's Liberation: An Oxymoron," *Quarterly Journal of Speech* 59 (1973): 74–86.
8. Paula Rabinowitz, *They Must Be Represented: The Politics of Documentary* (New York: Verso, 1994), 7.
9. Jan Rosenberg, *Women's Reflections: The Feminist Film Movement* (Ann Arbor, MI: UMI Research Press, 1983), 9.
10. Ruth McCormick, "Women's Liberation Cinema," *The Documentary Tradition,* ed. Lewis Jacobs, 2nd ed. (New York: W.W. Norton & Co., 1979), 523. For more on the distinctions between these various branches of the women's movement, see also Jo Freeman, "The Origins of the Women's Movement," *American Journal of Sociology,* 78 (1973); Maren Lockwood Carden, *The New Feminist Movement* (New York: Russell Sage, 1973); and Rosenberg, *Women's Reflections,* 9–20.
11. McCormick, "Women's Liberation," 523.
12. Rosenberg, *Women's Reflections,* 10.
13. McCormick, "Women's Liberation," 524.
14. Rosenberg, *Women's Reflections* 10.
15. McCormick, "Women's Liberation," 524.
16. Rosenberg, *Women's Reflections,* 18.
17. Lewis Jacobs, *The Documentary Tradition,* 2nd ed. (New York: W. W. Norton & Co, 1979), 376.
18. Rosenberg, *Women's Reflections,* 17.
19. Lewis Jacobs, *The Documentary,* 516–517.
20. Rosenberg, *Women's Reflections,* 2.
21. Erens, "Women's Documentary," 555; Eric Barnouw, *Documentary: A History of the Non-Fiction Film,* 2nd rev. ed. (New York: Oxford University Press, 1983), 297.
22. Erens, "Women's Documentary," 564.
23. Erens, "Women's Documentary," 565.
24. Many of these filmmakers were following the calls of some feminist film theorists, such as Laura Mulvey, who advocated "a politically and aesthetically avant-garde cinema" capable of "leaving the past behind without rejecting it, transcending outworn or oppressive forms, or daring to break with normal pleasurable expectations in order to conceive a new language of desire." See Laura Mulvey, "Visual Pleasure and Narrative Cinema," *Issues in Feminist Film Criticism,* ed. Patricia Erens (Bloomington: Indiana University Press, 1990), 30.
25. Lesage, "The Political Aesthetics," 229.
26. Lesage, "The Political Aesthetics," 224.
27. Karlyn Kohrs Campbell, "Femininity and Feminism: To Be or Not To Be A Woman," *Communication Quarterly* 31 (1983): 104.
28. Rosenberg, *Women's Reflections,* 3.
29. Annette Kuhn, *Women's Pictures: Feminism and Cinema,* 2nd ed. (New York: Verso, 1994), 183.
30. Rosenberg, *Women's Reflections,* 77–82; Erens, "Women's Documentary," 563.
31. Claire Johnston, "Introduction," *Notes on Women's Cinema,* ed. Claire Johnston (Lon-

don: Society for Education in Film and Television, 1973), 2.
32. Julia Lesage, et al., "New Day's Way," *Jump Cut* 9 (1975): 22; Kuhn, *Women's Pictures*, 181-182.
33. Alice Lynd and Staughton Lynd, eds., *Rank and File: Personal Histories by Working-Class Organizers* (Boston: Beacon Press, 1973).
34. Lynd and Lynd, *Rank and File*, 5.
35. Julia Reichert and James Klein, "Union Maids," *The Documentary Conscience: A Casebook in Filmmaking*, ed. Alan Rosenthal (Berkeley: University of California Press, 1980), 317.
36. Reichert and Klein, "Union Maids," 325.
37. Clarke Taylor, "Film Shorts Spark N.Y. Festival," *L.A. Times* 9 Oct. 1978: 19.
38. Clarke, "Film Shorts," 19.
39. Rev. of *With Babies and Banners*, dir. Lorraine Gray. *Variety* 11 Apr. 1979: 34.
40. Linda Gordon, "*Union Maids*: Working Class Heroines," *Jump-Cut* 14 (1977): 34-35.
41. Judith Mayne, "Feminist Film Theory and Criticism," *Multiple Voices in Feminist Film Criticism*, ed. Diane Carson, Linda Dittmar, and Janice R. Welsch (Minneapolis: University of Minnesota Press, 1994), 59.
42. E. Ann Kaplan, *Women and Film: Both Sides of the Camera* (New York: Methuen, 1983), 126.
43. Judith Mayne, "Visibility and Feminist Film Criticism," *Film Reader* 5 (1982): 123.
44. Alexandra Juhasz, "They Said We Were Trying to Show Reality—All I Want to Show Is My Video: The Politics of the Realist Feminist Documentary," *Collecting Visible Evidence*, ed. Jane M. Gaines and Michael Renov (Minneapolis: University of Minnesota Press, 1999), 194.
45. Kuhn, *Women's Pictures*, 151.
46. Such theorists include Claude Lévi-Strauss, Jacques Lacan, Christian Metz, Roland Barthes, Julia Kristeva, and Louis Althusser.
47. Mayne, "Feminist Film," 50.
48. E. Ann Kaplan, "Theories and Strategies of the Feminist Documentary," *New Challenges for Documentary*, ed. Alan Rosenthal (Berkeley: University of California Press, 1988), 89.
49. Eileen McGarry, "Documentary, Realism and Women's Cinema," *Women and Film* 2 (1975): 51.
50. Claire Johnston, "Women's Cinema as Counter-Cinema," *Notes on Women's Cinema*, ed. Claire Johnston (London: Society for Education in Film and Television, 1973), 28.

51. Johnston, "Women's Cinema," 28.
52. Johnston, "Women's Cinema," 29.
53. See Mary Ann Doane, Patricia Mellencamp, and Linda Williams, "Feminist Film Criticism: An Introduction," *Re-Vision: Essays in Feminist Film Criticism*, ed. Mary Ann Doane, Patricia Mellencamp, and Linda Williams (Frederick, MD: University Publications of America, 1984), 8; and Manhola Dargis and Amy Taubin, "Double Take," *Village Voice* 21 Jan. 1992: 56. In the *Village Voice* article, for example, Dargis writes, "Could it be that once these messy, activist, earnest works were banished to the dustbin, attention would be paid to the sort of filmmaking that neatly mirrored the same concerns of a certain, emerging academic feminism?"
54. Christine Gledhill, "Developments in Feminist Film Criticism," *Re-Vision: Essays in Feminist Film Criticism*, ed. Mary Ann Doane, Patricia Mellencamp, and Linda Williams (Frederick, MD: University Publications of America, 1984), 22.
55. Kaplan, *Women and Film*, 140.
56. See Juhasz, "They Said," 194.
57. Erens, "Women's Documentary," 558.
58. Rosenberg, *Women's Reflections*, 88. Rosenberg made this statement about *Union Maids* in particular, but I would argue that it applies to both films.
59. Lesage, "The Political Aesthetics," 229.
60. Bill Nichols, *Introduction to Documentary* (Bloomington: Indiana University Press, 2001), 123.
61. Kuhn, *Women's Pictures*, 144.
62. Michel, "Feminism, Film, and Public History," 241.
63. For more on this argument, see Barbara Halpern Martineau, "Talking About Our Lives and Experiences: Some Thoughts About Feminism, Documentary and 'Talking Heads,'" *"Show Us Life": Toward a History and Aesthetics of the Committed Documentary*, ed. Thomas Waugh (Metuchen, NJ: The Scarecrow Press, 1984), 258-263.
64. Lesage, "The Political Aesthetics," 234.
65. Juhasz, "They Said," 203.
66. For more on this view, and filmmakers' discussion of their perspectives on narrative, see Jeffrey Youdelman, "Narration, Invention, & History: A Documentary Dilemma," *Cineaste* 7.2 (1982): 9-15.
67. Bill Nichols, *Representing Reality: Issues and Concepts in Documentary* (Bloomington: Indiana University Press, 1991), 48.
68. Joris Ivens quoted in Yoduleman, "Narrative, Invention," 11.
69. See similar arguments in Kuhn, *Women's Pictures*, 150.

70. Michel, "Feminism, Film, and Public History," 242.
71. Susan Reverby, "'With Babies and Banners': A Review," *Radical America* 13.5 (1979): 63.
72. The soundtrack of *Union Maids* was comprised of songs, such as "Union Maid" and "Join the Union" by Pete Seeger and the Almanac Singers and "Sweet Home Chicago" by Taj Mahal and the Pointer Sisters, while *With Babies and Banners* included "I am a Union Woman" by Mary McCasin and "Rebel Girls" by Hazel Dickens.
73. Reverby, "'With Babies,'" 64.
74. For more on the re-writing of social history through the construction of "women's history," see Keith Tribe, "History and the Production of Memories," *Screen* 18.4 (1978): 9–23.
75. Michel, "Feminism, Film, and Public History," 242.
76. Kaplan, *Women and Film*, 131.
77. Kaplan, *Women and Film*, 131.
78. Juhasz, "They Said," 194.
79. See Juhasz, "They Said," 205. It is also significant to note that most feminist film theorists argued for dismantling female identity as a viable response to Hollywood and the patriarchal discourses that construct women's identity in film. The feminist filmmakers responsible for the feminist film movement believed reconstruction of women's identity was a more fruitful place to begin.
80. Kuhn, *Women's Pictures*, 130.
81. Kaplan, *Women and Film*, 136.
82. E. Ann Kaplan, "Theories and Strategies of the Feminist Documentary" *New Challenges for Documentary*, ed. Alan Rosenthal (Berkeley: University of California Press, 1988): 96–99.
83. See parallel claims offered in Maurice Charland, "Finding a Horizon and Telos: The Challenge to Critical Rhetoric," *Quarterly Journal of Speech* 77 (1991): 73. Charland is referencing the debate between rhetoric and cultural studies, and makes a similar accusation that Critical Rhetoricians have sacrificed phronesis and its desired political action by neglecting the challenge of reaching a broad public audience.
84. Juhasz, "They Said," 196.
85. Barbara Susan, "About My Consciousness Raising," *Voices From Women's Liberation*, ed. Leslie B. Tanner (New York: Signet, 1970), 242.
86. Reverby, "'With Babies,'" 67.
87. Reichert and Klein, "Union Maids," 326.
88. B. Ruby Rich, *Chick Flicks: Theories and Memories of the Feminist Film Movement* (Durham: Duke University Press, 1998), 307.
89. Gary Crowdus, rev. of *With Babies and Banners*, dir. Lorraine Gray, *Cineaste*, 9 (Fall 1978): 45.

Chapter 4

1. Winifred D. Wandersee, *On the Move: American Women in the 1970s* (Boston: Twayne Publishers, 1988), 173.
2. *Norma Rae*, dir. Martin Ritt, perf. Sally Field, Ron Liebman, Beau Bridges, Twentieth Century–Fox, 1979 and *Silkwood*, dir. Mike Nichols, perf. Meryl Streep, Kurt Russell, Cher, Twentieth Century–Fox, 1983.
3. See Peter Lev, *American Films of the 70s: Conflicting Visions* (Austin: University of Texas Press, 2000), 185.
4. Martin Scorcese told *The New York Times* in 1997 that "The end of the 70s was the last golden period of cinema in America." Cited in Lev, *American Films*, 183. This sentiment was also expressed by film critic Pauline Kael in a 1991 interview, in which she proclaimed the early 1970s as Hollywood's single authentic Golden Age. Pauline Kael, interview, *Weekend Edition*, Natl. Public Radio, WHYY, Philadelphia, 9 March 1991.
5. Diane Jacobs, *Hollywood Renaissance* (South Brunswick, NJ: A. S. Barnes, 1977), 1.
6. Geoff Gilmore, "The State of Independent Film," *National Forum* 77.4 (1997): 10.
7. Robert Phillip Kolker, *A Cinema of Loneliness*, 2nd ed. (New York: Oxford University Press, 1988), 5.
8. Robert Sklar, *Movie-Made America: A Cultural History of American Movies*, rev. ed. (New York: Vintage Books, 1994), 324.
9. Kolker, *A Cinema*, 5.
10. Sklar, *Movie-Made*, 324.
11. Sklar, *Movie-Made*, 322.
12. Sklar, *Movie-Made*, 323.
13. Kolker, *A Cinema*, 8.
14. Robert B. Ray, *A Certain Tendency of the Hollywood Cinema, 1930–1980* (Princeton: Princeton University Press, 1985), 267.
15. H. Wayne Schuth, *Mike Nichols* (Boston: Twayne Publishers, 1978), 160.
16. Gabriel Miller, *The Films of Martin Ritt: Fanfare for the Common Man* (Jackson: University Press of Mississippi, 2000), 172.
17. Ray, *A Certain Tendency*, 267.
18. See Penelope Gilliatt, rev. of *Norma Rae*, dir. Martin Ritt, *The New Yorker* 19 Mar. 1979: 128; and David Ansen, rev. of *Norma Rae*, dir. Martin Ritt, *Newsweek* 5 Mar. 1979: 105.

19. Jack Kroll, rev. of *Silkwood*, dir. Mike Nichols, *Newsweek* 12 Dec. 1983: 108.
20. Henry P. Liefermann, *Crystal Lee: A Woman of Inheritance* (New York: Macmillan Publishing, 1975).
21. Robert Brent Toplin, *History By Hollywood: The Use and Abuse of the American Past* (Urbana: University of Illinois Press, 1996), 207–208.
22. Toplin, *History*, 210.
23. Quoted in Miller, *The Films*, 177.
24. "Real Life Norma Rae Feels Snubbed By Field," *Variety* 14 Aug. 1985: 2.
25. Charles Sawyer, rev. of *Silkwood*, dir. Mike Nichols, *Films in Review* Mar. 1984: 178.
26. See Elizabeth Stone, "'Norma Rae': The Story They Could Have Told," *Ms.* May 1979: 28–33.
27. See Pat Aufderheide, "A Mensch for All Seasons," *In These Times* 16–22 Apr. 1980: 15–16.
28. See Clarke Taylor, "The On-Camera, Off-Camera Drama of Crystal Lee Jordan," *L. A. Times* 4 Mar. 1979, calendar: 5; and Aufderheide, "A Mensch," 16.
29. Taylor, "The On-Camera," 5.
30. Aufderheide, "A Mensch," 16.
31. Eric Leif Davin, "Crystal Lee," *In These Times* 15–18 Mar. 1980: 16–17.
32. Anna Mayo, "Cashing In on Karen," *Village Voice* 21 Feb. 1984: 28, 55.
33. Angela Bonavoglia, rev. of *Silkwood*, dir. Mike Nichols, *Cineaste* 13.3 (1984): 40.
34. Mayo, "Cashing In," 28.
35. Stone, "'Norma Rae': The Story," 29.
36. Ansen, rev. of *Norma Rae* 105; Richard Schickel, "Strike Busting," *Time* 12 Mar. 1979: 76.
37. See Tom O'Brien, "Uncertain Verdict: 'Silkwood,'" *Commonweal* 9 Mar. 1984: 146–147; and Suzanne Gordon, "Silkwood On-Screen: Rebel Without a Cause?," *Ms.* Feb. 1984: 30–32.
38. Tom Hoffer and Richard Alan Nelson have described docudrama as: "A unique blend of fact and fiction which dramatizes events and historic personages from our recent memory .... The accuracy and comprehensiveness of such a recreation ... can vary widely and is conditioned not only by intent but also by factors such as budget and production time." See Tom W. Hoffer and Richard Alan Nelson, "Docudrama on American TV," *Journal of the University Film Association* 30.2 (1978): 21.
39. Steve Lipkin, "Defining Docudrama: In the Name of the Father, Schindler's List, and JFK," *Why Docudrama? Fact-Fiction on Film and TV*, ed. Alan Rosenthal (Carbondale: Southern Illinois University Press, 1999), 370.
40. For more on melodrama, see Christine Gledhill, ed. *Home is Where the Heart Is: Studies in Melodrama and the Women's Film* (London: BFI Publishing, 1987); Thomas Elsaesser, "Tales of Sound and Fury," *Monogram* 4 (1972): 2–15; and Charles Affron, *Cinema and Sentiment* (Chicago: University of Chicago Press, 1982).
41. Lipkin, "Defining Docudrama," 370.
42. Tom Doherty, rev. of *Silkwood*, dir. Mike Nichols, *Film Quarterly* 38.4 (1984): 24.
43. Richard A. Blake, "Selective Memory," *America* 7 Apr. 1979: 286.
44. Terry Christensen, *Real Politics: American Political Movies from Birth of a Nation to Platoon* (New York: Basil Blackwell, 1997), 164. For a similar argument, see also David Sterritt, rev. of *Silkwood*, dir. Mike Nichols, *Christian Science Monitor* 5 Jan. 1984: 24.
45. Richard Schickel, rev. of *Silkwood*, dir. Mike Nichols, *Time* 19 Dec. 1983: 73.
46. Nora Ephron, "The Tie That Binds," *The Nation* 6 Apr. 1992: 453.
47. Miller, *The Films*, 177.
48. Doherty, rev. of *Silkwood*, 24.
49. Ray, *A Certain Tendency*, 296.
50. David Jon Wiener, "*Silkwood*," *American Cinematographer* (February 1984): 51.
51. Peter Stead, *Film and the Working Class: The Feature Film in British and American Society* (New York: Routledge, 1989), 223.
52. Annette Kuhn, *Women's Pictures: Feminism and Cinema*, 2nd ed. (New York: Verso, 1994), 142.
53. Ray, *A Certain Tendency*, 57.
54. Michael Ryan and Douglas Kellner, *Camera Politica: The Politics and Ideology of Contemporary Hollywood Film* (Bloomington: Indiana University Press, 1988), 109.
55. Pat Aufderheide, rev. of *Norma Rae*, dir. Martin Ritt, *Cineaste* 9.3 (1979): 42.
56. David Bordwell, Janet Staiger, and Kristin Thompson, *The Classical Hollywood Cinema: Film Style and Mode of Production to 1960* (New York: Columbia University Press, 1985), 82.
57. Diane Carson, "To Be Seen but Not Heard: The Awful Truth," *Multiple Voices in Feminist Film Criticism*, ed. Diane Carson, Linda Dittmar, and Janice R. Welsch (Minneapolis: University of Minnesota, 1994), 214.
58. Quoted in Bonavoglia, rev. of *Silkwood*, 40.
59. Christensen, *Reel Politics*, 164.
60. Toplin, *History By Hollywood*, 223.
61. Ray, *A Certain Tendency*, 18.
62. Philip Green, *Cracks in the Pedestal:*

Ideology and Gender in Hollywood (Amherst: University of Massachusetts Press, 1998), 1–2.
  63. Doherty, rev. of *Silkwood*, 24.
  64. Aufderheide, rev. of *Norma Rae*, 42.
  65. Green, *Cracks in the Pedestal*, 96.
  66. Jasmine Paul and Bette J. Kauffman, "Missing Persons: Working-Class Women and the Movies, 1940–1990," *Feminism, Multiculturalism, and the Media: Global Diversities*, ed. Angharad N. Valdivia (Thousand Oaks, CA: Sage, 1995), 173.

Chapter 5

  1. *Live Nude Girls Unite!* website, online, Internet, 23 Mar. 2002.
  2. See Gina Bellafante, "It's All About Me!" *Time* 29 June 1998. 10 February 2007 and Helene A. Shugart, Catherine Egley Waggoner, and D. Lynn O'Brien Hallstein, "Mediating Third-Wave Feminism: Appropriation as Postmodern Media Practice," *Critical Studies in Media Communication* 18 (2001): 194–210.
  3. See, for example, Katie Roiphe, *The Morning After: Sex, Fear and Feminism on Campus* (Boston: Little, Brown, 1993); Naomi Wolf, *Fire with Fire: The New Female Power and How It Will Change the 21st Century* (New York: Random House, 1993); and Christina Hoff-Sommers, *Who Stole Feminism? How Women Have Betrayed Women* (New York: Touchstone, 1994). For a rhetorical analysis of these books from an academic feminist perspective, see Lisa M. Griing-Pemble and Diane M. Blair, "Best-Selling Feminisms: The Rhetorical Production of Popular Press Feminists' Romantic Quest," *Communication Quarterly* 48 (2001): 360–379.
  4. For more information on postfemism/third-wave feminism and its representations in the media, see Angela McRobbie, "Postfeminism and Popular Culture," *Feminist Media Studies* 4.3 (2004): 255–264; Helene A. Shugart, "Isn't It Ironic?: The Intersection of Third-Wave Feminism and Generation X," *Women's Studies in Communication* 24 (2001): 165; Shugart, Waggoner, and Hallstein, "Mediating Third-Wave Feminism." For a greater discussion of the relationship between the second and third waves, including continuity and difference, see Cathryn Bailey, "Making Waves and Drawing Lines: The Politics of Defining the Vicissitudes of Feminism," *Hypatia* 12 (Summer 1997): 17–28.
  5. Karrin Vasby Anderson and Jessie Stewart, "Politics and the Single Woman: The 'Sex and the City Voter' in Campaign 2004," *Rhetoric and Public Affairs* 8.4 (2005): 595–616.
  6. Vasby and Stewart, 598.
  7. See Ann Brooks, *Postfeminisms: Feminism, Cultural Theory, and Cultural Forms* (New York: Routledge, 1997).
  8. Rebecca Walker, ed. *To Be Real* (New York: Anchor Books, 1995) and Barbara Findlen, ed. *Listen Up: Voices from the Next Feminist Generation* (Emeryville, CA: Seal Press, 1995).
  9. Lisa Marie Hogeland, "Fear of Feminism: Why Young Women Get the Willies," *Ms.* (November–December 1994): 18–21.
  10. Natalie Fixmer and Julia T. Wood, "The Personal is *Still* Political: Embodied Politics in Third Wave Feminism," *Women's Studies in Communication* 28 (Fall 2005): 251.
  11. Leslie Heywood and Jennifer Drake, eds. *Third Wave Agenda: Being Feminist, Doing Feminism* (Minneapolis: University of Minnesota Press, 1997): 2.
  12. Rory Dicker and Alison Piepmeier, eds. *Catching a Wave: Reclaiming Feminism for the 21st Century* (Boston: Northeastern University Press, 2003): 5.
  13. Amber E. Kinser, "Negotiating Spaces For/Through Third-Wave Feminism," *NWSA Journal* 16.3 (2004): 147.
  14. Quoted in Edward Guthman, "Union Activists Uncovered in 'Girls': Stripper Turns Her Advocacy into a Labor of Love," *San Francisco Chronicle* 1 Oct. 2000: 61.
  15. For more on the work of second-wave documentary, see Jennifer L. Borda, "Feminist Critique and Cinematic Counterhistory in the Documentary *With Babies and Banners*," *Women's Studies in Communication* 28 (Fall 2005): 157–182.
  16. A. O. Scott, "Throw Off the Yoke, But Keep the G-String," rev. of *Live Nude Girls Unite!*, dir. Julia Query and Vicki Funari, *The New York Times*, 20 Oct. 2000: E17.
  17. Amy Taubin, "Peep Shows and Prison Showmanship," rev. of *Live Nude Girls Unite!*, dir. Julia Query and Vicki Funari, *The Village Voice* 24 Oct. 2000: 146.
  18. Loren King, "Life, Love, Labor at the Lusty Lady," rev. of *Live Nude Girls Unite!*, dir. Julia Query and Vicki Funari, *Boston Globe* 19 Jan. 2001: D8; Saul Austerlitz, rev. of *Live Nude Girls Unite!*, dir. Julia Query and Vicki Funari, *Cineaste* 27.1 (2001): 64.
  19. See Karlyn Kohrs Campbell, "Gender and Genre: Loci of Invention and Contradiction in the Earliest Speeches by U.S. Women," *Quarterly Journal of Speech* 81 (1995): 479–495 and Karlyn Kohrs Campbell, "The Rhet-

oric of Women's Liberation: An Oxymoron," *Quarterly Journal of Speech* 59 (1971): 74–86.
20. Shugart, "Isn't It Ironic?," 133.
21. See Heywood and Drake, 8.
22. Heywood and Drake, *Third Wave Agenda*, 8.
23. For more on how the third wave feminist movement may be characterized through its contradictions, see Heywood and Drake, *Third Wave Agenda*, 1–20.
24. Amanda D. Lotz, "Communication Third-Wave Feminism and New Social Movements: Challenges for the Next Century of Feminist Endeavor," *Women and Language* 26 (2003): 6.
25. Dicker and Piepmeier, *Catching a Wave*, 16.
26. Shugart, Waggoner, and Hallstein, "Mediating," 195.
27. Sura Wood, "Lusty Ladies," *SF Weekly* 26 April–2 May, 2000, *Live Nude Girls Unite!* website, online, Internet, 23 Mar. 2002.
28. Catherine M. Orr, "Charting the Currents of the Third Wave," *Hypatia* 12 (Summer 1997): 34, 33.
29. Mary Douglas Vavrus, *Postfeminist News: Political Women in Media Culture* (Albany: State University of New York Press, 2002): 2.
30. King, "Life, Love, Labor," D8.
31. Orr, "Charting the Currents," 34.
32. Shugart, "Isn't It Ironic?," 133.
33. Shugart, Waggoner, and Hallstein, "Mediating," 195.
34. Heywood and Drake, *Third Wave Agenda*, 7.
35. Shawn J. Parry-Giles, "Image-Based Politics, Feminism and the Consequences of their Convergence," *Critical Studies in Mass Communication* 15 (December 1998): 460, 462.
36. Bonnie J. Dow, "If There's No Such Thing As Reality, Has Elvis Really Left the Building?" *Critical Studies in Mass Communication* 15 (December 1998): 472.

Chapter 6

1. Bonnie J. Dow, *Prime Time Feminism: Television, Media Cutlure, and the Women's Movement Since 1970* (Philadelphia: University of Pennsylvania Press, 1996): 207.
2. For more on the feminist quest and lifestyle feminism portrayed in the media, see Bonnie J. Dow, "*Ally McBeal*, Lifestyle Feminism, and the Politics of Personal Happiness," *The Communication Review* 5 (2002): 263.
3. Dow, *Prime Time*, 209.
4. Susan Douglas, *Where the Girls Are: Growing Up Female with the Mass Media* (New York: Three Rivers Press, 1995): 291.
5. Jennifer Drake, "Third Wave Feminisms," *Feminist Studies* 23 (Spring 1997): 108.
6. Jasmine Paul and Bette J. Kauffman, "Missing Persons: Working-Class Women and the Movies, 1940–1990," *Feminism, Multiculturalism, and the Media: Global Diversities*, ed. Angharad N. Valdivia (Thousand Oaks, CA: Sage, 1995), 174.
7. See Jerry White, "Union Membership in U.S. at Lowest Level in 60 Years," *World Socialist Web Site*, 26 Feb. 2001, online, Internet, 24 Mar. 2002; Jefferson Cowie, "Solidarity Strikes Out," *The American Prospect* 1–14 Jan. 2002: 41–45; Leigh Strope, "Organized Labor Setbacks Could Provide Opportunity," *Delaware County Daily Times* 3 Sept. 2001: 15.
8. Sklar, Robert. *Movie-Made America: A Cultural History of American Movies*, rev. ed. (New York: Random House, 1994), 341–343. For a greater discussion of the relationship between the Reagan administration and Hollywood film and their joint participation as influential institutional voices in the cultural dialogue, see Dale Bertelsen, "Rhetorical Privation as Cultural Praxis: Implicit Rhetorical Theory in Presidential Oratory and Contemporary Hollywood Films," diss., Penn State U, 1989, 170.
9. Sklar, *Movie-Made America*, 343.
10. Michael Ryan and Douglas Kellner, *Camera Politica: The Politics and Ideology of Contemporary Hollywood Film* (Bloomington: Indiana University Press, 1988), 11.
11. Susan Jeffords, *Hard Bodies: Hollywood Masculinity in the Reagan Era* (New Brunswick: Rutgers University Press, 1994), 25.
12. Susan Faludi, *Backlash: The Undeclared War Against American Women* (New York: Crown Publishers, 1991), 113. See also Elizabeth G. Traube, *Dreaming Identities: Class, Gender, and Generation in the 1980s Hollywood Movies* (Boulder, CO: Westview Press, 1992).
13. Sklar, *Movie-Made America*, 374.
14. Claudia Puig, "Declarations of Independents at the Sundance Film Festival," *USA Today* 21 Jan. 1999, online, Internet, 29 Mar. 2002: 2.
15. Puig, "Declaring Independents," 2.
16. Susannah Grant, *Erin Brockovich: The Shooting Script* (New York: Newmarket Press, 2000), 126.
17. Quoted in Grant, *Erin*, 126.
18. Grant, *Erin*, 126.
19. Kenneth Turan, "The Smile Wins the

Day," *The Los Angeles Times* 17 Mar. 2000, *laTimes.com*, Internet, 23 Mar. 2002.

20. Ansen, "A Trash-Talking," 60; Ebert, "Erin Brockovich."

21. Peter Travers, rev. of *Erin Brockovich*, dir. Steven Soderbergh, *Rolling Stone.com*, online, Internet, 30 Mar. 2002.

22. Joe Morgenstern, "'Erin Brockovich' Has Both Beauty and Brains," *The Wall Street Journal* 17 Mar. 2000: W1.

23. See imdb.com.

24. David Edelstein, "Charlize and the Chauvinist Factory," rev. of *North Country*, dir. Nikki Caro, *Slate* online, 20 Oct. 2005, online, Internet, 7 June 2007.

25. Roger Ebert, "*North Country*: A Mine of Oscar-caliber Performances," rev. of *North Country*, dir. Nikki Caro, *Chicago Sun Times* 21 Oct. 2005, online, Internet, 7 June 2007.

26. Steve Persall, "A Victim Rises Up," rev. of *North Country*, dir. Nikki Caro, *St. Petersburg Times* 20 Oct. 2005, online, Internet, 7 June 2007; Manohla Dargis, "A Few Women at a Mine, Striking a Blow for All," rev. of *North Country*, dir. Nikki Caro, *The New York Times* 21 Oct. 2005, online, Internet, 7 June 2007.

27. David Rooney, "North Country," rev. of *North Country*, dir. Nikki Caro, *Variety*, 15 Sept. 2005, online, Internet, 7 June 2007.

28. Grant, *Erin*, iv–v.

29. Turan, "The Smile."

30. Ruthe Stein, "One Stunning Miner Manages to Extract Emotion from a Dismal Situation," rev. of *North Country*, dir. Nikki Caro, *San Francisco Chronicle* 21 Oct. 2005, online, Internet, 7 June 2007. Kenneth Turan, "'North Country,'" rev. of *North Country*, dir. Nikki Caro, *Los Angeles Times* 21 Oct. 2005, online, Internet, 7 June 2007.

31. Ansen, "A Trash-Talking," 60.

32. Thomas Dougherty, rev. of *Erin Brockovich*, dir. Steven Soderbergh, *Cineaste* 25.3 (2000): 40.

33. Ansen, "A Trash-Talking," 60.

34. Travers, rev. of *Erin Brockovich*.

35. Turan, "The Smile."

36. Yvonne Tasker, *Working Girls: Gender and Sexuality in Popular Cinema* (New York: Routledge, 1998), 3.

37. Ebert, rev. of *Erin Brockovich*; Ansen, "A Trash-Talking," 60.

38. Stein, "One Stunning."

39. Brandon French, *On the Verge of Revolt: Women in American Films of the Fifties* (New York: Frederick Ungar Publishing, 1978), xxiv.

40. *Erin Brockovich*, dir. Steven Soderbergh, perf. Julia Roberts, Albert Finney, Aaron Eckhart, Universal Pictures and Columbia Pictures, 2000; *Live Nude Girls Unite!*, dir. Julia Query and Vicki Funari, perf. Julia Query and workers at the Lusty Lady, First Run Features, 2000.

41. David Ansen of *Newsweek* and Wesley Morris of the *San Francisco Examiner* both compared *Erin Brockovich* to *Norma Rae* and Roger Ebert applauds Julia Query, the subject of *Live Nude Girls Unite!*, as a "spirited Union Maid." See David Ansen, "A Trash Talking Crusader: Move Over, Norma Rae," rev. of *Erin Brockovich*, dir. Steven Soderbergh, *Newsweek* 13 Mar. 2000: 60; Wesley Morris, "Roberts Is Sassy, Brassy in 'Erin,'" rev. of *Erin Brockovich*, dir. Steven Soderbergh, *San Francisco Examiner*, 17 Mar. 2000, online, Internet, 23 Mar. 2002; Roger Ebert, rev. of *Live Nude Girls Unite!*, dir. Julia Query and Vicky Funari, *Chicago Sun Times* 22 Jun. 2001, online, Internet, 23 Mar. 2002.

Chapter 7

1. Ty Burr, "Women on the Verge," *Entertainment Weekly* 19 Feb. 2001: 43.

2. Burr, "Women," 43.

3. Burr, "Women," 43.

4. David Bordwell, Janet Staiger, and Kristin Thompson, *The Classical Hollywood Cinema: Film Styles and Mode of Production to 1960* (New York: Columbia University Press, 1985), xii.

Bibliography

A Crime to Fit the Punishment. Dir. Stephen Mack and Barbara Moss. Narrator Lee Grant. Mack and Moss, 1982.

Affron, Charles. *Cinema and Sentiment*. Chicago: University of Chicago Press, 1982.

Alpert, Hollis. "Enough! Enough!" *Saturday Review* 17 Nov. 1956: 29.

Altman, Rick R. *The American Film Musical*. Bloomington: Indiana University Press, 1987.

———, ed. *Genre: The Musical*. Boston: Routledge & Kegan Paul, 1981.

Anderson, Karrin Vasby, and Jessie Stewart. "Politics and the single woman: The 'sex and the city voter' in campaign 2004." *Rhetoric and Public Affairs* 8 (2005): 595–616.

Ansen, David. Rev. of *Norma Rae*, dir. Martin Ritt. *Newsweek* 5 Mar. 1979: 105.

———. "A Trash Talking Crusader: Move Over, Norma Rae." Rev. of *Erin Brockovich*, dir. Steven Soderbergh. *Newsweek* 13 Mar. 2000: 60.

Arbuthnot, Lucie, and Gail Seneca. "Pretext and Text in *Gentleman Prefer Blondes*." *Issues in Feminist Film Criticism*. Ed. Patricia Erens. Bloomington: Indiana University Press, 1990. 112–125.

Aufderheide, Pat. "A Mensch for All Seasons." *In These Times* 16–22 Apr. 1980: 15–16.

———. Rev. of *Norma Rae*, dir. Martin Ritt. *Cineaste* 9.3 (1979): 42–43.

Auslander, Philip. *Performing Glam Rock: Gender & Theatricality in Popular Music*. Ann Arbor: The University of Michigan Press, 2006.

Auster, Al, et al. "Hollywood and the Working Class: A Discussion." *Socialist Review* 9 (1979): 109–121.

Austerlitz, Saul. Rev. of *Live Nude Girls Unite!*, dir. Julia Query and Vicki Funari. *Cineaste* 27.1 (2001): 64.

Bailey, Catherine. "Making Waves and Drawing Lines: The Politics of Defining the Vicissitudes of Feminism." *Hypatia* 12 (Summer 1997): 17–28.

Barnes, Harper. "'Live Nude Girls' Starts Slow But Gets Quite Good." Rev. of *Live Nude Girls Unite!*, dir. Julia Query and Vicki Funari. *St. Louis Post-Dispatch* 16 Mar. 2001: E2.

Barnouw, Eric. *Documentary: A History of the Non-Fiction Film*. 2nd rev. ed. New York: Oxford University Press, 1983.

Barsam, Richard M. *Nonfiction Film: A Critical History*. Rev. ed. Bloomington: Indiana University Press, 1992.

Benson, Edward, and Sharon Hartman Strom. "Crystal Lee, Norma Rae, and All Their Sisters." *Film Library Quarterly* 12 (1979): 18–23.

Benson, Thomas W. "The Rhetorical Structure of Frederick Wiseman's *Primate*." *Quarterly Journal of Speech* 71 (1985): 204–217.

———, and Carolyn Anderson. *Reality Fictions: The Films of Frederick Wiseman*. Carbondale: Southern Illinois University Press, 1989.

Berg, Chariles Ramírez. *Cinema of Solitude: A Critical Study of Mexican Film, 1967–1983*. Austin: University of Texas Press, 1992.

Bertelsen, Dale. "Rhetorical Privation As Cultural Praxis: Implicit Rhetorical Theory in Presidential Oratory and Contem-

porary Hollywood Films." Diss. Penn State University, 1989.
Biberman, Herbert. *Salt of the Earth: The Story of a Film*. Boston: Beacon Press, 1965.
Bissell, Richard. *7½ Cents*. Boston: Little, Brown, 1953.
Blake, Richard A. "Selective Memory." *America* 7 Apr. 1979: 286.
Bonavoglia, Angela. Rev. of *Silkwood*, dir. Mike Nichols. *Cineaste* 13.3 (1984): 38–40.
Borda, Jennifer L. "Feminist Critique and Cinematic Counterhistory in the Documentary *With Babies and Banners*." *Women's Studies in Communication* 28 (Fall 2005): 157–182.
Bordwell, David. *Narration in the Fiction Film*. Madison: University of Wisconsin Press, 1985.
____, Janet Staiger, and Kristin Thompson. *The Classical Hollywood Cinema: Film Style and Mode of Production to 1960*. New York: Columbia University Press, 1985.
Britton, Andrew. "Stars and Genre." *Stardom: Industry of Desire*. Ed. Christine Gledhill. New York: Routledge, 1991. 198–206.
Brooks, Ann. *Postfeminisms: Feminism, Cultural Theory, and Cultural Forms*. New York: Routledge, 1997.
Brunsdon, Charlotte, ed. *Films for Women*. London: British Film Institute, 1986.
Burr, Ty. "Women on the Verge." *Entertainment Weekly* 19 February 2001: 43–48.
Byars, Jackie. *All That Hollywood Allows: Re-reading Gender in 1950s Melodrama*. Chapel Hill: University of North Carolina Press, 1991.
Campbell, Karlyn Kohrs. "Femininity and Feminism: To Be or Not To Be A Woman." *Communication Quarterly* 31 (1983): 101–108.
____. "Gender and Genre: Loci of Invention and Contradiction in the Earliest Speeches by U.S. Women." *Quarterly Journal of Speech* 81 (1995): 479–495.
____. "The Rhetoric of Women's Liberation: An Oxymoron." *Quarterly Journal of Speech* 59 (1973): 74–86.
Canby, Vincent. "Sally Field's 'Norma Rae' Is a Triumph." *New York Times* 11 Mar. 1975: 19+.
Candelaria, Cordelia. "Social Equity in Film Criticism." *Chicano Cinema: Research, Reviews, and Resources*. Ed. Gary D. Keller. Binghampton, NY: Bilingual Review/Press, 1985. 64–70.
Carden, Maren Lockwood. *The New Feminist Movement*. New York: Russell Sage, 1973.
Cargill, Jack. "Empire and Opposition: The 'Salt of the Earth' Strike." *Labor in New Mexico: Unions, Strikes, and Social History Since 1881*. Ed. Robert Kern. Albuquerque: University of New Mexico Press, 1983. 183–267.
Carson, Diane. "To Be Seen But Not Heard: *The Awful Truth*." *Multiple Voices in Feminist Film Criticism*. Ed. Diane Carson, Linda Dittmar, and Janice R. Welsch. Minneapolis: University of Minnesota, 1994. 213–225.
____, Linda Dittmar, and Janice R. Welsch, eds. *Multiple Voices in Feminist Film Criticism*. Minneapolis: University of Minnesota Press, 1994.
Ceplair, Larry, and Steven Englund. *The Inquisition in Hollywood: Politics in the Film Community 1930–1960*. Garden City, NY: Anchor Press/Doubleday, 1980.
Christensen, Terry. *Real Politics: American Political Movies from Birth of a Nation to Platoon*. New York: Basil Blackwell, 1997.
Churchill, Winston. "Sinews of Peace." Westminster College. Fulton, Missouri. 5 Mar. 1946. Online. George Washington University Speech and Transcript Center. Internet. 16 July 2001.
Cohan, Steven. "Case Study: Interpreting *Singin' In the Rain*." *Reinventing Film Studies*. Ed. Christine Gledhill and Linda Williams. New York: Oxford University Press. 53–75.
Collins, Jim. "Toward Defining a Matrix of the Musical Comedy: The Place of the Spectator Within the Textual Mechanisms." *Genre: The Musical*. Ed. Rick Altman. Boston: Routledge & Kegan Paul, 1981.
Condit, Celeste. "The Rhetorical Limits of Polysemy." *Critical Studies in Mass Communication* 6 (1989): 103–122.
Cook, Pam. "Border Crossings: Women and Film in Context." *Women and Film: A Sight and Sound Reader*. Eds. Pam Cook and Philip Dodd. Philadelphia: Temple University Press, 1993. ix–xxiii.
____. *Screening the Past: Memory and*

Nostalgia in Cinema. New York: Routledge, 2005.
_____. "Star Signs." *Screen* 20.3/4 (1980): 80–88.
Cowie, Jefferson. "Solidarity Strikes Out." *The American Prospect* 1–14 Jan. 2002: 41–45.
Crowdus, Gary. Rev. of *With Babies and Banners*, dir. Lorraine Gray. *Cineaste* 9 (Fall 1978): 43–45.
Crowther, Bosley. "'Salt of the Earth' Opens at the Grande — Filming Marked by Violence." Rev. of *Salt of the Earth*, dir. Herbert Biberman. *The New York Times* 15 Mar. 1954: 20.
Davin, Eric Leif. "Crystal Lee." *In These Times* 15–18 Mar. 1980: 16–17.
de Beauvoir, Simone. *The Second Sex*. Trans. and Ed. H.M. Parshley. New York: Vintage Books/Random House, 1952.
de Cordova, Richard. *Picture Personalities: The Emergence of the Star System in America*. Urbana: University of Illinois Press, 1990.
Dicker, Rory, and Alison Piepmeier, eds. *Catching a Wave: Reclaiming Feminism for the 21st Century*. Boston: Northeastern University Press, 2003.
Dittmar, Linda. "The Articulating Self: Difference as Resistance in *Black Girl*, *Ramparts of Clay*, and *Salt of the Earth*." *Multiple Voices in Feminist Film Criticism*. Ed. Diane Carson, Linda Dittmar, and Janice R. Welsch. Minneapolis: University of Minnesota, 1994. 391–405.
Doane, Mary Anne, Patricia Mellencamp, and Linda Williams. "Feminist Film Criticism: An Introduction." *Re-Vision: Essay in Feminist Film Criticism*. Ed. Mary Ann Doane, Patricia Mellencamp, and Linda Williams. Frederick, MD: University Publications of America, 1984. 1–17.
Doherty, Thomas. Rev. of *Erin Brockovich*, dir. Steven Soderbergh. *Cineaste* 25.3 (2000): 40.
Doherty, Tom. Rev. of *Silkwood*, dir. Mike Nichols. *Film Quarterly* 38.4 (1984): 24–26.
Dollinger, Sol, and Genora Johnson Dollinger. *Not Automatic: Women and the Left in the Forging of the Auto Workers' Union*. New York: Monthly Review Press, 2000.
Dow, Bonnie. *Prime-Time Feminism: Television, Media Culture, and the Women's Movement Since 1970*. Philadelphia: University of Pennsylvania Press, 1996.
Dowdy, Andrew. *The Films of the Fifties: The American State of Mind*. New York: William Morrow, 1973.
Dyer, Richard. *Heavenly Bodies: Film Stars and Society*. New York: St. Martin's Press, 1986.
_____. *Stars*. Rev. ed. London: British Film Institute, 1999.
Ebert, Roger. Rev. of *Live Nude Girls Unite!*, dir. Julia Query and Vicky Funari. *Chicago Sun Times* 22 Jun. 2001. Online. Internet. 23 Mar. 2002. Available URL: http://www.suntimes.com/ebert/ebert_reviews/2001/06/062205.html.
Eckert, Charles. "Shirley Temple and the House of Rockefeller." *Stardom: Industry of Desire*. Ed. Christine Gledhill. New York: Routledge, 1991. 60–73.
Ellis, Jack C. *The Documentary Idea: A Critical History of English-Language Documentary Film and Video*. Englewood Cliffs, NJ: Prentice-Hall, 1989.
_____. *A History of Film*. Englewood Cliffs, NJ: Prentice-Hall, 1979.
Elsaesser, Thomas. "Tales of Sound and Fury." *Monogram* 4 (1972): 2–15.
Ephron, Nora. "The Tie That Binds." *The Nation* 6 Apr. 1992: 453–455.
Erens, Patricia. "Women's Documentary Filmmaking: The Personal Is Political." *New Challenges for Documentary*. Ed. Alan Rosenthal. Berkeley: University of California Press, 1988. 554–555.
Erin Brockovich. Dir. Steven Soderbergh. Perf. Julia Roberts, Albert Finney, Aaron Eckhart. Universal Pictures and Columbia Pictures, 2000.
Faludi, Susan. *Backlash: The Undeclared War Against American Women*. New York: Crown Publishers, 1991.
"Fear Reads May Season 'Salt of the Earth' With Paprika in Foreign Showings." *Variety* 17 Mar. 1954: 1+.
Fehr, Richard, and Frederick G. Vogel. *Lullabies of Hollywood: The Movie Music and the Movie Musical, 1915–1992*. Jefferson, North Carolina: McFarland, 1993.
Feuer, Jane. *The Hollywood Musical*. 2nd ed. London: The Macmillan Press, 1993.

Findlen, Barbara, ed. *Listen Up: Voices from the Next Feminist Generation*. Emeryville, CA: Seal Press, 1995.

Fine, Sidney. *Sit-down: The General Motors Strike of 1936–1937*. Ann Arbor: The University of Michigan Press, 1969.

Flynn, Elizabeth Gurley. "What 'Salt of the Earth' Means to Me." *Political Affairs* 33 (June 1954): 63–65.

Foster, James C., ed. *American Labor in the Southwest: The First One Hundred Years*. Tucson: University of Arizona Press, 1982.

Freeman, Jo. "The Origins of the Women's Movement." *American Journal of Sociology* 78 (1973): 124–132.

French, Brandon. *On the Verge of Revolt: Women in American Films of the Fifties*. New York: Frederick Ungar, 1978.

Fried, Richard M. *Nightmare in Red: The McCarthy Era in Perspective*. New York: Oxford University Press, 1990.

Friedlander, Mira. Rev. of *The Pajama Game* stage play, dir. Simon Callow. *Variety* 17 May 1999.

Garafola, Lynn. "Hollywood and the Myth of the Working Class." *Radical America* 14 (1980): 7–15.

Gelb, Alan. *The Doris Day Scrapbook*. New York: Grosset & Dunlap, 1977.

Georgakas, Dan. "Union-Sponsored Radical Films." *Encyclopedia of the American Left*. Ed. Mari Jo Buhle, Paul Buhle, and Dan Georgakas, 2nd ed. New York: Oxford University Press, 1998.

Geraghty, Christine. "Re-examining Stardom: Questions of Texts, Bodies, and Performance." *Reinventing Film Studies*. Ed. Christine Gledhill and Linda Williams. New York: Oxford University Press. 183–202.

Gilliatt, Penelope. "About Rebellion: Two Fine Documentaries." *The New Yorker* 16 May 1977: 97–98.

———. Rev. of *Norma Rae*, dir. Martin Ritt. *The New Yorker* 19 Mar. 1979: 128.

Gilmore, Geoff. "The State of Independent Film." *National Forum* 77.4 (1997): 10–12.

Gledhill, Christine. "Developments in Feminist Film Criticism." *Re-Vision: Essays in Feminist Film Criticism*. Ed. Mary Ann Doane, Patricia Mellencamp, and Linda Williams. Frederick, MD: University Publications of America, 1984. 18–47.

———. *Home is Where the Heart Is: Studies in Melodrama and the Women's Film*. London: BFI, 1987.

———. "Introduction." *Stardom: Industry of Desire*. Ed. Christine Gledhill. New York: Routledge, 1991. xiii–xx.

———. "Image and Voice: Approaches to Marxist-Feminist Film Criticism." *Multiple Voices in Feminist Film Criticism*. Ed. Diane Carson, Linda Dittmar, and Janice R. Welsch (Minneapolis: University of Minnesota, 1994. 109–123.

———. "Pleasurable Negotiations." *Female Spectators*. Ed. Deidre Pribram. New York: Verso, 1988. 64–89.

———. "Signs of Melodrama." *Stardom: Industry of Desire*. Ed. Christine Gledhill. New York: Routledge, 1991. 207–232.

Gomery, Douglas. *The Hollywood Studio System*. New York: St. Martin's, 1986.

Gómez-Quiñones, Juan. *Mexican American Labor, 1790–1990*. Albuquerque: University of New Mexico Press, 1994.

Gordon, Linda. "*Union Maids*: Working Class Heroines." *Jump-Cut* 14 (1977): 34–35.

———. "What's New in Women's History." *Feminist Studies Critical Studies*. Ed. Teresa de Lauretis. Bloomington: Indiana University Press, 1986.

Gordon, Suzanne. "Silkwood On-Screen: Rebel Without a Cause?" *Ms*. Feb. 1984: 30–32.

Grant, Susannah. *Erin Brockovich: The Shooting Script*. New York: Newmarket Press, 2000.

Green, Philip. *Cracks in the Pedestal: Ideology and Gender in Hollywood*. Amherst: University of Massachusetts Press, 1998.

Griing-Pemble, Lisa M., and Diane M. Blair. "Best-Selling Feminisms: The Rhetorical Production of Popular Press Feminists' Romantic Quest." *Communication Quarterly* 48 (2001): 360–379.

Guthman, Edward. "Union Activists Uncovered in 'Girls': Stripper Turns Her Advocacy into a Labor of Love." Rev. of *Live Nude Girls Unite!*, dir. Julia Query and Vicki Funari. *San Francisco Chronicle* 1 Oct. 2000: 61.

Guynn, William. *A Cinema of Nonfiction*. London: Associated University Presses, 1990.

Harris, Thomas. "The Building of Popular

Images: Grace Kelley and Marilyn Monroe." *Stardom: Industry of Desire.* Ed. Christine Gledhill. New York: Routledge, 1991. 40–44.

Haskell, Molly. *From Reverence to Rape: The Treatment of Women in the Movies.* 2nd ed. Chicago: The University of Chicago Press, 1987.

———. *Holding My Own in No Man's Land: Women and Men and Film and Feminists.* New York: Oxford University Press, 1997.

Hershfield, Joanne. *Mexican Cinema/Mexican Woman, 1940–1950.* Tucson: The University of Arizona Press, 1996.

Heywood, Leslie, and Jennifer Drake, eds. *Third Wave Agenda: Being Feminist, Doing Feminism.* Minneapolis: University of Minnesota Press, 1997.

Hitchens, Gordon. "Notes on a Blacklisted Film: 'Salt of the Earth.'" *Film Culture* 50–51 (1970): 79–81.

Hoff-Sommers, Christina. *Who Stole Feminism? How Women Have Betrayed Women.* New York: Touchstone, 1994.

Hoffer, Tom W., and Richard Alan Nelson. "Docudrama on American TV." *Journal of the University Film Association* 30.2 (1978): 20–23.

Hogeland, Lisa Marie. "Fear of Feminism: Why Young Women Get the Willies." *Ms.* (November-December 1994): 18–21.

Hotchner, A. E. *Doris Day: Her Own Story.* New York: William Morrow and Company, 1976.

Jackson, Carlton. *Picking Up the Tab: The Life and Movies of Martin Ritt.* Bowling Green, OH: Bowling Green State University Popular Press, 1994.

Jacobs, Diane. *Hollywood Renaissance.* South Brunswick, NJ: A. S. Barnes, 1977.

Jacobs, Lea, and Richard de Cordova. "Spectacle and Narrative Theory." *Quarterly Review of Film Studies* 7 (1982): 293–302.

Jacobs, Lewis. *The Documentary Tradition.* 2nd ed. New York: W. W. Norton & Co, 1979. 516–517.

James, David and Rick Berg, eds. *The Hidden Foundation: Cinema and the Question of Class.* Minneapolis: University of Minnesota Press, 1996.

Jarrico, Paul, and Herbert Biberman. "Breaking Ground: The Making of *Salt of the Earth."* *Celluloid Power: Social Film Criticism from The Birth of a Nation to Judgment at Nuremberg.* Ed. David Platt. Metuchen, NJ: The Scarecrow Press, 1992. 478–484.

"Jarrico Sees 'Illegal Conspiracy' Vs. 'Salt'; To Sue Solons, Pixites," *Variety* 29 July 1953: 19.

Jeffords, Susan. *Hard Bodies: Hollywood Masculinity in the Reagan Era.* New Brunswick, NJ: Rutgers University Press, 1994.

Johnston, Claire. "Introduction." *Notes on Women's Cinema.* Ed. Claire Johnston. London: Society for Education in Film and Television, 1973. 2–4.

———. "Women's Cinema as Counter-Cinema." *Notes on Women's Cinema.* Ed. Claire Johnston. London: Society for Education in Film and Television, 1973. 24–31.

Johnston, Eric. "Utopia is Production." *Screen Actor* 14 (April 1946): 7.

Jones, Dorothy B. "Communism in the Movies: A Study of Film Content." *Report on Blacklisting: Vol. I — the Movies.* John Cogley. New York: Fund for the Republic, 1956. 196–233.

Jowett, Garth. *Film: The Democratic Art.* Boston: Little, Brown, 1976.

Juhasz, Alexandra. "They Said We Were Trying to Show Reality — All I Want to Show Is My Video: The Politics of the Realist Feminist Documentary." *Collecting Visible Evidence.* Ed. Jane M. Gaines and Michael Renov. Minneapolis: University of Minnesota Press, 1999. 190–215.

Kael, Pauline. *I Lost It At the Movies.* Boston: Little, Brown, 1965.

———. Interview. *Weekend Edition.* Natl. Public Radio. WHYY, Philadelphia. 9 March 1991.

Kaplan, E. Ann. "The Case of the Missing Mother: Maternal Issues in Vidor's *Stella Dallas." Feminism and Film.* Ed. E. Ann Kaplan. New York: Oxford University Press, 2000. 466–478.

———. *Looking for the Other: Feminism, Film, and the Imperial Gaze.* New York: Routledge, 1997.

———. "Theories and Strategies of the Feminist Documentary." *New Challenges for Documentary.* Ed. Alan Rosenthal. Berkeley: University of California Press, 1988. 78–102.

_____. "Theory and Practice of the Realist Documentary Form in *Harlan County, U.S.A.*" *"Show Us Life": Toward a History and Aesthetics of the Committed Documentary.* Ed. Thomas Waugh. Metuchen, NJ: The Scarecrow Press, 1984. 212–222.

_____. *Women and Film: Both Sides of the Camera.* New York: Methuen, 1983.

Kasdan, Margo. "'Why Are You Afraid to Have Me at Your Side?': From Passivity to Power in *Salt of the Earth*." *The Voyage In: Fictions of Female Development.* Ed. Elizabeth Abel, Marianne Hirsch, and Elizabeth Langland. Hanover, NH: University Press of New England, 1983. 258–351.

Keller, Gary D. *Hispanics and United States Film: An Overview and Handbook.* Tempe, AZ: Bilingual Review/Press, 1994.

_____. "The Image of the Chicano In Mexican, United States, and Chicano Cinema: An Overview." *Chicano Cinema: Research, Reviews, and Resources.* Ed. Gary D. Keller. Binghampton, NY: Bilingual Review/Press, 1985. 13–58.

Kellner, Douglas. *Media Culture: Cultural Studies, Identity and Politics Between the Modern and the Postmodern* (New York: Routledge, 1995): 2.

Kemp, Sandra, and Judith Squires, eds. *Feminisms.* New York: Oxford University Press, 1997.

Kernan, Lisa. "'Keep Marching, Sisters': The Second Generation Looks at *Salt of the Earth*." *Nuestro* 9 (May 1985): 23–25.

King, Barry. "Articulating Stardom." *Stardom: Industry of Desire.* Ed. Christine Gledhill. New York: Routledge, 1991. 167–182.

King, Loren. "Life, Love, Labor at the Lusty Lady." Rev. of *Live Nude Girls Unite!*, dir. Julia Query and Vicki Funari. *Boston Globe* 19 Jan. 2001: D8.

King, Noel. "Recent 'Political Documentary': Notes on 'Union Maids' and 'Harlan County, USA.'" *Screen* 22.2 (1981): 7–18.

Kingsolver, Barbara. *Holding the Line: Women in the Great Arizona Mine Strike of 1983.* Ithaca: IRL Press, 1989.

Kinser, Amber E. "Negotiating Spaces For/Through Third-Wave Feminism." *NWSA Journal* 16.3 (2004): 147.

Klevan, Andrew. *Film Performance: From Achievement to Appreciation.* New York: Wallflower Press, 2005.

Kolker, Robert Phillip. *A Cinema of Loneliness.* 2nd ed. New York: Oxford University Press, 1988.

Kozloff, Sarah. *Invisible Storytellers: Voice-Over Narration in American Fiction Film.* Berkeley: University of California Press, 1988.

Kroll, Jack. Rev. of *Silkwood*, dir. Mike Nichols. *Newsweek* 12 Dec. 1983: 108.

Kuhn, Annette. *Women's Pictures: Feminism and Cinema.* 2nd ed. New York: Verso, 1994.

Lafferty, William. "A Reappraisal of the Semi-Documentary in Hollywood, 1945–1948." *The Velvet Light Trap* 20 (1983): 22–26.

Lawrence, Amy. *Echo and Narcissus: Women's Voices in Classical Hollywood Cinema.* Berkeley: University of California Press, 1991.

Lawson, John Howard. *Film in the Battle of Ideas.* New York: Masses and Mainstream, 1953.

Leab, Daniel J. "'The Iron Curtain' (1948): Hollywood's First Cold War Movie." *Historical Journal of Film, Radio and Television* 8 (1988): 153–181.

_____. "Writing History With Film: Two Views of the 1937 Strike Against General Motors By the UAW." *Labor History* 21 (1979–1980): 102–112.

Lesage, Julia, et al. "New Day's Way." *Jump Cut* 9 (1975): 21–22.

_____. "The Political Aesthetics of the Feminist Documentary Film." *Issues in Feminist Film Criticism.* Ed. Patricia Erens. Bloomington: Indiana University Press, 1990. 222–237.

Lev, Peter. *American Films of the 70s: Conflicting Visions.* Austin: University of Texas Press, 2000.

Liefermann, Henry P. *Crystal Lee: A Woman of Inheritance.* New York: Macmillan Publishing, 1975.

Lipkin, Steve. "Defining Docudrama: *In the Name of the Father*, *Schindler's List*, and *JFK*." *Why Docudrama? Fact-Fiction on Film and TV.* Ed. Alan Rosenthal. Carbondale: Southern Illinois University Press, 1999. 370–383.

Lipsitz, George. "Herbert Biberman and the Art of Subjectivity." *Telos* 32 (1977): 174–182.

Live Nude Girls Unite! Dir. Julia Query and Vicki Funari. Perf. Julia Query and workers at the Lusty Lady. First Run Features, 2000.

Live Nude Girls Unite! website. Online. Internet. 23 Mar. 2002. Available URL: http://www.livenudegirlsunite.com

Lorence, James J. *The Suppression of Salt of the Earth: How Hollywood, Big Labor, and Politicians Blacklisted a Movie in Cold War America.* Albuquerque: The University of New Mexico Press, 1999.

Lynd, Alice, and Staughton Lynd, eds. *Rank and File: Personal Histories by Working-Class Organizers.* Boston: Beacon Press, 1973.

Macdonald, Dwight. *On Movies.* New York: Berkeley-Medallion Edition, 1971.

Mackey-Kallis, Susan. *Oliver Stone's America: "Dreaming the Myth Outward."* Boulder, CO: Westview Press, 1996.

Maltby, Richard. "Made for Each Other: The Melodrama of Hollywood and the House Committees on Un-American Activities, 1947." *Cinema, Politics, and Society in America.* Ed. Philip Davies and Brian Neve. Manchester: Manchester University, 1981.

Marcus, Millicent. *Italian Film and the Light of Neorealism.* Princeton: Princeton University Press, 1986.

Margolies, Ken. "Silver Screen Tarnishes Unions: Hollywood Movies Have Given Workers a Black Eye." *Screen Actor* 23 (1981): 43–52.

Martineau, Barbara Halpern. "Talking About Our Lives and Experiences: Some Thoughts About Feminism, Documentary and 'Talking Heads.'" *Show Us Life": Toward a History and Aesthetics of the Committed Documentary.* Ed. Thomas Waugh. Metuchen, NJ: The Scarecrow Press, 1984. 252–273.

Mast, Gerald. *Can't Help Singin': The American Musical on Stage and Screen.* Woodstock, NY: The Overlook Press, 1987.

_____, and Bruce F. Kawin. *A Short History of the Movies.* 6th ed. Boston: Allyn and Bacon, 1996.

Matthew-Walker, Robert. *From Broadway to Hollywood: The Musical and the Cinema.* London: Sanctuary Publishing, 1996.

Mattina, Anne. "'Rights as Well as Duties': The Rhetoric of Leonora O'Reilly." *Communication Quarterly* 42 (1994): 196–205.

May, Larry. "Movie Star Politics: The Screen Actors' Guild, Cultural Conversion, and the Hollywood Red Scare." *Recasting America: Culture and Politics in the Age of the Cold War.* Ed. Larry May. Chicago: University of Chicago Press, 1989. 125–153.

Mayne, Judith. *Cinema and Spectatorship.* New York: Routledge, 1993.

_____. "Feminist Film Theory and Criticism." *Multiple Voices in Feminist Film Criticism.* Ed. Diane Carson, Linda Dittmar, and Janice R. Welsch. Minneapolis: University of Minnesota Press, 1994. 48–64.

_____. "Review Essay: Feminist Film Theory and Criticism." *Signs* 11 (1985): 81–100.

_____. "Visibility and Feminist Film Criticism." *Film Reader* 5 (1982): 120–124.

_____. *The Woman at the Keyhole: Feminism and Women's Cinema.* Bloomington: Indiana University Press, 1990.

Mayo, Anna. "Cashing In on Karen." *Village Voice* 21 Feb. 1984: 28+.

McCarthy, Patrick. "*Salt of the Earth*: Convention and Invention of the Domestic Melodrama." *Rendezvous: Journal of Arts and Letters* 19 (1983): 22–32.

McCormick, Ruth. Rev. of *Salt of the Earth*, dir. Herbert Biberman. *Cineaste* 5 (Fall 1973): 53–55.

_____. Rev. of *Union Maids*, dir. Julia Reichert, James Klein, and Miles Mogulescu. *Cineaste* 8 (Summer 1977): 50–51.

_____. "Women's Liberation Cinema." *The Documentary Tradition.* Ed. Lewis Jacobs, 2nd ed. New York: W.W. Norton & Co., 1979.

McGarry, Eileen. "Documentary, Realism and Women's Cinema." *Women and Film* 2 (1975): 50–59.

McLean, Adrienne L. *Being Rita Hayworth: Labor, Identity and Hollywood Stardom.* New Brunswick: Rutgers University Press, 2004.

McRobbie, Angela. "Post-feminism and Popular Culture." *Feminist Media Studies* 4.3 (2004): 255–264.

Medhurst, Martin J., and Thomas W. Benson, eds. *Rhetorical Dimensions In Media: A Critical Casebook*. 2nd ed. Dubuque: Kendall/Hunt, 1991. 443–445.

Mellencamp, Patricia. "Spectacle and Spectator: Looking through the American Musical Comedy." *Ciné-tracts* 1 (1977): 27–35.

Michel, Sonya. "Feminism, Film, and Public History." *Issues in Feminist Film Criticism*. Ed. Patricia Erens. Bloomington: Indiana University Press, 1990. 238–249.

Miller, Gabriel. *The Films of Martin Ritt: Fanfare for the Common Man*. Jackson: University Press of Mississippi, 2000.

Miller, Tom. "Class Reunion: *Salt of the Earth* Revisited." *Cineaste* 13.3 (1984): 31–36.

_____. Rev. of *The Suppression of Salt of the Earth: How Hollywood, Big Labor, and Politicians Blacklisted a Movie in Cold War America*, by James J. Lorence. *Cineaste* 25.3 (2000): 59–60.

Monroy, Douglas. "Fence Cutters, Sedicioso, and First-Class Citizens: Mexican Radicalism in America." *The Immigrant Left in the United States*. Ed. Paul Buhle and Dan Georgakas. Albany: State University of New York Press, 1996. 11–44.

Mora, Carl J. *Mexican Cinema: Reflections of a Society 1896–1988*. Rev. ed. Berkeley: University of California Press, 1989.

Mordden, Ethan. *Movie Star: A Look at the Women Who Made Hollywood*. New York: St. Martin's Press, 1983.

Morgenstern, Joe. "'Erin Brockovich' Has Both Beauty and Brains." Rev. of *Erin Brockovich*, dir. Steven Soderbergh. The Wall Street Journal 17 Mar. 2000: W1.

Morris, Peter. "*Salt of the Earth*." *Celluloid Power: Social Film Criticism from The Birth of a Nation to Judgment at Nuremberg*. Ed. David Platt. Metuchen, NJ: The Scarecrow Press, 1992. 485–490.

Morris, Wesley. "Roberts Is Sassy, Brassy in 'Erin.'" Rev. of *Erin Brockovich*, dir. Steven Soderbergh. San Francisco Examiner, 17 Mar. 2000. Online. Internet. 23 Mar. 2002. Available URL: http://www.sfgate.com/cgi-bin/artcle.cgi?f=/e/a/2000/03/17/WEEKEND6120.dtl

Mulvey, Laura. "Visual Pleasure and Narrative Cinema." *Issues in Feminist Film Criticism*. Ed. Patricia Erens. Bloomington: Indiana University Press, 1990. 28–40.

Musser, Charles, and Robert Sklar. "Introduction." *Resisting Images: Essays on Cinema and History*. Ed. Robert Sklar and Charles Musser. Philadelphia: Temple University Press, 1990. 3–11.

Neve, Brian. *Film and Politics in America: A Social Tradition*. New York: Routledge, 1992.

Nichols, Bill. *Introduction to Documentary*. Bloomington: Indiana University Press, 2001.

_____. *Representing Reality: Issues and Concepts in Documentary*. Bloomington: Indiana University Press, 1991.

Nielsen, Mike, and Gene Mailes. *Hollywood's Other Blacklist: Union Struggles in the Hollywood System*. London: British Film Institute, 1995.

Noriega, Chon, ed. *Chicanos and Film: Essay on Chicano Representation and Resistance*. New York: Garland, 1992.

Noriega, Chon. "Citizen Chicano: The Trials and Titillations of Ethnicity in the American Cinema, 1935–1962." *Social Research* 58 (1991): 413–438.

Norma Rae. Dir. Martin Ritt. Perf. Sally Field, Ron Liebman, Beau Bridges. Twentieth Century–Fox, 1979.

North Country. Dir. Nikki Caro. Perf. Charlize Theron, Woody Harrelson, Frances McDormand, Sissy Spacek. Warner Brothers, 2005.

O'Brien, Tom. "Uncertain Verdict: 'Silkwood.'" Rev. of *Silkwood*, dir. Mike Nichols. *Commonweal* 9 Mar. 1984: 146–147.

Ogintz, Eileen. "The Strike That Made Labor History." *Chicago Tribune* 19 Oct. 1978: 1+.

One of the Hollywood Ten. Dir. Karl Francis. Perf. Jeff Goldblum and Greta Scacchi. Alibi Films International, 2000.

The Pajama Game. Dir. George Abbott and Stanley Donen. Perf. Doris Day, John Raitt, Eddie Foy Jr., Carol Haney. Warner Bros., 1957.

Paul, Jasmine, and Bette J. Kauffman. "Missing Persons: Working-Class Women and the Movies, 1940–1990." *Feminism, Multiculturalism, and the Media: Global Diversities*. Ed. Angharad N. Valdivia. Thousand Oaks, CA: Sage, 1995. 163–184.

Plantinga, Carl R. *Rhetoric and Representation in Nonfiction Film*. New York: Cambridge University Press, 1997.

Powers, Stephen, David J. Rothman, and Stanley Rothman. *Hollywood's America: Social and Political Themes in Motion Pictures.* Boulder, CO: Westview Press, 1996.

Prince, Stephen. "Political Film in the Nineties." *Film Genre 2000: New Critical Essays.* Ed. Wheeler Winston Dixon. Albany: State University of New York Press, 2000. 63–76.

Puette, William J. *Through Jaundiced Eyes: How the Media View Organized Labor.* Ithaca: IRL Press, 1992.

Puig, Claudia. "Declarations of Independents at the Sundance Film Festival." *USA Today* 21 Jan. 1999. *USAToday.com.* Online. 29 Mar. 2002.

Rabinowitz, Paula. *They Must Be Represented: The Politics of Documentary.* New York: Verso, 1994.

Ray, Robert B. *A Certain Tendency of the Hollywood Cinema, 1930–1980.* Princeton: Princeton University Press, 1985.

"Real Life Norma Rae Feels Snubbed By Field." *Variety* 14 Aug. 1985: 2.

"Reds in the Desert." *Newsweek* 2 Mar. 1953: 27–28.

Reichert, Julia, and James Klein. "Union Maids." *The Documentary Conscience: A Casebook in Filmmaking.* Ed. Alan Rosenthal. Berkeley: University of California Press, 1980.

Renov, Michael, ed. *Theorizing Documentary.* New York: Routledge, 1993.

Return of the Secaucus 7. Dir. John Sayles. Perf. Mark Arnott, Gordon Clapp, Maggie Cousineau-Arndt. Libra/Specialty, 1980.

Rev. of *The Pajama Game,* dir. George Abbott and Stanley Donen. *Time* 9 Sept. 1957: 110.

Rev. of *With Babies and Banners,* dir. Lorraine Gray. *Variety* 11 Apr. 1979: 34.

Reverby, Susan. "'With Babies and Banners': A Review." *Radical America* 13.5 (1979): 63–69.

Riambau, Esteve, and Casimiro Torreiro. "This Film Is Going to Make History: An Interview with Rosaura Revueltas." *Cineaste* 19 (December 1992): 50–51.

Rich, B. Ruby. *Chick Flicks: Theories and Memories of the Feminist Film Movement.* Durham, Duke University Press, 1998.

_____. "In the Name of Feminist Film Criticism." *Issues in Feminist Film Criticism.* Ed. Patricia Erens. Bloomington: Indiana University Press, 1990. 268–287.

Roberts, Shari. "'The Lady in the Tutti-Frutti Hat': Carmen Miranda, A Spectacle of Ethnicity." *Cinema Journal* 32.3 (1993): 3–23.

Robinson, Lillian S. "Out of the Mine and into the Canyon: Working-Class Feminism, Yesterday and Today." *The Hidden Foundation: Cinema and the Question of Class.* Ed. David E. James and Rick Berg. Minneapolis: University of Minnesota Press, 1996. 172–192.

Roffman, Peter, and Jim Purdy. *The Hollywood Social Problem Film: Madness, Despair, and Politics from the Depression to the Fifties.* Bloomington: Indiana University Press, 1981.

Roiphe, Katie. *The Morning After: Sex, Fear and Feminism on Campus.* Boston: Little, Brown, 1993.

Rosen, Marjorie. *Popcorn Venus: Women, Movies and the American Dream.* New York: Coward, McCann & Geoghegan, 1973.

Rosenberg, Jan. *Women's Reflections: The Feminist Film Movement.* Ann Arbor, MI: UMI Research Press, 1983.

Rosenfelt, Deborah Silverton. *Salt of the Earth.* Old Westbury, NY: The Feminist Press, 1978.

Rosenthal, Alan, ed. *The Documentary Conscience: A Casebook in Filmmaking.* Berkeley: University of California Press, 1980.

_____, and John Corner, eds. *New Challenges for Documentary.* Berkeley: University of California Press, 1988.

Ross, Steven J. *Working-Class Hollywood: Silent Film and the Shaping of Class in America.* Princeton: Princeton University Press, 1998.

Ruiz, Vicki L. *From Out of the Shadows: Mexican Women in Twentieth-Century America.* New York: Oxford University Press, 1998.

Ryan, Michael, and Douglas Kellner. *Camera Politica: The Politics and Ideology of Contemporary Hollywood Film.* Bloomington: Indiana University Press, 1988.

"Salt & Pepper." Rev. of *Salt of the Earth,* dir. Herbert Biberman. *Time* 29 Mar. 1954: 92.

Salt of the Earth. Dir. Herbert Biberman. Perf. Rosuara Revueltas and Juan Chacón. Independent Production Company, 1954.

"'Salt'—One Brand." Rev. of *Salt of the Earth*, dir. Herbert Biberman. *Newsweek* 29 Mar. 1954: 87.

Sawyer, Charles. Rev. of *Silkwood*, dir. Mike Nichols. *Films in Review* Mar. 1984: 178.

Sayre, Nora. *Running Time: Films of the Cold War.* New York: The Dial Press, 1978.

Scheuer, Philip K. "Fast, Furious Musical Film Made of Stage Hit." Rev. of *The Pajama Game*, dir. George Abbott and Stanley Donen. *Los Angeles Times* 30 Aug. 1957: 6.

Schickel, Richard. Rev. of *Silkwood*, dir. Mike Nichols. *Time* 19 Dec. 1983: 73.

———. "Strike Busting." *Time* 12 Mar. 1979: 76.

Schumach, Murray. *The Face on the Cutting Room Floor: The Story of Movie and Television Censorship.* New York: Harper and Row, 1964.

Schuth, H. Wayne. *Mike Nichols.* Boston: Twayne, 1978.

Scott, A. O. "Throw Off the Yoke, But Keep the G-String." Rev. of *Live Nude Girls Unite!*, dir. Julia Query and Vicki Funari. *The New York Times* 20 Oct. 2000: E17.

Shochat, Ella, and Robert Stam. "The Cinema After Babel: Language, Difference, Power." *Screen* 26.3 (1985): 35–58.

Shugart, Helene A., Catherine Egley Waggoner, and D. Lynn O'Brien Hallstein, "Mediating Third-Wave Feminism: Appropriation as Postmodern Media Practice." *Critical Studies in Media Communication* 18 (2001): 194–210.

"Silver City Troubles." *Newsweek* 16 Mar. 1953: 43–44.

Silkwood. Dir. Mike Nichols. Perf. Meryl Streep, Kurt Russell, Cher. Twentieth Century-Fox, 1983.

Sklar, Robert. *Movie-Made America: A Cultural History of American Movies.* Rev. ed. New York: Vintage Books, 1994.

Sorlin, Pierre. *Italian National Cinema 1896–1996.* New York: Routledge, 1996.

Stacey, Jackie. "Feminine Fascinations: Forms of Identification in Star-Audience Relations." *Stardom: Industry of Desire.* Ed. Christine Gledhill. New York: Routledge, 1991. 141–163.

Stam, Robert, and Louise Spence. "Colonialism, Racism and Representation." *Screen* 24.2 (1983): 2–20.

Stead, Peter. *Film and the Working Class: The Feature Film in British and American Society.* New York: Routledge, 1989.

Stern, Leslie. "Feminism and Cinema-Exchanges." *Screen* 20.3/4 (1980): 89–105.

Sterritt, David. Rev. of *Silkwood*, dir. Mike Nichols. *Christian Science Monitor* 5 Jan. 1984: 24.

Stone, Elizabeth. "'Norma Rae': The Story They Could Have Told." *Ms.* May 1979: 28–33.

Stricker, Frank. "Hollywood Meets the Unions." *New Labor Review* 2 (Fall 1978): 111–118.

Strope, Leigh. "Organized Labor Setbacks Could Provide Opportunity." *Delaware County Daily Times* 3 Sept. 2001: 15.

Suber, Howard. "Politics and Popular Culture: Hollywood at Bay, 1933–1953." *American Jewish History* 68 (1979): 517–533.

Susan, Barbara. "About My Consciousness Raising." *Voices from Women's Liberation.* Ed. Leslie B. Tanner. New York: Signet, 1970. 238–243.

Sutton, Martin. "Patterns of Meaning in the Musical." *Genre: The Musical.* Ed. Rick Altman. Boston: Routledge & Kegan Paul, 1981.

Tasker, Yvonne. *Working Girls: Gender and Sexuality in Popular Cinema.* New York: Routledge, 1998.

Taubin, Amy. "Peep Shows and Prison Showmanship." Rev. of *Live Nude Girls Unite!*, dir. Julia Query and Vicki Funari. *The Village Voice* 24 Oct. 2000: 146.

Taylor, Clarke. "Film Shorts Spark N.Y. Festival." *L.A. Times* October 9, 1978: 19.

———. "The On-Camera, Off-Camera Drama of Crystal Lee Jordan." *L. A. Times* 4 Mar. 1979, calendar: 5.

Thomas, Paul. "'I Could Have Been A Contender': Hollywood Discovers the Working Class?" *Film Library Quarterly* 12 (1979): 58–63.

Thornham, Sue, ed. *Feminist Film Theory: A Reader.* Washington Square, New York: New York University Press, 1999.

Tonn, Mari Boor. "Militant Motherhood: Labor's Mary Harris 'Mother' Jones." *The Quarterly Journal of Speech* 82 (1996): 1–21.

Toplin, Robert Brent. *History by Hollywood: The Use and Abuse of the American Past.* Urbana: University of Illinois Press, 1996.

Traube, Elizabeth G. *Dreaming Identities: Class, Gender, and Generation in the 1980s Hollywood Movies.* Boulder, CO: Westview Press, 1992.

Travers, Peter. Rev. of *Erin Brockovich*, dir. Steven Soderbergh. *Rolling Stone.com.* Online. 30 Mar. 2002.

Tribe, Keith. "History and the Production of Memories." *Screen* 18.4 (1978): 9–23.

Turan, Kenneth. "Doris Finally Gets Her Day." *The Los Angeles Times* 18 Jan. 2001: 6.

____. "The Smile Wins the Day." *The Los Angeles Times* 17 Mar. 2000. *latimes.com.* Internet. 23 Mar. 2002.

Union Maids. Dir. Julia Reichert, James Klein, and Miles Mogulescu. Perf. Stella Nowicki, Sylvia Woods, and Christine (Kate) Ellis. New Day Films, 1976.

Vasby Anderson, Karen, and Jessie Stewart, "Politics and the Single Woman: The 'Sex and the City Voter' in Campaign 2004." *Rhetoric and Public Affairs* 8.4 (2005): 595–616.

Vavrus, Mary Douglas. *Postfeminst News: Political Women in Media Culture.* Albany: State University of New York Press, 2002.

Vorse, Mary Heaton. *Labor's New Millions.* New York: Arno & The New York Times, 1969.

Waldman, Diane, and Janet Walker, eds. *Feminism and Documentary.* Minneapolis: University of Minnesota Press, 1999.

Walker, Rebeccda, ed. *To Be Real.* New York: Anchor Books, 1995.

Walsh, Andrea S. *Women's Film and Female Experience 1940–1950.* New York: Praeger, 1984.

Walsh, Frank R. "The Films We Never Saw: American Movies View Organized Labor, 1934–1954." *Labor History* 27 (1986): 564–580.

Wandersee, Winifred D. *On the Move: American Women in the 1970s.* Boston: Twayne Publishers, 1988.

Warren, Charles, ed. *Beyond Document: Essays on Nonfiction Film.* Hanover: University Press of New England, 1996.

White, Jerry. "Union Membership in U.S. at Lowest Level in 60 Years." *World Socialist Web Site.* 26 Feb. 2001. Online. Internet. 24 Mar. 2002. Available URL: http://www.wsws.org/articles/2001/feb 2001/afl-f26.shtml.

Wiener, David Jon. "*Silkwood.*" Rev. of *Silkwood*, dir. Mike Nichols. *American Cinematographer* (February 1984): 50–54.

Williams, Linda. "'Something Else Besides a Mother': *Stella Dallas* and the Maternal Melodrama." *Feminism and Film.* Ed. E. Ann Kaplan. New York: Oxford University Press, 2000. 479–504.

____. "Type and Stereotype: Chicano Images in Film." *Chicano Cinema: Research, Reviews, and Resources.* Ed. Gary D. Keller. Binghampton, NY: Bilingual Review/Press, 1985. 59–63.

With Babies and Banners. Dir. Lorraine Gray. Perf. Genora Johnson and members of the Women's Emergency Brigade. New Day Films, 1978.

Wolf, Naomi. *Fire with Fire: The New Female Power and How It Will Change the 21st Century.* New York: Random House, 1993.

Wolf, Stacy. *A Problem Like Maria: Gender and Sexuality in the American Musical.* Ann Arbor: The University of Michigan Press, 2002.

Wood, Sura. "Lusty Ladies." *SF Weekly* 26 April–2 May, 2000. Live Nude Girls Unite! website. Online. Internet. 23 Mar. 2002. Available URL: http://www.livenudegirlsunite.com.

Youdelman, Jeffrey. "Narration, Invention, & History: A Documentary Dilemma." *Cineaste* 7.2 (1982): 9–15.

Zaniello, Tom. *Working Stiffs, Union Maids, Reds, and Riffraff.* Ithaca: IRL Press, 1996.

Zieger, Gay P., and Robert H. Zieger. "Unions on the Silver Screen: A Review Essay on *F.I.S.T., Blue Collar,* and *Norma Rae.*" *Labor History* 23 (Winter 1982): 67–78.

Zinsser, William K. Rev. of *The Pajama Game*, dir. George Abbott and Stanley Donen. *New York Herald Tribune* 30 Aug. 1957: 6.

Index

Numbers in **_bold italics_** indicate pages with photographs.

Abbott, George 56, 204*n*32
academic feminism 85–86, 143–45; *see also* scholarship
Academy Awards 109, 170, 189
actors and actresses 8, 24, 89, 109, 188, 189, 191, 192; *see also* star persona; *see under* specific actor or actress name
Adler, Richard 204*n*32
advertising and publicity 24–26, 48, **_92_**, 104, 106, 169–70, 173
aesthetics 8, 9, 10, 190–91; *see also under* title of movie
agency 9, 11, 37–38; capitalism and 151; musicals and 49, 63–64, 69; patriarchy and 146, 151–52; structure/agency duality 7
Ally McBeal 143
Alonzo, John 115
Alpert, Hollis 52
Altman, Rick 56, 57, 65
ambition 50, 52, 71–72, 102, 164
American dream (ideal) 164–65, 177, 182
American Dream (movie) 147
American Federation of Labor (AFL) 24
American Movie Awards 109
Anderson, Karrin Vasby 144
Ansen, David 106, 112, 171, 178, 181, 184
Arlen, Alice 110, 114
Asseyeu, Tamara 107–8
Astaire, Fred 65
audience *see* spectatorship
Aufderheide, Pat 111, 127, 139
Auslander, Philip 71
Austerlitz, Saul 147
avant-garde cinema 28, 79, 86, 95, 203*n*48, 206*n*24
awards 81, 82, 109, 170, 172, 189

Baby Boom 168
Beauvoir, Simone de 205*n*57
Benson, Edward 199*n*11
Benson, Thomas 8, 200*n*24
Bessie, Alvah 202*n*23

Biberman, Herbert 15, 23, 24, 29, 200*n*1, 202*n*23
Bingham, Clara 171
biopics 13; *see also* docudramas
Bissel, Richard 48, 55–56, 67, 204*n*32
blacklisting *see* "Hollywood Ten"
Blake, Richard 113
Bocelli, Arnaldo 30
Bodnar, John 4
Bonavoglia, Angela 111
Bordwell, David 58, 132, 192
Brandon, Liane 81
Brecht, Bertolt 22
Brewer, Roy 20–21, 22, 24
Bridges, Beau 107
Bridget Jones 143
Broadcast News 168
Brockovich, Erin 170; *see also Erin Brockovich*
The Brothers McMullen 169
Burr, Ty 189
Byars, Jackie 47, 48

cable-TV 104, 146, 168, 200*n*1
Cannes Film Festival 109
Cano, Larry 110
capitalism **_172_**; American dream and 164–65, 177, 182; Communism vs. 21; effects of collective action on 153, 161; female agency and 151; Marxist feminists vs. 77; personal growth vs. critique of 117, 136, 166, 183–84, 186, 196; triumph of 6, 67–68, 69–70, 189, 194, 196
Capra, Frank 104–5
Caro, Nikki 171
Carson, Diane 6, 135
Catching the Wave: Reclaiming Feminism for the 21st Century (Dicker/Peipmeier) 145
censorship 26
Ceplair, Larry 21
Chacón, Juan 17, 24
character development 9; *see also under* title of movie

225

Cher 109
children 38, 97, 98, 154; caring for 119, 124, 129, 130, 152, 164, 165–66; custody battles 109, 111, 120–21; legacy and 43; picketing by 92; single parenthood 107, 176, 177, 178, 182
Christensen, Terry 113, 135
Churchill, Winston 21, 201*n*19
cinematic techniques 9, 11, 58; classical Hollywood style and 192–93; documentaries 90–91, 96; musicals and 205*n*44; objectification and 151, 181–82, 193; realism and 29–30, 31–32, 84–86, 94, 115–16, 191; *see also under* specific technique; title of movie
A Civil Action 171
Class Action: The Story of Lois Jensen and the Landmark Case That Changed Sexual Harassment Law (Bingman) 171
class oppression 30–31, 103, 116
classical Hollywood style: cinematic techniques 192–93; depictions of independence in 55, 59–60, 61–62, 173–74; deviation from 27–28; docudramas and 112–15, 136–37, 174, 187, 192–93; documentaries vs. 73–74, 78, 136; narrative of 55, 58, 69, 147, 173–74, 187, 192–93; post-feminist depictions 14, 164–65; realism vs. 8, 147, 174, 187, 191; status quo and 85–86, 136–37
Clerks 169
close-up: as a device 9, 115; documentaries and 90–91, 96; realism and 191; visual linking 33
coalition politics 143, 145, 146, 147–53, 160–63, 187; *see also* collective action
Cold War 18–27, 167, 201*n*19; *see also* Communism
Cole, Lester 202*n*23
collective action 14, 58, 182; effects of on capitalism 153, 161; Marxist feminists and 77; as a means to an end 166, 173–74; necessity of 125; potential of 36, 42, 84, 96–97, 143, 146, 193, 197; social problem films 23; third-wave feminism and 146, 148–50, 153, 158–63; *see also* coalition politics
Collins, Jim 63
Columbia Pictures 108
Communism 2, 16, 18, 19–27, 167, 201*n*19, 203*n*52; *see also* "Hollywood Ten"; House Un-American Activities Committee (HUAC)
Communist Infiltration in the United States (U.S. Chamber of Commerce) 201*n*21
Communist Party 22, 23
Conference of Studio Unions 20–21
Congress of Industrial Organizations (CIO) 24

consciousness-raising: feminist politics and 51, 73–75, 79–80, 81, 95–97, 140, 161; of spectatorship 10, 12–13, 17–18, 30, 94–98
conservatism 7, 166–75, 186, 190, 193, 195; commercial expectations and 106, 111, 114, 136; musicals and 49, 57, 58, 62–63; Reagan/Bush era 144–45, 166–69; responses to 18, 27; third-wave feminism and 163
Cook, Pam 51, 71
Cooper, Gary 21
corporatism 102, 103–5
Crawford, Joan 48
A Crime to Fit the Punishment 16
crosscutting 32–33, 177
Crowdus, Gary 99
Crowther, Bosley 26
Crystal Lee: A Woman of Inheritance (Liefermann) 107–8
cultural context 1–2, 9; *see also under* title of movie

Dargis, Manohla 173
Davin, Eric Leif 111
Davis, Bette 48
Day, Doris **53**, **68**, 206*n*65; femininity and 11–12; proto-feminist identity of 49, 70–71; star persona of 49–55, 58, 64, 70–72, 184, 188, 195
deconstructionism 58, 86, 94–95
de Cordova, Richard 51, 63–64
defiance: body language depicting 120, 132, 133; consequences of 136, 189–90; musical as a venue for 55, 65; *see also* rebellion
De Sica, Vittorio 30
De Vito, Danny 170
Dicker, Rory 145
Dies, Martin 201*n*21
direct address 9, 58, 63–64, 66, 84, 87, 149–50, 205*n*44
directors, status of 104–5
Disney, Walt 21; *see also* Walt Disney Corporation
distribution 80–81, 104, 105, 168–69
Dittmar, Linda 6, 27, 203*n*69
Dmytryk, Edward 202*n*23
docudramas 13, 112–40; characterization 121–36; classical Hollywood style 112–15, 136–37, 174, 187, 192–93; defined 112–13, 209*n*38; dominant culture/ideology and 114–15, 117, 136–37; double bind of 113; heroism in 125–36; individualism vs. collective 117–21, 139–40; melodrama and 112–13, 114, 173–74, 187, 192–93; narrative and 113, 114, 117, 132–33; power and 135, 137; realism in 14–17; relationships in 125–33
documentaries 5, 12–13, 195–96, 201*n*7; cinematic techniques 90–91, 96; classical Hollywood style vs. 73–74, 78, 136;

Index

dominant culture/ideology and 85–86, 89, 91, 162, 196; growth of 78; historical record and 75; realism and 75, 82–100, 163, 191–92, 201*n*7; social authenticity of 187; *see also* feminist filmmaking
Doherty, Thomas 113, 114, 181
domestic violence 41–42, 135, 177
domesticity 49, 189–90, 193–94; depictions of 29–30, 32; melodramas and 45; men and 19, 35–36, 178, 182–83; public sphere vs. 60, 69–70, 129–31; star persona and 71, 206*n*65; as a "women's issue" 44
dominant culture/ideology 5, 17–18, 43–44, 143, 190–91, 192, 196–97; docudramas and 114–15, 117, 136–37; documentaries and 85–86, 89, 91, 162, 196; independent films and 201*n*7; status quo and 7–8, 58, 85–86; women's movement and 76–78; *see also* patriarchy; popular culture/media; status quo
domination/resistance 7–8, 36, 42, 43–46, 57–68. *see also* defiance; feistiness; rebellion; spiritedness
Donen, Stanley 56
double bind 90, 95, 113
"double shift" 74, 130
"double text" 48
Douglas, Susan 165
Dow, Bonnie 2, 162–63, 164, 165
Dowdy, Andrew 56–57
Drake, Jennifer 145, 148, 160, 165
Dunaway, Faye 109
Dyer, Richard 50–51, 54

Ebert, Robert 171, 172–73, 184
economic context 5, 6, 7–8, 9, 10, 13, 190; *see also under* title of movie
Edelstein, David 172
Ellis, Christine (Kate) 81
Ellis, Jack 201*n*9
Empire Zinc 23–24
empowerment 12, 43, 153–63, 191; as defined by third-wave feminists 160; disempowerment 3, 137, 164–65, 174; interviews as a device of 89; sexuality as a tool for 143, 144, 147, 151–53, 155, 156, 182
Englund, Steve 21
Ephron, Nora 110, 114, 135
Erens, Patricia 73
Erin Brockovich 164–97, *172*, 189–97; advertising and publicity 169–70; aesthetics 173; awards 170; character development 165, 174–78, 182–88; cinematic technique 169, 174, 181–82; economic context 167; historical context 14, 164–65, 166; narrative structure 165, 166, 175; plot 170, 173; political context 166–69, 186; production history 170–71, 173; profits 170; realism in 169, 174, 191–92; reviews 171, 172, 181, 184; rhetorical influence 183–84, 185–88; star personas 195; style 169–70; themes 165–66
escapism 4, 19, 28, 56
Europe, motion picture industry in 29, 30–31
Exotic Dancers Alliance (EDA) 142
experimental cinema 28, 79, 86, 95, 203*n*48, 206*n*24
exploitation 31, 42, 147, 153, 161, 162, 165–66, 186

Faludi, Susan 168
fandom 50–51; *see also* star persona
Fatal Attraction 168
Fehr, Richard 55, 56, 204*n*28
feistiness 50, 54–55, 59–60, 118; *see also* spiritedness
femininity: double bind and 90; feminist depictions of 73–74; power and *53*, 59; second-wave feminism and 147–48, 156; third-wave feminism and 145; traditional depictions of 11–12, 13, 49–50, 52, *53*, 55, 60–61, 66, 103, 131, 194
feminism 2, 8–9, 14, 76–78, 143–145; contradictions in 181–84; images of 162–63; political action and 153–58; "popular press feminists" 143–47; populist vision of 101–2, 136–40; *see also* first-wave feminism; post-feminism; proto-feminism; second-wave feminism; third-wave feminism; women's movement
feminist emergence: domination/resistance and 43–46; narrative subjectivity and 36–43; self-identity and 38–39, 40, 41, 44, 50, 64, 65, 136, 203*n*69
feminist filmmaking 12–13, 73–100; advantages of 78–79; distribution 80–81; goals 74, 79–80; mobilizing aspect of 75, 80; origins 73–75, 77–78; patriarchy and 80, 85–86, 89–90; power and 89, 90–91, 96; rhetorical influence 75, 76, 79–80, 94–98, 208*n*83; rise of 78–79; scholarship 6–7, 82–83, 84–86, 94–95, 206*n*24, 208*n*79, 208*n*83; skill-sharing aspect of 81; spectatorship and 73–74, 75, 79–80, 94–98, 208*n*83; status quo and 77–78, 190, 191, 193; subgenres 79
feminist identity 44, 50, 68, 102–3, 162–63, 165, 166
Feuer, Jane 57, 58, 63, 204*n*44
Field, Sally 13, *108*, 109, 139, 184, 188, 195
Fifth Amendment 202*n*24
film/film industry *see* motion picture industry
Findlen, Barbara 144–45
First Amendment 110, 202*n*24
first-wave feminism 2, 147–48
Fixmer, Natalie 145, 153

Index

Fonda, Jane 109
Ford, John 104–5
form 9–10, 11, 12–13, 74, 83, 113–17, 190
Fosse, Bob 204n32
Foy, Eddie, Jr. 204n32
Frank, Harriet, Jr. 108–9, 111
French, Brandon 47, 184–85
Funari, Vicki 142

gaze 63–65, 66, 181–82, 193
gender roles 3, 6, 31, 32–36, 39–43, 47–48, 95, 97–98, 199n11; *see also* domesticity; femininity; masculinity
genres of film 28; *see also* specific genre
Gilliatt, Penelope 106
Gilmore, Geoff 103
Gledhill, Christine 43–44, 50–51, 86
Golden Globe Awards 109
Goldfarb, Lyn 74, 82
Gordon, Linda 82
Gordon, Suzanne 112
Grant, Susannah 170, 173
Gray, Lorraine 74, 82
Green, Philip 136–37, 140
Greer, Will 24

Hallstein, D. Lynn O'Brien 152
Haney, Carol 204n32
Harlan County, U.S.A 147
Harrelson, Woody 171
Haskell, Molly 48, 54–55, 61, 206n65
Hawks, Howard 104–5
Hayworth, Rita 51
heroism 166, 184–97; consequences of 120, 129, 134–35, 136, 189–90, 193–94; docudramas and 125–36; feminist contradictions and 181–84; outlaw 13, 102–3, 118–22, 136–40, 174, 193; "women's pictures" 5–6, 47–48
Herstory 80–81
heterosexuality 58, 61, 67–68, 152
"Hey There" (song) 66
Heywood, Leslie 145, 148, 160
Hirsch, Buzz 110
historical context 1–2, 3–4, 9; *see also under* title of movie
historical revisionism 75
historicity 91–92
Hoff-Sommers, Christina 143, 164
Hoffer, Tom 209n38
Hogeland, Lisa Marie 144–45
Hollywood *see* classical Hollywood style; motion picture industry
"Hollywood Ten" 22, 23, 201n21, 202n23
House Un-American Activities Committee (HUAC) 21–22, 25, 27, 201n11, 201n21, 202n24

"I Figured It Out" (song) 66

identity *see* feminist identity; self–identity
independence 197; classical Hollywood style 55, 59–60, 61–62, 173–74; consequences of 129, 193–94; men's resistance to 36, 40, 107; musicals and 49, 50, 65, 69; negative presentations of 121–22; 1950s depictions 184–85; 1980s depictions 168; post-feminist depictions 164–65; second-wave feminism and 154, 156; star persona and 71–72; 21st century depictions 174–75; *see also* defiance; feistiness; rebellion; spiritedness
independent films 18, 23, 27, 166, 185–97; defined 201n7; distribution 80, 104, 105, 168–69; dominant culture/ideology and 201n7; growth of in the 1980s 168–69; mainstream films vs. 7–8, 9, 185–88, 189–97; *see also* documentaries; feminist filmmaking
Independent Productions Corporation (IPC) 23, 25
individualism 58; community vs. 17, 31, 34, 162, 182, 196; in docudramas 117–21, 139–40; post-feminism and 143–44, 146, 164–66
International Alliance of Theatrical Stage Employees (IATSE) 20–21, 22, 24
intertextuality 50, 71–72; *see also* star persona
interviewing, as a technique 74, 86–91, 152
"Iron Curtain" speech (Churchill) 21
"It Goes Like It Goes" (song) 115
It Happens to Us 90
Italian cinema 29, 30–31, 83; *see also* Neo-realism

Jackson, Donald 25
Jacobs, Diane 103
Jacobs, Lea 63–64
Jacobs, Lewis 78
Jarrico, Paul 23, 24, 26, 29
Jaws 104
Jeffords, Susan 168
Jencks, Clinton 25
Jenkins, Richard 177
Jersey Films 170
Johnston, Claire 81, 85–86, 94, 95
Johnston, Eric 21, 22, 27
Jones, Dorothy 19, 201n11
Jordan, Crystal Lee 107, 110–11, 112, 114
Jordan, Larry "Cookie" 110
Jowett, Garth 204n28
Juhasz, Alexandra 84, 90, 94, 96

Kael, Pauline 26, 208n4
Kaplan, E. Ann 83, 85, 95
Kasdan, Margo 36–37
Kauffman, Bette J. 140, 167
Kawin, Bruce 30

Index

Keaton, Diane 109
Keller, Gary 45
Kellner, Douglas 7, 117, 168
King, Loren 146
Kinser, Amber E. 145–46
Klein, James 74, 81–82, 98–99
Klevan, Andrew 52
Kolker, Robert 104, 105
Kopple, Barbara 147
Kroll, Jack 106
Kuhn, Annette 43, 80, 84, 95, 117

labor activism 83–84; entry of women into 74–75; expectations of female activists 6; rhetorical tensions of cinematic representations of 8; romanticization of 106
labor movement 196; decline of 2, 14, 166, 167; in the 1930s 75, 83–84, 185
labor unions 4–5, 67, 142; decline of 2, 166, 167; feminist filmmaking and 74; in the motion picture industry 20–21, 24, 26
Lafferty, William 201n9
language 203n60
Lardner, Ring, Jr. 202n23
Lawson, John Howard 201n7, 202n23
Leno, Jay 146
Lesage, Julia 74, 79, 80, 87, 89
Lev, Peter 102
liberal feminism 76–78, 143–45; *see also* second-wave feminism
liberalism 7, 102, 114, 117
"liberated woman" 2
liberationists 76–78; *see also* radical feminists
Liebman, Ron 107
Liefermann, Henry P. 107–8
Lipkin, Steve 112–13
Listen Up (Findlen) 144
litigation 110–11
Live Nude Girls Unite! 141–63, **159**, 182, 189–97; aesthetics 147; cinematic techniques 146, 151; construction of 150; cultural context 147; economic context 154–55; historical context 14; narrative structure 149–50, 155; plot 141–42, 148–50, 154–58; political context 143–49, 162–63; production history 142, 146–47, 186–87; profits 146; realism in 191–92; reviews 147; rhetorical influence 143, 144, 147–48, 152–53, 157, 162–63, 163, 185–88; social context 143–47, 153; spectatorship 146, 151
Lorence, James 23
Lynd, Alice 81
Lynd, Staughton 81

Macdonald, Dwight 54
mainstream films: depictions of feminism in 76, 94–95, 136–40; from realism to escapism 4, 19, 28, 56; independent films vs. 7–8, 9, 185–88, 189–97
Maltby, Richard 22
Maltz, Albert 202n23
Marcus, Millicent 203n56
Margolies, Ken 5, 67
marriage 32, 38, 44, 58, 67–68, 69, 107, 168; patriarchy and 61–62, 68, 70, 72, 194
Marxism 30, 32, 77, 95, 161, 203n52
Marxist feminists 77
masculinity 13, 34, 90, 103, 131, 168
mass media 8, 44, 101; media construct 2, 76–78; post-feminism and 14, 143–44, 153–54, 162, 163, 164–65; *see also* advertising and publicity; popular culture/media; television
Mast, Gerald 30, 55
Matthew-Walker, Robert 57, 204n24
Mattina, Anne 6
Mayne, Judith 6–7, 9–10
Mayo, Anna 111
McDormand, Frances 172
McGarry, Eileen 85
McLean, Adrienne 51, 69
meaning-making 8–10, 189–97, 200n24; *see also* rhetorical influence
Medhurst, Martin 8
media construct 2, 76–78
Mellencamp, Patricia 61
melodramas: docudramas and 112–13, 114, 173–74, 187, 192–93; domesticity and 45; good vs. evil 28; stereotypes 102
men: domesticity and 19, 35–36, 178, 182–83; resistance to women's independence and 36, 40, 107; *see also* masculinity
Mexican Americans 16, 18, 24, 26, 44, 203n60
Meyer, Louis B. 21
Michel, Sonya 5, 89, 93
middle-class 4, 16, 22, 132
militancy **17**, 22, 43, 62, 91–92, 97–98, 184, 193
Miller, Gabriel 106
Miller, Tom 16
Miramax 169
Mogulescu, Miles 74, 81
Monroe, Marilyn 51
montage 29–30, 115, 176
Montgomery, Robert 22
Mordden, Ethan 54
Morgenstern, Joe 171
Motion Picture Alliance for the Preservation of American Ideals (MPA) 21, 22
Motion Picture Association 110
motion picture industry 3, 7, 8–9; advertising and publicity 24–26, 48, **92**, 104, 106, 169–70, 173; corporatism 102, 103–5; distribution 80–81, 104, 105, 168–69; during the 1930s 20; during the 1940s 45, 47–48;

during the 1950s 19–23, 28, 45, 48–50, 55, 61, 184–85, 201*n*7, 201*n*11; during the 1960s 103–6; during the 1970s 101–9, 185, 208*n*4; during the 1980s 101–3, 166–69; during the 1990s 164–65; during the 21st century 166, 185–88; litigation 110–11; package-unit system 105, 192; profits 104, 109, 146, 169–70; studio system 11, 18, 49, 103–5; unionization of 20–21, 24, 26
Motion Picture Producers' Association (MPPA) 21, 22, 27
Mulvey, Laura 64, 205*n*54, 206*n*24
music, as an aural support 91
musicals 55–70; agency and 49, 63–64, 69; cinematic techniques 205*n*44; conservatism and 49, 57, 58, 62–63; effects on spectatorship 50, 63–64; independence in 49, 50, 65, 69; narrative and 50, 58, 63; re-emergence of 204*n*28; spiritedness in 57; status quo and 11, 57, 58, 66–67, 69–70

narrative: classical Hollywood style 55, 58, 69, 147, 173–74, 187, 192–93; docudramas and 113, 114, 117, 132–33; musicals and 50, 58, 63; situation-complication-resolution model 27–28; subjectivity 36–43; visual codes 51, 56; *see also* public vs. private narrative
National Labor Relations Board (NLRB) 142
National Organization of Women (NOW) 76
naturalism 29, 86
Nelson, Craig T. 123
Nelson, Richard Alan 209*n*38
Neorealism 10, 11, 29–36, 83, 203*n*56; defined 30
Neve, Brian 27
"New American Cinema" 114
"new American Way" 27
New Day Films 81, 82
New York Film festival 82
newspaper clippings 74, 89, 91, 93, 150
newsreels 74, 87, 91, 93, 150, 192
Nichols, Bill 87, 90
Nichols, Mike 105–6, 110
Norma Rae 101–40, **108**, 165, 171, 178, 185, 189–97, 199*n*11; awards 109; character development 102–3, 117–22, 124–28, 175; cinematic techniques 115–17; cultural context 101–2; economic context 13, 103–4, 106, 116, 140; form 13, 113–14, 117; historical context 13; narrative structure 102–3, 106–7, 113, 125, 132–33, 136; plot 13, 101, 102, 107, 125, 133; political context 13; production history 102, 107–9, 110–11, 114; profits 109; realism in 115–17; reviews 106, 112; rhetorical influence 13, 185, 187–88;

social context 13, 136–37; star personas 13, 109; themes 117
North Country 164–97, **180**; advertising and publicity 173; aesthetics 173; award nominations 172; character development 165, 174–88; cinematic technique 174; economic context 167, 172–73; historical context 14, 164–65, 166; narrative structure 165, 166; plot 173, 175, 179–81, 182; political context 166–69, 186; production history 171–72; profits 172; realism in 174, 191–92; reviews 172–74, 184; rhetorical influence 183–84, 185–88; star personas 171; style 169; themes 165–66
Nowicki, Stella 81

objectification 61, 64, 79, 83, 89; cinematic techniques and 151, 181–82, 193; subjectivity vs. 8, 131, 151–52, 157, 182
O'Brien, Tom 112
On Movies (Macdonald) 54
On the Waterfront 201*n*11
Ondricek, Miroslav 116
oppression 136–37; class and 30–31, 103, 116; consciousness-raising and 96–97; deconstructionism and 85–86; Marxist perspective of 77; power structure of society and 41; third-wave feminism and 142–43, 146, 157, 163, 197
oral history 87, 89
Ornitz, Samuel 202*n*23
Orr, Catherine 154, 157
outlaw heroism 13, 102–3, 118–22, 136–40, 174, 193; *see also* defiance; rebellion

package-unit system 105, 192
Paige, Janis 204*n*32
The Pajama Game 11–12, 47–72, **53**, **68**, 189–97; aesthetics 49; character development 61–68, 174–75, 184–85, 187–88; cinematic techniques 58, 63–64, 66, 193; economic context 47; historical context 11, 12; narrative structure 10–11, 49, 50, 57–68, 69; plot 11, 48–49, 56, 58–61, 62–63, 66–67; production history 55–56; reviews 56, 57; rhetorical influence 11, 58, 67–68, 70–71, 184–85, 187–88; social context 47–50, 52, 69–70; spectatorship 11–12, 50, 63–65, 66, 70; star personas 11–12, 49–55, 63–64, 70–72, 195; themes 49, 58, 65
paradigm system 192
parallel shots 33–34
Paramount Studios 169
Parry-Giles, Shawn 162
Participant Productions 171
Pathé Laboratory 25
patriarchy 6–7, 9, 51, 193, 195, 197, 208*n*79; agency and 146, 151–52; feminist film

Index

making and 80, 85–86, 89–90; marriage and 61–62, 68, 70, 72, 194; Marxist feminists and 77; post-feminism and 164, 166, *172*, 182; third-wave feminism and 146, 151–52, 153, 161; working within 136, 143
Paul, Jasmine 140, 167
Peipmeier, Alison 145
"performative spectatorship" 63
Persall, Steve 173
personal vs. political 79–80, 138–39, 142, 148, 153–54, 165
photographs 74, 87, 89, 91–93, 154
phronesis 208n83
Pidgeon, Walter 24–25
plot 9; *see also under* title of movie
political context 3, 5, 7–8, 9; *see also under* title of movie
"politicos" 77
popular culture/media 8, 89, 136, 182; function of 2, 3; media construct 2, 76–78; post-feminism and 14, 143–44, 162, 163, 164–65; *see also* dominant culture/ideology
"popular press feminists" 143–47
postcolonialism 144
post-feminism 2, 184; classical Hollywood style and 14, 164–65; independence and 164–65; individualism and 143–44, 146, 164–66; lifestyle choice vs. political identity 14, 143–44, 165, 166, 186; mass media and 14, 143–44, 153–54, 162, 163, 164–65; patriarchy and 164, 166, *172*, 182; power and 164–65; second-wave feminism vs. 164–66; third-wave feminism vs. 143–47, 154, 164
postmodernism 144
poststructuralism 84–85, 95, 144
power 7, 41–42, 68, *180*, 197; collective action and 36, 42, 96–97, *108*, 143, 153; containment of 61–62; docudramas and 135, 137; femininity and *53*, 59; feminist filmmaking and 89, 90–91, 96; Marxist feminists and 77; post-feminism and 164–65; revisionist perspective of 75; third-wave feminism and 143, 144, 147, 160, 163, 182; *see also* empowerment
"power feminism" *see* post-feminism
Powers, Stephen 44
Prime-Time Feminism (Dow) 2
production contexts 9–10, 13; *see also* cultural context; economic context; historical context; political context; social context
production history *see under* title of movie
pro-filmic events 85
profits 104, 109, 146, 169–70
proto-feminism 44, 49, 50, 52, 55, 57, *68*, 70–71
psychoanalysis 84–85
public space, creation of 83–84

public vs. private narrative 11, 13, 59–60, 62–63, 192, 194, 195–96, 197; docudramas and 103, 113, 116, 117, 129–40, 173, 182–84, 185, 187–88; documentaries and 80, 95–97, 143, 149, 185, 187–88; social problem films and 45; third-wave feminism and 153–54, 163
publicity *see* advertising and publicity
Puig, Claudia 169
Purdy, Jim 4

Query, Julia 141–42, 146, 152, 188, 194–95

Rabinowitz, Paula 75
race/racism 15, 19, 28–29, 31, 32, 36, 43, 144, 168
radical feminists 76–77, 145
radicalism 6, 21, 195
Raitt, John *53*, *68*, 204n32
Rambo 168
Rand, Ayn 23
Rank and File: Personal Histories of Working-Class Organizers (Lynd) 81
Rapping, Elayne 7
Ravetch, Irving 108–9, 111
Ray, Robert 105, 106, 114, 117, 118, 136
Reagan, Ronald 22, 24
Reagan/Bush era 144–45, 166–69
realism 12, 169, 191–92, 204n11; cinematic technique and 29–30, 31–32, 84–86, 94, 115–16, 191; classical Hollywood style and 8, 147, 174, 187, 191; defined 191; docudramas and 114–17; documentaries and 75, 82–100, 163, 191–92, 201n7; escapism and 4, 19, 28, 56; spectatorship and 94–98; *see also* Neorealism
rebellion 62, 71, 118, *172*; consequences of 120, 135, 136, 189–90; outlets for 177–78; *see also* defiance
Redford, Robert 168
Reichert, Julia 74, 81–82, 98–99
relationships 103, 125–33, 138–39, 205n57; *see also* children; marriage
Reporters' Committee for Freedom of the Press 110
resistance *see* domination/resistance
Return of the Secaucus 7 15
Reverby, Susan 91, 93, 97
Reveultas, Rosaura 24, 25
Reynolds, Debbie 54
rhetorical influence 1–2, 5–6, 8–10, 189–97, 200n24, 208n83; *see also under* title of movie
Rich, B. Ruby 99
Ritt, Martin 105–6, 107–9, 110–11, 112, 114, 124
Roberts, Julia 170, *172*, 184, 188
Roberts, Shari 70

Robinson, Lillian 37
Roffman, Peter 4
Rogers, Ginger 65
Roiphe, Katie 143, 164
Rooney, David 173, 174
Rose, Alex 107-8
Rosen, Marjorie 44, 47-48, 54
Rosenberg, Jan 76, 77, 86
Rosenfelt, Deborah Silverton 36, 44
Ross, Jerry 204*n*32
Ross, Steven 4
Rossellini, Roberto 30
Rothman, David 44
Rothman, Stanley 44
Rothschild, Amalie 81
Russell, Kurt 109
Russell, Rosalind 48
Ryan, Michael 117, 168

Salt of the Earth 15-46, *17*, 189-97, 199*n*11; advertising and publicity 24-26; aesthetics 17, 28; censorship of 26; character development 43-46; cinematic techniques 11, 28, 29-30, 31-34, 42-43, 192-93; cult following of 16-17, 200*n*1; cultural context 10, 29-30, 43-46, 203*n*60; economic context 10, 16-17, 27, 29, 30-31, 38; historical context 15-16, 29-30; narrative structure 10-11, 18, 27-28, 31-32, 35, 36-43; Neorealism in 10, 11, 29-36, 191; plot 10, 15, 18-19, 28-29, 42, 192-93; political context 10, 16-27, 38, 203*n*52; production history 16, 23-26; release of 16, 26, 45; reviews 26-27; rhetorical influence 10, 11, 15-18, 16-18, 27-28, 184-85, 188; spectatorship 10, 17, 27-28; themes 10, 16-18, 27-28, 31, 33, 34-36
Sauvage, Cécile 205*n*57
Sayles, John 15
Sayre, Nora 202*n*53
Scheuer, Philip K. 57
Schickel, Richard 112, 113
scholarship 199*n*11; critiques of realist tradition 82-83, 94-95; feminist filmmaking 6-7, 82-83, 84-86, 94-95, 206*n*24, 208*n*79; post-feminism vs. third-wave 143-45; rhetoric vs. cultural studies 208*n*83; self-identity 208*n*79; social problem films 3-6; star personas 50-51
Schuth, H. Wayne 106
Scott, A.O. 147
Scott, Adrian 23, 202*n*23
Screen Actor's Guild 21, 24-25
Screen Guide for Americans (Rand) 23
The Second Sex (Beauvoir) 205*n*57
second-wave feminism 2, 12, 182; consciousness-raising and 51, 73-75, 79-80, 81, 95-97, 140, 161; independence and 154, 156; "personal is political" 79-80, 138-39, 142, 148, 153-54, 165; post–feminism vs. 164-66; third-wave feminism vs. 14, 142, 143-49, 153-63
Sefcovic, Enid M.I. 199*n*11
Seitzman, Michael 171
self-identity 205*n*57; in docudramas 102-3, 117-18, 136, 138, 139, 186; in documentaries 79-80, 83, 95, 96, 97, 147; dualities of 47-48, 60-62, 66, 70-71; emergence of 38-39, 40, 41, 44, 50, 64, 65, 136, 203*n*69; feminist 44, 50, 68, 102-3, 162-63, 165, 166; Marxist vs. liberationist feminists 77; post–feminism and 14, 143-44, 165, 166, 186; proto-feminism and 44, 49, 50, 52, 55, 57, *68*, 70-71; retaining of 66, 68, 69-70, 156; scholarship and 208*n*79; third-wave feminism and 147, 148-49, 151, 153-54, 157; *see also* personal vs. political
selfishness 120, 121, 122, 178
semiology 84-86
sentimentality 106, 115, 117, 139, 149, 170
setting 9, 83
sex industry 143, 147, 151-55, 157, 161, 163, 195-96
sex, lies and videotape 169
sexism 15, 27, 36, 90, 97-98, 172, 179, 186; *see also* gender roles
sexual harassment 74, 90, 152, 166, 172-73, *180*, 182
sexuality 122, 139, *172*, 176, 181-82, 186; as a tool for empowerment 143, 144, 147, 151-53, 155, 156, 182
Shamberg, Carlos Santos 170
Shamberg, Michael 170
Sher, Stacey 170
Shipp, Cameron 52, 54
Shochat, Ella 203*n*60
Shugart, Helene 148, 152, 158, 160
Silkwood 101-40, *122*, 165, 178, 189-97; award nominations 109; character development 102-3, 117-18, 120-24, 128, 175, 189, 193; cinematic techniques 116-17; cultural context 101-2; economic context 13, 103-4, 106, 140; form 13, 113-17; historical context 13; narrative structure 102-3, 106, 113, 125, 132-33, 136; plot 13, 101, 102, 109-10, 133; political context 13; production history 102, 110-11, 114; profits 109; realism in 191-92; reviews 106, 112; rhetorical influence 13, 185, 187-88; social context 13, 136-37; star personas 13; themes 117
Silkwood, Bill 111
Silkwood, Karen 111
Silver, Ron 110
"Sinews of Peace" (Churchill) 201*n*19
situation-complication-resolution model 27-28

Sklar, Robert 104–5, 167–68
Sloan, Kay 4
social context 3–4, 7–8; *see also under* title of movie
social problem films 3–6, 19–20, 23, 45, 106, 201n11; *see also* "women's pictures"
socialism 3, 7, 12, 77, 161, 166, 190–91, 194, 203n52
Soderbergh, Steven 169–70
songs *53*, 66, 115; *see also* musicals
Spacek, Sissy 171, 177
spectatorship: consciousness-raising of 10, 12–13, 17–18, 30, 94–98; direct address 9, 58, 63–64, 66, 84, 87, 149–50, 205n44; effects of musicals on 50, 63–64; feminist filmmaking and 73–74, 75, 79–80, 94–98, 208n83; meaning-making and 8–10, 189–97; popular culture/media and 3; realism and 94–98; spectoral gaze 63–65, 66, 181–82, 193; *see also* direct address; rhetorical influence; star persona
Speilberg, Steven 104
spiritedness 121–22, 175; consequences of 135, 136; musicals and 57; star persona and 55; *see also* feistiness
Staiger, Janet 192
Stam, Robert 203n60
star persona 13, 48; as a distraction 139, 184, 188, 195; independence and 71–72; scholarship and 50–51; spectoral gaze and 63–64; *see also* specific person
"star text" 50–51, 70, 71
Stars (Dyer) 50–51
status quo 45–46, 194, 197; classical Hollywood style and 85–86, 136–37; dominant culture/ideology and 7–8, 58, 85–86; effects of challenges to 102, 135, 188; feminist filmmaking and 77–78, 190, 191, 193; musicals and 11, 57, 58, 66–67, 69–70
Stead, Peter 117
Steiger, Janet 132
Stein, Ruthe 173–74, 184
stereotypes 73–74, 187
Stewart, Jessie 144
Stone, Elizabeth 112
Streep, Meryl 13, 109, *122*, 139, 184, 188, 195
Strom, Sharon Hartman 199n11
structural elements 31; *see also* plot; theme
structuralism/poststructuralism 84–86, 94–95, 144
Student Nonviolent Coordinating Committee 16
studio system 11, 18, 49, 103–5
stylistic elements 9; *see also* docudramas; documentaries; independent films; mainstream films; Neorealism
subjectivity 36–43, 85, 187, 191; Dyer's emphasis on 51; interviews and 87; objectification vs. 8, 131, 151–52, 157, 182

Sundance Institute 168
Susan, Barbara 96
Sutton, Martin 67

Tasker, Yvonne 181
Taubin, Amy 147
Taylor, Robert 22
technology 78, 104, 167
television 16, 104, 146, 168, 200n1
Tenney, Jack 201n21
Terminator 168
textual analysis/negotiation 7–10, 52, 71–72, 84–86, 94–95, 200n24; *see also* production contexts; "star text"
theme 9, 117, 190; *see also under* title of movie
"There Once Was a Man" (song) *53*, 65–66
Theron, Charlize 171, *180*, 184, 188, 195
Third Wave Agenda: Being Feminist, Doing Feminism (Heywood/Drake) 145
third-wave feminism 143–66; collective action and 146, 148–50, 153, 158–63; conservatism and 163; definition of empowerment 160; oppression and 142–43, 146, 157, 163, 197; patriarchy and 146, 151–52, 153, 161; post-feminism vs. 143–47, 154, 164; power and 143, 144, 147, 160, 163, 182; public vs. private narrative 153–54, 163; second-wave feminism vs. 14, 142, 143–49, 153–63; self-identity and 147, 148–49, 151, 153–54, 157
Thomas, J. Parnell 22
Thompson, Kristin 192
Thomson, Kristin 132
"to-be-looked-at-ness" 64, 205n54
To Be Real (Walker) 144
Tonn, Mari Boor 6
Travers, Peter 171, 181
Trumbo, Dalton 202n23
Turan, Kenneth 54, 171, 173, 174
20th Century-Fox 108

union activism, in the motion picture industry 20–21, 24, 26
Union Maids 12–13, 73–100, 189–97; aesthetics 78, 83; award nominations 81; cinematic techniques 74, 84, 91–93; construction of 74–75, 98–99; historical context 12; narrative structure 75, 83–84, 86–87, 91, 99–100; plot 12, 74, 87–88; political context 12; production history 81–82; realism in 75, 82–100, 191–92; reviews 82; rhetorical influence 13, 74–75, 84, 99–100, 185, 188; social context 12; spectatorship 13, 81–82, 94–100; themes 84, 89–90
unions *see* labor unions
United Artists 108
United Auto Workers (UAW) 82

U.S. Chamber of Commerce 201*n*21
U.S. Court of Appeals 110
U.S. Immigration and Naturalization Service. 25

VCRs 104, 168
victim feminism 70, 72, 103, 143, 151–52, 164–65, 178
viewers *see* spectatorship
Visconti, Luchino 30
visual codes 51, 56
Vogel, Frederick G. 55, 56, 204*n*28
voice-over 32, 40, 42–43, 90, 98, 149

Waggoner, Catherine Egley 152
Walker, Alice 144–45
Walker, Rebecca 144
Wallace, Dr. Joyce 155–56
Walt Disney Corporation 169
Wandersee, Winifred 101
Warner, Jack L. 21
Warner Bros. 55–56, 108, 169
Warnes, Jennifer 115
Welsch, Janice R. 6
Wilson, Michael 23, 24
With Babies and Banners 12–13, 73–100, **92**, 189–97; aesthetics 78; award nominations 82; cinematic techniques 74, 84, 89, 91–93, 98; construction of 74–75, 99; historical context 12; narrative structure 75, 83–84, 86–87, 88–89, 91, 97–98, 99–100; plot 12, 74, 88–89, 98; political context 12; production history 82; realism in 82–94, 191–92; reviews 82, 99; rhetorical influence 13, 74–75, 84, 99–100, 185, 188; social context 12; spectatorship 13, 94–100; themes 84, 89–90
Wolf, Naomi 143, 164
Wolf, Stacy 58, 61–62, 63, 69
Women Make Movies 80–81
"women on the verge" 189–90
Women's Emergency Brigade (UAW) 82
Women's Film Festival 82
Women's Film Project 80–81
Women's Labor History Project 82
women's movement 76–78, 199*n*11; changing ideologies 49, 99, 142–48; evolution of 2, 73; momentum of 101; *see also* feminism; first-wave feminism; post–feminism; proto-feminism; second-wave feminism; third-wave feminism
"women's pictures" 5–6, 47–48
Wood, Julia T. 145, 153
Woods, Sylvia 81
working-class culture 2, 3–4, 103, 165–66, 199*n*11
Working Girl 168
Writer's Guild 110

Zivkovich, Eli 110

www.ingramcontent.com/pod-product-compliance
Lightning Source LLC
Chambersburg PA
CBHW032049300426
44116CB00007B/660